Spoken Records

Third Edition

by

Helen Roach

The Scarecrow Press, Inc.
Metuchen, N.J.   1970

To My Mother.

Be not afeared, the Isle is full of noises,
Sounds, and sweet airs, that give delight and
    hurt not:
Sometimes a thousand twangling instruments
Will hum about mine ears; and sometimes
    voices,
That if I then had wak'd after long sleep,
Will make me sleep again, and then in dream-
    ing,
The clouds methought would open, and show
    riches
Ready to drop upon me, that when I wak'd
I cried to dream again.

                                    The Tempest, III, ii

Acknowledgements

The author wishes to express her thanks to the libraries in which she has worked and to commercial firms which have been most helpful in providing lists and review copies of records not otherwise available.

In conclusion the author wishes to express her gratitude to Mary and Margaret Murray for encouragement and helpful criticism, and to Caroline Doerflinger for secretarial and editorial assistance far beyond the call of duty in the preparation of the final manuscript.

Portion of a letter from Robert Frost, Feb. 22, 1914, to John T. Bartlett reprinted from Selected Letters of Robert Frost edited by Lawrence Thompson by permission of the Estate of Robert Frost and Holt, Rinehart and Winston, Inc. Copyright (c) 1964 by Holt, Rinehart and Winston, Inc.

"Two Records" from Shakespeare and Company, (c) 1956, 1959 by Sylvia Beach. Reprinted by permission of Harcourt, Brace & World, Inc., and Faber and Faber, Ltd.

From The Oral Study of Literature by Algernon Tassin. Copyright renewed (c) 1966, Meredith Corporation. Reprinted by permission of Appleton-Century-Crofts.

Preface

A great teacher of speech, and that is what Professor Roach is, must have an ear for the written as well as the spoken word. The page speaks to her in the inevitable style of its writer; and her sense of what is fit exacts a strict reading of its hard-won perfections. Like a good musician reading a score, she hears the eloquent variations in her mind.

It is toward imparting that skill that this book is directed. Professor Roach here provides us with touchstones, standards of excellence with which she means to help us reach the fine pitch of discernment which her years of sensitive listening have brought her.

That discernment ought not to be dismissed as a pleasing but essentially frivolous accomplishment. A great text makes its demand of truth on audience as well as performers: we must prepare to listen as they must prepare to read, by bringing ourselves to a reverent sense of that text's full nature.

Such preparation must, of necessity, deepen our judgment and our pleasure, and teach us to honor, as this book does, language, that blessed gift which separates us from the beasts.

Kirkland House   William Alfred
Harvard University

Table of Contents

Chapter I

An Introduction to Spoken Records

What has happened in the field of spoken recording in the years since its inception at the close of the last century is not generally known. Educators and students are aware of records as valuable oral complements to the study of drama and poetry. Parents are familiar with records as a source of entertainment. But there are all kinds of records available today which would interest many adults if they knew about them. Indeed many records have in recent years become commercially available both on disc and on tape. Tapes, however, are not a part of the content of this volume.

During the 1930's and 1940's, a few major record companies, universities and libraries were instrumental in processing a limited number of spoken records. Then, after World War II, Caedmon Records pioneered a program concentrating on high level spoken records. A few other companies soon followed their leadership accelerating the movement toward its present avalanche in production.

As surprising as some of the inclusions in the repertory of spoken recordings that are now available are some of the omissions. One cannot come to this territory expecting to find what he wants, as is the case for music.

Perhaps not so surprising in a pioneering field is the fact that many records have not been well done. New listeners have been turned away by the poor recordings before hearing others which make for rewarding listening. Some records are indeed works of art.

There are basic elements present on any good recording. Basic, of course, is the matter of interest. Personalities, speeches, interviews and discussions, and events make up much of what is to be found on documentary recording. Literature is recorded most.

9

When material is memorized or read it must come through readers who are aware that what is in the mind tends to be communicated in speech. They must understand that the role of the recording artist is that of a non-intrusive medium of transmission for something different from himself. This artist's work stems from the same accurate center as that of the original writer at the peak of his realization and is directed towards the terminus of the original conception.

A frequent cause of poor recordings has been failure to adapt to the new medium. Even actors with considerable stage experience have not always made the adjustment. Some actors have been guilty of histrionic readings when dealing with non-dramatic works on records.

Self-listening is a common temptation for the inexperienced before the microphone, whether he be amateur or professional. It is the pitfall of attempting to be speaker and listener, artist and critic at the same time. The experienced listener knows when this is happening. He also knows when the performer identifies everything with himself instead of becoming a medium of transmission for the creation of something different from himself. An experienced listener quickly recognizes a performer's intrusion with personal feelings of shyness, indifference, resentment, tiredness or laziness. He knows, too, when the performer, instead of being concerned with meaning, is thinking of the way he is doing it, the way he sounds, or of some other aspect of his craft.

But the root reason for weaknesses in spoken recordings has been poorly taught reading. The educational system of the present century has so concentrated attention on silent reading that oral reading and an awareness of its inherent value have been completely neglected.

The professor of Shakespeare does the reading aloud, but the tongues of the students before him remain without that experience in depth for themselves. The fruits are evident on such a deadening and mechanical recording as Shakespeare's Sonnets by the Marlowe Society of Cambridge. It takes supervised experience, much like that acquired in a chemistry lab, to develop the skill needed to

bring life to material embalmed in print.   Anyone who reads Shakespeare with the eye must feel the temptation to speak the lines.
The urge is not to be confused with a desire to "ham," a form of
untruth, of exhibitionism.   It is a normal human desire to let
Shakespeare speak again.

One articulate defender of oral reading as a discipline in the
college curriculum was Professor Algernon Tassin of Columbia College, himself a Harvard graduate:

> ... The oral study of literature... will secure ... accu-
> rate thinking... the subtler the literature the more neces-
> sary is vocal embodiment to point it out... That this is
> an unpoetic age may not be entirely because it is a scien-
> tific one.   It may well be because the beauty of verse as
> verse lies in its rhythmic utterance, and we no longer
> utter it... If the appreciation of poetry is as rare as the
> ability to establish orally its sound and sense values... no
> wonder this is not a poetry reading age... Rich and varied
> illustrations can nowhere be got at so inexpensively as in
> reading aloud passages from literature... If the student
> reads aloud the passages himself, his grasp on the prin-
> ciples is surer.   What we do ourselves we know better
> than when we are merely told it by others... Sympathetic
> reading aloud is a fine art, and it is the only fine art
> within the gifts and opportunities of every student.   To
> many, it affords the only esthetic and spiritual develop-
> ment they ever receive in college, or--in the realm of
> art--in their lives for that matter.   To this end, lectures
> about literature are important, but they are not so impor-
> tant as reading literature.   They will of themselves only
> inform the mind; they will not enrich the spirit.   Nor will
> reading literature do so unless it is read with co-opera-
> tion...
>
> The student who achieves a reading of Shakespeare un-
> known to him before, a meaning which may be implied but
> is not asserted by the author, is a creator.   He has made
> something new out of old material, and Shakespeare could
> do no more than that.   Such artistic creation--the imagi-
> native co-operation with what he reads--is the birthright
> of every child, and that he should lose it just as creation
> widens on his view is pitiable...
>
> The theory of reading aloud can be entirely summed up in
> one statement.   The reader is taking the place of the
> writer and simply talking what he has to say.   Literature
> is talk made permanent.   In the pithy contemporary
> phrase, it is 'canned talk.'   The objects of the reader,
> then, are the same as the objects of the talker... True,
> it may sometimes happen that he will fail to deliver the

meaning when he has got it. But that is merely because
the customary attitude of people in speaking printed words
is absurdly different from their attitude in speaking their
own. He fails to deliver the meaning he has seen because
he really is not talking, he is only pronouncing...the oral
reader often fails to communicate. This is because of his
vocal monotony. No voice can communicate for more than
a sentence or two without movement. The ear of the listener becomes dulled. It is in reading aloud that the difference in the general attitude toward the printed and the
spoken word is most glaring. Few students would be content to talk in the unanimated voices in which they read.
If they were, their hearers would not let them continue
long. Every normal talking voice has movement, its ups
and downs. The rise and fall in the voice is called modulation. It is dictated by the attitude of the speaker toward
what he says, and is regulated by his intention in the
words he uses. By reason of the artificial attitude the
oral reader takes toward the printed word--that is to say,
no attitude at all--he neglects to employ the movement that
all voices must take when naturally used and consequently
what he says is largely unintelligible... The rises and
falls in the voice should be dictated by the conscious intention. If they are not, the utterance gets into a pattern of
ups and downs, like song, and the sense is defeated...On
the subject of faithfulness to the mood of the writer, it
may be pointed out that there is a kind of inaccuracy which,
faithful enough to the ideas if they were really yours, is
destructive to his. The average reader, student or adult,
is unwilling to let a writer speak for himself. He puts
his own valuation on the words according to his temperament, not remembering that the set of emotional associations intended by the writer may be different... A sentimental reading is not one which exhibits sentiment, but
which exhibits the wrong sentiment or the right one out of
proportion to the author's intention.

There is another kind of incomplete accuracy which destroys effectiveness. The listener gets the separate affirmations but is at a loss to discern their general aim.
What is he to get out of this bundle of interesting ideas
you give him? What is the central idea, the backbone to
which all the others must be fitted? The reader must size
up not only the general mood of the writer but his general
aim. There is not only a point to the sentence and to the
paragraph and stanza, there is, even more importantly, a
point to the entire passage. This is where the value...of
the one-sentence statement of the meaning comes in. Here
lies the central idea--all the rest is subsidiary. Find it
and try in your reading to make it stand out. Unless it
does so, the listener will again be seeing details too closely; in short, failing to see the wood for the trees...

> ...illuminative oral reading should be taught because it is
> not only cultural but creative. It is the sole creative art
> which the average man has a chance at. Work of inter-
> pretation is work of creation for the worker. The differ-
> ence is only one of degree and of the permanence of the
> concrete material result--the permanence of the spiritual
> result is the same. The interpreter, like the creator,
> gives shape and expression to something which was there
> before but had hitherto existed unperceived by him...
>
> Not until somewhat late in life... did I realize how slip-
> shod a reader I had been... When I reflect how many
> years it was after I left college before I came to recog-
> nize the fact that I did not know how to read, I am
> tempted to indict an educational system which, in assum-
> ing that I already knew how, although it knew very well[1]
> to the contrary, taught me Hamlet with Hamlet left out.

The direction of a recording is important. Poor direction or
the complete lack of it explains some failures in spoken recordings.
Many have been hurt by enthusiastic but ill-equipped directors, competent directors unaccustomed to the milieu, and even able directors
who, in the rush to publication, have not taken time to establish
rapport with the performers, much less to rehearse or re-do recordings.

That so many good recordings do exist is due in large part
to the good directors experienced in the medium. The director
(Caedmon) with the most credits for excellence of output and with
the widest range of undertaking is Howard O. Sackler, the poet and
dramatist.   Among other notable directors are V. C. Clinton Baddeley (Jupiter), George Rylands (Argo), Arthur Luce Klein (Spoken
Arts) and Douglas Cleverdon of the B. B. C.   Under such leadership,
standards of excellence have been established and new frontiers
opened up.   These directors have contributed knowledge, experience
and a pioneering spirit without which so much that is valuable in
spoken recording might not have been achieved.

Some Comments on the Selection of Spoken Records

Because a poet or a piece of literature is great does not
mean that a record is good.   Neither does material culled for sleeve
notes or the brochure included with many albums mean the recording
is good.   The advertising blurbs for a record may claim more for

execution than is warranted. Because of the possibility of poor execution on spoken recordings and the morass of competitive claims,
it is difficult to distinguish a good recording from a poor one without hearing it.

Very limited space is given to the reviewing of spoken records in learned journals, magazines, and the public press. It does
not adequately cover the large output in this country and has rarely
touched on the best from abroad unless the latter has an American
distributor. Moreover, the assignment to review or compile lists
of spoken records often goes to those for whom this area is of pe-
ripheral interest. There are many lists which serve to perpetuate
the bad records.

The above comments about spoken record reviews do not hold
for a small group of publications which for many years have been
seriously engaged in reviewing spoken records. The most venerable
of these is The Gramophone, Harrow, Middlesex, England, published by the company which made such a disc as the Orthological
Society pressing of the James Joyce recording. Besides regular reviews of spoken word recordings, the Gramophone Company has for
the past five years issued an annual Spoken Word and Miscellaneous
Catalogue (priced at five shillings). It has over 100 pages of in-
dexes for authors, artists, anthologies, titles, recordings in foreign
languages, recordings for children, miscellaneous entertainment,
documentary and instructional records, sound effects, etc. It is the
only catalogue of its kind with a very useful compilation by successive editors: Cecil Bellamy, Charles Fox, and Albert McCarthy.

Spoken records as yet are not easily available for examination by the studious listener, educator, researcher, or connoisseur.
Few college and university libraries have developed collections.
And the generally limited collections of the few public libraries
which offer spoken records are quickly disfigured by user abuse.

Because of these difficulties the purpose here has been to
call attention to worthwhile achievement in this little known world
and to indicate much that is well done which might otherwise be
missed. Selections for inclusion have been made on the basis of
excellence in execution, literary or historical merit, interest and

entertainment value.   There has been an attempt to include those
items which may prove to be of permanent value.

Records discussed are not of equal merit either in content or
execution.   While all omissions do not constitute an adverse judgment, some omissions do.   Some older records have been super-
seded but in a few cases known out-of-prints have been included.
An attempt has been made to suggest the size and range of output
to date.   While the dearth of material in some areas is noticeable,
frontiers are constantly opening up and new discoveries are being
made about the world of sound to extend those frontiers.   Although
record companies come and go and titles can become O. P. inside a
year, they are sometimes revived by other organizations.   Here the
Gramophone Spoken Word and Miscellaneous Catalogue, and to a
lesser degree the Schwann Catalog, may help.   There has been an
effort here, though incomplete, to catch some interesting outcrop-
pings if only to take note of the inventive minds concerned with
spoken recording.

Looking hopefully towards the future, one can say that among
the best spoken records today is an elite group which communicates
more than entertainment.   These contain essential soundings in spok-
en language which, because of the long-time exclusiveness of writing
in our educational pattern, have become increasingly absent from the
American oral tradition.   The better records can and do carry implicit ear training and incentives to more distinguished use of spoken
language than adults of the present generation have generally been
exposed to in their schooling.   Some of the poorer records, best described in the words of Henry James as "vague and formless in
their utterance," and unresponsive to sound and meaning in speech,
provide the same incentive by default.

Suggestions for a Basic Spoken Record Library

There are some spoken records whose excellence makes them
favorites.   Disregarding specialized tastes, the following group of
records would provide a good basic library.   Detailed descriptions
of all of these records are to be found in the text in the appropriate chapters.

1. John Gielgud, The Ages of Man.   Scenes and sonnets from
     Shakespeare.

2. John Barrymore Reads Shakespeare with Commentary.

3. James Joyce: A Portrait of the Artist as a Young Man, read
     by Cyril Cusack.

4. Animal Tales Told in the Gullah Dialect by Albert H. Stoddard
     of Savannah, Georgia.

5. The Jupiter Book of Ballads.

6. The Wind in the Willows by Kenneth Grahame.

7. John Masefield, O. M. Reads A Fox's Day.

8. The Yale Series of Recorded Poets: Robert Frost.

9. An Evening With Dylan Thomas.

10. Here Today.   Forty-five Living English Poets.

11. A Recorded Anthology of Scottish Verse.   Part One - Poems
      of Robert Burns.   Read by Harold Weightman.

12. Poems by W. B. Yeats, spoken according to his own directions.

13. Lawrence Durrell Reading from "Grecian Echoes," "Bitter
      Lemons," "Prospero's Cell" and "Reflections on a Marine
      Venus."

14. Proust, Remembrance of Things Past.   "Swann in Love."

15. Jean Genet, Readings by the Author and Cast.

16. Roddy McDowall Reads the Horror Stories of H. P. Lovecraft.

17. Jeeves, by P. G. Wodehouse.

18. Five British Sculptors Talk.

19. Road Recordings: Of Whaling and Shipwreck.

20. John F. Kennedy: A Self-Portrait.   The Gallant Warrior of
      the Thousand Days.

21. I Can Hear It Now, Vols. I and II.   Prepared by Edward R.
      Murrow and Fred W. Friendly.

22. Hark! The Years! A recorded scrapbook of famous personali-
      ties and historic events.

23. The School for Scandal.   Tennent Production.

24. Cyrano de Bergerac.

25. The Art of Ruth Draper, Vol. I.

26. Milton's Paradise Lost, read by Anthony Quayle.

27. Poetry of Lord Byron, read by Peter Orr.

28. Murder in the Cathedral, with Paul Scofield.

29. Blind Willie Johnson, his story told, annotated and documented by Samuel B. Charters.

30. A Knock at Midnight, a sermon by Dr. Martin Luther King, Jr.

31. The Incredible Year Produced by CBS News and "A Review of '68" from BBC.

32. The Hungarian Revolution Narrated by the Commander-in-Chief of the Freedomfighter Forces, Major General Bela K. Kiraly.

33. Miracles, Poems Written by Children. Collected by Richard Lewis. Read by Julie Harris and Roddy McDowall.

34. Children Talking. From the famous B.B.C. series of interviews with Harold Williamson.

35. Laurence Olivier in Othello.

36. The Jungle Books by Rudyard Kipling, Read by Christopher Casson and Eve Watkinson.

37. J. R. R. Tolkien: Poems and Songs of Middle Earth.

38. Macbeth. Old Vic Company with Alec Guinness and Pamela Brown.

39. A Gathering of Great Poetry for Children. Edited by Richard Lewis.

40. Homer: The Iliad, Books 15-18; and Homer: The Odyssey, Books 9-12. Translated by Richard Lattimore. Read by Anthony Quayle.

Reference

1. Tassin, Algernon, The Oral Study of Literature, (Crofts, New York, 1947) Introduction.

Chapter II

Documentaries, Lectures, Interviews and Speeches

Early Recordings

In the late 1880's Thomas Edison commissioned Colonel
George E. Gouraud to record living personalities abroad with the
new phonograph.   The retired army officer was to get on record the
voices of such dignitaries as Queen Victoria, Pope Leo XIII and Alfred Lord Tennyson.   Some of these recordings can still be heard.
That of Alfred Lord Tennyson caught the poet recording "The Charge
of the Light Brigade" but not too seriously.   Much better are the
voices of Edwin Booth and the tiny wisp from Florence Nightingale.

Since that time, collectors and scholars in many fields have
moved fast to record people and sounds while they can be heard.
Stores of oral archives never before possible are being accumulated.
Some of this material, previously transmitted through radio and TV,
has been collected on cylinders and tapes and many of these await
the time and skill needed for distillation of the precious contents onto records.

Early in the business of recording famous personalities was
a boy scout, G. Robert Vincent, who in 1912 persuaded Teddy Roosevelt, then in the midst of his presidential campaign, to record
something.   The result is on Hark! The Years!, [1] the most competently executed commercial recording of this kind, giving a sampling of
events and personalities of the first sixty years of recording.

Expert in choice and length of selections, arrangement, musical fitness and the brief, non-obtrusive comment of Frederic March,
it is a good digest, in a nostalgic, sentimental, and romantic spirit,
of the available material.   "... Literally hundreds of old cylinders,
disc records, transcriptions and sound tracks were auditioned;
countless hours of research and selection, re-recording and filter-
ing, writing and editing went into its making."

18

It took a whole year of uninterrupted work for G. Robert
Vincent, whose "love for collecting the voices of famous personalities made this work possible." What was involved can be hinted at
in the description of how one item, the trumpet call at Balaklava,
on the opening selection of <u>Hark! The Years</u>!, was eventually salvaged. The record opens with the charge as it was sounded at
Balaklava on October 25, 1854. It was recorded, with the permission of the British Museum, on the trumpet used at Waterloo, by
the surviving trumpeter of the Balaklava charge, Kenneth Landfrey,
in London, August 2, 1890, through Colonel Gouraud, Thomas Edison's representative.

In 1935 Robert Vincent and a friend visited Walter H. Miller,
formerly director of the Edison Recording Division, at his home in
South Orange, New Jersey. In the cellar were many old wax cylinders including the one with the Balaklava trumpeter's call. With
this treasure in their possession they made their way back to New
York on the ferry and up to Vincent's work studio on Broadway.
By 7:30 p. m. work had begun and, with the help of a few more
friends who stayed through the night, the proper sapphire stylus was
ground and a filtered electrical duplication made on a disc. At
3:00 a. m. they heard the clear trumpet call. "We felt like sound
archeologists and celebrated the feat by going to an all-night drugstore for chocolate sodas."

After the trumpet charge, one hears the voice of Florence
Nightingale, in her seventies, feeble and compassionate in the loving
message: "God bless my old comrades of Balaklava and bring them
safe to shore." A late recording of Thomas Edison is heard:
"When I look around at the resources of the electrical field today, I
feel I would be glad to begin again as an electrician..."

Nat Shilkret, the famous conductor and composer, prepared
the musical score and conducted the orchestra for the many transitions on the record. There are, in addition to musical bits which
fit into the chronology, parts of recordings by Caruso, Lillian Russell and W. C. Handy containing many nostalgic memories for those
who lived then.

One hears Commander Robert E. Peary give his bleak de-

scription of the discovery of the North Pole in 1909. There is a
section of William Jennings Bryan's "Cross of Gold" speech and the
recording of Teddy Roosevelt secured when twelve-year-old Vincent
visited his friend at Oyster Bay with his phonograph equipment. He
asked for a message for his boy's club who were expectantly await-
ing the result of his trip back in New York. Roosevelt complied
with the wish: "... to see you boys act as good citizens in the same
way I'd expect any one of you to act in a football game..."

There are also the voices of Woodrow Wilson, distinguished
in speech and sentiment; Mahatma Gandhi, humbly declaring his belief in peace as he was led to prison; the tired young Charles Lind-
bergh; Calvin Coolidge, New Englander; the great opera star and hu-
manitarian, Madame Schumann-Heink; and the leader for women's
rights, Mrs. Carrie Chapman Catt.

The saga of G. Robert Vincent's early interest in recording
voices and a description of his work as founder and curator of The
National Voice Library at Michigan State University will be found in
the Appendix.

In 1924, when only musical records were commercially fea-
sible, Sylvia Beach of Shakespeare and Company had a recording of
a part of Ulysses made by James Joyce at H. M. V. in Paris at her
own expense. The passage from Aeolus in Ulysses "expressed
something he wanted said and preserved his own voice." Only thirty
copies were made and these were distributed to Joyce's family and
friends. One copy was placed in the Musée de la Parole in Paris.

Soon after this first effort, Miss Beach brought Joyce and
C. K. Ogden of the University of Cambridge together for the recording of about seven minutes of "Anna Livia Plurabelle" on the then
superior equipment at the studio of the Orthological Society in Cambridge. A kind of Rosetta Stone for future readers, this fragmen-
tary recording demonstrates Joyce's extraordinary vocal gifts.
Transcending what scholars may eventually say, it provides for every man a basis of judgment and an experience to be remembered
with awe akin to that recalled by those who "saw Nijinsky dance."
Through it, Joyce directly communicates his symphony of words.
The music of his spoken language has been captured here, albeit

briefly, beyond the expectation and experience of most men.

We hear Joyce's realization behind "... Throw your cobwebs from your eyes, woman, and spread your washing proper..." and once again in "Dear Dirty Dumpling..." And we wonder at the magic which can so imperceptibly open another world in the onsweeping pattern of the last section, "I can't hear with the waters of... Tell me, tell me..."

This fragment is on the closing section of a recording of the Meeting of the James Joyce Society at the Gotham Book Mart, New York City, on October 23, 1951,[2] where the program consisted of comments and reminiscences by Joyce scholars and friends (Joseph Campbell, Padraic Colum, Dr. Schwartz) and the reverential playing of this short moment of the master's voice. (A fuller description of the evolution of Joyce recordings is to be found in Shakespeare and Company by Sylvia Beach.)

Sounds of the Times. First Part of the Century

Gouraud, Vincent, and Sylvia Beach had enterprising and courageous followers. England Before the First Great War,[3] a recent compilation from old records by H. P. Court of Toronto "is an attempt to convey some of the atmosphere in England during the reign of Edward VII." Background noises make for periods of uncomfortable listening but anyone willing to take these in stride will hear speeches made in 1909 by Asquith, Lloyd George and Winston Churchill. Also to be heard, but briefly, are the voices of General Booth, Cardinal Bourne, Josiah Wedgewood, Robert Baden-Powell and Henry Morton Stanley. Most interesting and satisfying is Sir Ernest Shackleton's description of the dash for the South Pole in 1909. He had come within ninety miles of success at that time and gratefully names each of the men who took part in the expedition.

Several bits from the theatre are also heard. Little Tich and Marie Lloyd sing. The latter does her famous "Woman's Opinion of Man." Especially valuable is the impersonation by Bransby Williams of Irving doing the Dream Scene from The Bells. H. P. Court writes in accompanying notes: "There is no listenable record available of the greatest of the late Victorian actors, Sir Henry Irv-

ing.   Perhaps the nearest we can come is this record of Bransby
Williams..."   (More information about Bransby Williams and the
recordings he made is contained in the Appendix.)

The Russian Revolution, [4] one of the C. B. S. Legacy Collection, has brought together a number of eye-witnesses of the 1917
events who, at their own request, remain unidentified.   They recall
such matters as the workers' unrest, starvation and revolt.   There
are also songs, announcements, the voice of Lenin with an accompanying translation, and voices of other politicians as well as foreign observers.   Among these last were Sir Bruce Lockhart and
Professor W. Lyon Blease in transcriptions from their reports on
the B. B. C.   It is a dimensional experience giving the feel of the times
and of suffering by those who did not die.

The Russian Revolution sampling gives some idea of the high
quality of the C. B. S. Legacy series.   Among other documentary
titles are The Bad Men, The Irish Revolution and The Greatness of
Israel.

Volume I of Edward R. Murrow: A Reporter Remembers, [5]
dealing with the years 1934-48, contains a stirring report of the
Blitz, recorded in a bomber over Berlin.   Murrow safely returned
to file, along with his own report, those of two other reporters
whose bombers did not return.   The record was originally issued
alone but is now available only through the three-record album,
Old Time Radio, put out by Columbia Records.

Edward R. Murrow: A Reporter Remembers, [6] Vol. II covers
the years 1948-61.   It is made up of excerpts from his broadcasts
from 1948 to the close of his career with C. B. S. News when he was
appointed head of the United States Information Agency by the late
President Kennedy.   The excerpts represent such varied facets of
his reporting talent as the Berlin Blockade, Salk Vaccine and the
Summation Broadcast on Senator Joseph R. McCarthy.   They illustrate well the historical perspective and informed background from
which he spoke.

A chronicle of the Second World War and of the years following and preceding it is told in the sounds and voices of the men who
made the history on the I Can Hear It Now [7] series prepared by Mur-

row and Fred Friendly. Typical of what was involved in the undertaking is a description of the preparation of Volume I, 1933-45, for
which the editors "... spent the better part of two years listening to
more than five hundred hours of old broadcasts. More than one
hundred hours were transferred onto magnetic tape and it was from
these that the forty-five minutes of I Can Hear It Now were dis-
tilled." The fruits of their labors were released on November 7,
1949.

　　　　The material on these records is selected and arranged with
a minimum of transitional narrative to tie the parts together. There
is great craft in this achievement. The events of an era are now
preserved on fine recordings which are more vivid than most printed
page accounts could be.

　　　　Years of broadcasting major events of the world in which
they lived brought to Edward R. Murrow and Fred W. Friendly a
unique sense of the form and pressure of the times. They were in
a position to make a selective compilation from the oral records of
the period. That they found the energy says much for their dedication, and the resulting albums are a monument to their vision and
sense of responsibility to history.

　　　　From the rich B. B. C. store of events and voices which have
made history comes the record, The Sounds of Time, [8] first issued
in November, 1949. "... Months of patient labor reduced the amount
of potential material to nearly two hundred hours of recordings. The
task of distilling less than forty-five minutes of indispensable sound
... occupied further months of painstaking selection and timing... "
Written by Frederic Mullally, the samplings are brief but varied.
Sometimes one wishes for more than one or two sentences, e. g. ,
from such speakers as King George V, Mussolini, Hitler, and Tommy Handley.

　　　　The great bells of St. Paul's are heard as well as a nightingale in a Surrey wood and a Cockney taxi driver. The absorbing
character of the material may be guessed at from some of the major headings: "The giant airship Hindenburg bursts into flames at
Lakehurst, May 6, 1937" (The cataclysmic effect of this catastrophe
on the broadcaster is also heard on the I Can Hear It Now series);

"King Edward VIII abdicates for 'The Woman I Love.'"; "J. B. Priestley broadcasts his famous postscript to the epic of Dunkirk"; "A liberated victim of a Nazi concentration camp meets his mother"; "General 'Ike' Eisenhower becomes a Freeman of the City of London and addresses fellow citizens from the mansion house steps."

On Europe Since the War: The Story of Ten Years of European Cooperation, [9] narrator Lord Boothby introduces the recorded voices of Sir Winston Churchill, General George Marshall, The Rt. Hon. Ernest Bevin, Dr. Eugen Gerstenmaier, M. André Philip, Lord Morrison of Lambeth, M. Finn Moe, Mr. Eamonn De Valera, Count Sforza, M. Robert Schumann, The Rt. Hon. Harold Macmillan, Sir David Maxwell-Fyfe (Viscount Kilmuir), M. Paul-Henri Spaak, Dr. Konrad Adenauer, Dr. Johan Willem Beyen, The Rt. Hon. Reginald Maudling, M. Jean Rey, Dr. Ludwig Erhard, The Rt. Hon. John Edwards, The Rt. Hon. Selwyn Lloyd. The range of this list suggests the scope of the record. Although most of the speeches are in English, some are in other languages. These sections are printed on the sleeve with their translations.

Report with Soundings [10] is a recording from down under of material originally presented in a radio broadcast to mark the centenary, in 1959, of the Province of Marlborough in New Zealand. Port Underwood, once the scene of huge whaling operations, was eventually to become country which grew a prize white clover where nothing would grow before. Descendants of the early settlers tell of the drive in 1847 of the first flock of sheep landed from Australia. Maori history and songs are interwoven. The record is interesting and indicative of much more which might have been salvaged than the M. C. of the original radio program had time for in his interviews. Because of the comparative newness of the settlers of New Zealand, this country's history would appear to be virgin territory for collecting spoken records of unusual significance.

Hitler's Inferno, [11] in words and music, is on two records. On Volume I, Adolf Hitler speaks in Rome, 1937; Joseph Paul Goebbels introduces Adolf Hitler, 1935; Adolf Hitler speaks in Vienna, 1939; and the defendants, Goering, Hess, von Ribbentrop and others plead "Not Guilty" at the Nuremberg War Crime Trial. Volume II

includes a German Youth Rally in Berlin, 1933; an address to a
"Worker Service Men" Munich rally, 1934; and an address to a Nazi
party Congress in Nuremberg in 1935.

One can read of the power of marching songs and rallies and
speeches as propaganda tools but listening to these two records
brings an overwhelming realization of that power. Speeches shouted
out to huge crowds, bands playing, stirring theme songs set to Wag-
nerian music, and waves of tremendous sounds as the audience responded are the sounds one hears on these records of terrible power.
It is a documentary with many implications.

Those interested in more voices might wish to hear Voices
of History, Spoken Arts SA 1011-12; The Little Flower, Fiorello
LaGuardia, Audio Fidelity AFLP 710; and from the growing list of
B. B. C. Radio Enterprises: British Prime Ministers Speaking;
Tribute to Ludwig Koch, which includes recordings of Von Hinden-
burg and Kaiser Wilhelm, c. 1914; As I Remember, recollections of
Baroness Asquith; speeches on Sir Malcolm Sargent's My Beloved
Promenades; and The Story of the Aeroplane.

Discourses Ltd. , another British company, has made available three B. B. C. Scrapbooks: 1914, 1940, and 1945. The same
company is also acting as distributor for several recent recordings
on the history of Wales produced by Wren Records of Wales. They
include not only histories of princes but also those of laboring men,
such as The Common Man in Stuart Wales. A catalogue request
to Wren Records will be rewarding to the specialist.

Harlem on My Mind[12] was used as a background for the controversial exhibit at New York's Metropolitan Museum of Art early
in 1969. Side 2 carries a Heritage Ensemble of Jazz. Side 1 is a
documentary of many voices speaking of early migrations from the
South, the conditions of escape (sometimes only by buying a return
ticket), the despair of relocation, revolt and new hope. Rarely does
one find impact so strong in such a short space of time. The record achieves what would be delayed and perhaps not so deeply sensed
in the slower process of reading. These are ungilded heroes,
people who lived a history.

The Coronation of Her Majesty Queen Elizabeth II,[13] recorded

by "His Master's Voice" in collaboration with the B. B. C., is the
official recording of the Coronation Ceremony of June 2, 1953. The
accompanying monograph written by the Rev. Edward C. Ratcliff,
Professor of Divinity at Cambridge University, gives the history and
meaning of the Coronation Service. There are also detailed notes
on the Coronation music, its history, the composers, directors and
performers. The introductory explanation of the Coronation Rite is
given by His Grace the Lord Archbishop of Canterbury, Dr. Fisher.
The commentators for B. B. C., Howard Marshall and John Snagge,
describe with unobtrusive brevity the action taking place.

It is an impressive recording with a Coronation Choir of over
four hundred singers drawn from all over the Commonwealth. Besides the organ of the Abbey there were many supporting instruments
the most exciting being the fanfares of massed trumpeters. The
words of the participants come through clearly as do such readings
as the epistle and gospel.

Another recording, The Coronation to Commemorate the
Crowning of Her Majesty Queen Elizabeth, [14] an Allegro Elite record
narrated by Marcus Morris, follows the main points of the ceremony. The words of the Archbishop of Canterbury, reenacted by
Martin Lewis, are dubbed. This record has captured the calls of
the excited crowds on the ride back to Buckingham Palace.

Behind the Lines, North Vietnam and the United States, with
Harrison E. Salisbury, [15] consists of selected eye-witness reports
on how the war in Vietnam looked from the other side. Harrison
E. Salisbury, journalist and editor of international standing, also
gives extemporaneous answers to questions about his experience and
what he believes to be the role and responsibility of a correspondent in a democratic society.

Rome and Canterbury [16] is a recording of the historic meeting between Pope Paul VI and Michael, Archbishop of Canterbury,
in 1966, at the Sistine Chapel of the Vatican. This was the first
meeting of highest ranking representatives of the Roman Catholic and
Anglican Churches in the four hundred years since the Reformation.
Greetings were exchanged with solemnity and warmth.

The spiritual significance of the meeting is discussed on the

second side by two Bishops, one from each of the communions represented.   They analyze the fruits of the meeting with understandable caution but hopefully.   The recording is one recently undertaken
by B. B. C. Radio Enterprises who are now making a number of
broadcasts of historic significance available on records.

Very Recent Documentaries

Following the model of early I Can Hear It Now albums,
"C. B. S. News looked back at the thousands of stories it reported
during 1968 and chose those which it felt best illustrated the unique
character of unexpectedness in this Unique Year." The Incredible
Year[17] is a production by Peter Wells and Joel Heller with Charles
Kuralt as narrator.   Side one includes Prologue and Pueblo; Jet;
Politics and the Martin Luther King Assassination; Dissent; the Pri-
maries and the Robert F. Kennedy Assassination.   Side two covers
the Conventions; the Campaign; Protest and the War; the World in
Turmoil; and Ring Around the Moon.

The many highlights of the year 1968 come back in the context of peoples and situations.   They were chosen as unforgettable
by those who covered the news.   It is difficult to listen to some of
them.   From Czechoslovakia we hear the cry, "Please inform...
please let the whole world know the truth."

A Review of "68," how the world seemed and sounded through
B. B. C. microphones in 1968, makes interesting comparative listening for the student of world affairs.   It is available through Discourses Ltd.

As this volume went to press, a new album came from the
record press: The Hungarian Revolution Narrated by the Commander-
in-Chief of the Freedom Fighter Forces, Major General Bela K.
Kiraly. [19]   Side one includes the Reform Movement; side two, From
Peaceful Reform to Revolution; side three, the Battle of Budapest;
side four, the Second Soviet Aggression.   Professor Kiraly narrates,
thirteen years later, what happened in Hungary in 1956, in a moving
account which will bring tears to the eyes of many a listener.   This
primary source material belongs where people may hear it and reflect on its lessons.   Well done, it is a great spoken document.

Lectures

The Distinguished Teachers Series was conceived, planned and directed by Arthur Luce Klein at the beginning of Spoken Arts. One of the early records, The Promise of Education, Robert M. Hutchins,[20] was made in 1956. President Hutchins' focus on the development of the intellectual powers of man as the essential purpose of education is still ammunition against those placing the major emphasis on interests, needs and adjustments.

Another of the Distinguished Teachers Series, Dr. Edward Teller: The Size and Nature of the Universe, The Theory of Relativity,[21] passes on the wit and engaging personality of the great physicist as he leads the listener to the point where he begins to believe that he might really be able to understand the theory of relativity. "... The reason for the difficulty of the theory is not because it is complicated. It is that it contradicts your previous ideas... not to understand relativity, not to understand science is something like not to understand music..."

A few years before his death three radio talks by Lord Birkett were processed on The Art of Advocacy.[22] "The Place of Advocacy in Our Society," as broadcast on May 28, 1961, is the first of these. It is a discourse on the nobility of the role of the advocate in a court of law. It establishes the place of the opinion of an advocate before the bar. Birkett closes the talk with winning advocacy for good speech and orderliness in the presentation of arguments.

Lord Birkett's reputation for after dinner speaking is supported by the two other talks on the record. One, "Cricketeers Everywhere," was delivered at the dinner in honor of Alec Bedser, at the Dorchester Hotel, London, September 22, 1960. The final talk on the record is one delivered at the Shakespeare Birthday Luncheon at Stratford-on-Avon, April 23, 1938.

Frank O'Connor's lecture on Irish Tradition[23] is preserved on the record by that name, and the text which is furnished with it gives not only poems and parts of the plays but also his complete remarks. The material ranges from poems of the golden age of early Irish medieval poetry to the plays of the modern Irish literary renaissance led by W. B. Yeats and the chief rebel, James Joyce.

There is a translation by O'Connor of a beautiful medieval poem: "The Scholar and The Cat," and Douglas Hyde's translation of a somewhat later one, "My Grief on the Sea." There are good dramatic readings from such plays as Yeats' On Bailie's Strand, Synge's Riders to the Sea and Playboy of the Western World, and Lady Gregory's The Gaol Gate. There are also passages from Joyce's Portrait of the Artist as a Young Man, Ulysses and Finnegans Wake. The passage from the first of these is read by O'Connor with spoken accommodation to Joyce's repetition of certain "death-associated" words toward which the listener's attention is directed in the lecture.

The usefulness of many recorded lectures is questionable, but this lecture by the late Frank O'Connor surely has value. It has, beyond what most lecturers could bring to the material, his sensitive insight and a justifiable native price in Irish tradition. It is a record by an authority, competent beyond scholarship, who was the contemporary of many of the major Irish writers and belonged to the Dublin tradition himself. It is skillful in selection and arrangement, and in its easy delivery of the material which is unusually at home with the music of spoken language. For anyone wanting more of the same, James Joyce by Frank O'Connor (Folkways #9834) will be of interest, as will Frank O'Connor Speaks (BBC Radio Enterprises, REGL 2M), with Frank O'Connor reading and talking about the art of writing.

The Story of Jazz, [24] narrated by Langston Hughes, tells of the beginnings of the blues with illustrations of the chief characteristics of jazz. Although brief, this is a most useful introduction to jazz and its place in the history of music. It is also titled The First Album of Jazz for Children.

The Glory of Negro History, [25] written and narrated by Langston Hughes, is a chronological narrative about the Negro in America. Using excerpts from writings and music, it provides excellent initial orientation for those new to Negro history. There is a warm rendering of Lawrence Dunbar's Little Brown Baby and a fiery declamation on freedom by Harriet Tubman. Some sections are spoken

by their authors, for example, Ralph Bunche on "The kind of world
we all long for." Moses Asch, founder of Folkways, was production director for the recording. The complete text accompanies the
record.

A recording which also reflects the American background is
Will Rogers Says. [26] America's favorite humorist and commonsense philosopher of the early 20th century talks about politics, the
cost of living, election campaigns, Mother's Day and himself. Excerpted from several of Will Rogers' broadcasts, the material is often so disappointingly short that it fails to communicate the relaxed
feeling one always had during a Will Rogers performance. The audience's delighted laughter is sometimes recorded and this testimony
from a few in-situation performances hints at the fun which longer
cuttings might have provided.

Good examples of Rogers' style of humor are the talks "On
God," "On Mother's Day," and "On the Pilgrims and Indians." In
this last, proud of his own Indian blood, he observes: "My ances-
tors didn't come over on the Mayflower - they met the boat." Then,
in logic as bold as Jonathan Swift's but without Swift's harsh bite,
he thinks aloud about the intruding settlers: "All they had to do to
get another hundred sixty acres was to shoot another Indian."

Invitation to Art by Brian O'Doherty, Research Fellow in
Education, The Museum of Fine Arts, Boston, [27] is another of the
very interesting Distinguished Teachers Series. The power and
strength of a reproduction of Michaelangelo's Christ at the Last
Judgment, Van Gogh's The Postman Roulin (pictured on the sleeve),
and Picasso's Guernica receive illuminative treatment in the discussion. The "introduction" encourages honest beginners who know
nothing about art to try to understand even abstract art. "It takes
courage and honesty to explore Modern Art just as it takes courage
and understanding to produce it."

Those interested in Ancient Civilization will welcome Edith
Hamilton: Echoes of Greece. [28] She is a most persuasive propo-
nent of classical studies on this record.

Two lectures were delivered expressly for recording before
students of the theatre in 1952 (two years before his death) by Ro-

bert Edmond Jones in the Lamont Library, Harvard College.   It
was Jones' sets for The Man Who Married A Dumb Wife in 1914
which began the modern revolution in American scene design.   The
lectures, processed as Robert Edmond Jones: Towards A New Theatre, [29] combine the confident experience of an old-timer with Jones'
hopes as he passes his dream on to a new generation.

In lecture #2, Jones presents his images of the theatre of
the future.   The photographic habit of mind is to be leavened by a
new awareness of the essential duality of man.   The drama of the
future will present life not as a simple melody but as a symphony
of the seen and unseen.

Ninety-nine copies of Edward Gordon Craig, Radio Talks, [30]
a three-record album with accompanying brochure, including eight
engravings for Hamlet reproduced here for the first time, were published for sale throughout the world by Discurio, London, on the occasion of Gordon Craig's ninetieth birthday, January 16, 1962.   By
now the album is a collector's item.   And by now there are also
enough ninetieth birthday recordings to form an exclusive club.

The album has seven of the fourteen talks Edward Gordon
Craig made for the British Broadcasting Corporation between 1951
and 1957.   He reminisces about trips to the theatre with his mother,
Ellen Terry, who "was trained for fully three years before she
learned how to speak properly for the stage."   Speaking of the training of an actor he says, "... eighteen months is not too much time
to train a man to learn to speak and walk properly for the stage."
The talks pour forth, as no printed page could, his idolization of
the "blazing genius" who taught him and it tells the joys of rehearsal in the presence of Ellen Terry and Henry Irving.   Irving would
go through a bit several times in different ways as he directed an
actor.   Craig describes one such rehearsal when as the Fool in
King Lear, Act Two, Irving "... feathered onto the stage... smiled
once and then blew out the smile."

A great moment in Craig's life is shared as he tells how
Salvini reacted to his stage designs: "These scenes liberate the
actor."   On this record, too, he recalls Isadora Duncan describing
"what it is to move."   On the third record a discussion of the

worth of masks in the theatre precedes the delightful "Celebrities I
Have Met," among them a bookloving bookseller. The series ends
with rollicking crackle over "How I played Hamlet in Salford, Lan-
cashire."

The B. B. C. producer says, aptly, in a quoted letter to
Craig: "of... many talks and talkers for the B. B. C. ... from none
did I learn so much or derive so much pleasure... the difference
between the spoken and written word, you took to instinctively."

Less Formal Talks and Interviews

The personal philosophies of ten living Americans with introductions by Edward R. Murrow are on This I Believe. [31] Four- to
five-minute statements by such notables as Ralph Bunche, Bernard
Baruch, and Helen Keller affirm their beliefs. Helen Keller's
speech, clarified in repetition by her companion, is a thought-pro-
ducing experience. Quotations from the writings of ten immortals,
from Socrates to Gandhi, Will Rogers and Marie Curie are read.
Madame Curie's is read by her daughter, and Gandhi's by a devoted
follower, S. Radhakrishnan.

Eleanor Roosevelt recalls her years with F. D. R. on My Husband and I. [32] It is spoken in a lower pitch than the high strained
one to which the public has become accustomed, and is a relaxing
listening experience as she meditatively recalls her early childhood,
the wedding, Campobello, polio, politics, nominations and victories,
White House life and the children, visits of dignitaries, World War
II and "the last time I saw Franklin Roosevelt."

The rebellious first lady who succeeded in running the White
House elevator herself also comments on the importance of not "taking yourself too seriously": "I don't think the wife of a President
should ever forget that it is he who is doing the important job and
that whatever she does must be a help to that job."

She remembers F. D. R. 's injunction to her after the slaying
of Mayor Cermack of Chicago while in his company: "... You cannot live with that on your mind all the time, otherwise life will be
impossible." This followed the statement from him "... Anyone who
does not mind getting caught can in spite of all the protection in the

world make an attempt on the President's life..."

Transition pauses and acoustic easing into new units keep a relaxed hold on the attention of the listener. Parts of the record-- we are not told which--were recorded only a few weeks before Mrs. Roosevelt's death in 1962. With deepened softness she closes the album: "The last time I remember seeing Franklin Roosevelt was in early April, 1945...I kissed him goodbye and wished him a restful holiday."

Human Rights[33] is an interview with Mrs. Eleanor Roosevelt on the United Nations' Declaration of Human Rights. The recording begins with Franklin Roosevelt's speech before Congress in 1941 on the Four Freedoms. The roll call vote on the Declaration of Human Rights is heard when it was passed eight years later. The remainder of the recording is taken up with the interview with Mrs. Eleanor Roosevelt, first Chairman of the United Nations Human Rights Commission. It is a record of some of the problems and difficulties which went into the drawing up of the final document. At the close Mrs. Roosevelt puts her finger on some of the leading problems and discusses the needs of the future. The accompanying booklet gives the complete text of the interview, the Universal Declaration of Human Rights and the draft of the International Covenants on Human Rights.

The Minority Party in America, Featuring an Interview with Norman Thomas[34] records Thomas early in 1960, then a man past 75 but still with the vocal power and distinction of a man half his age. He speaks of the educational and leavening force of the socialist party in the policitcal history of America. Giving credit to many others who were advocating similar reforms, he emphasizes the pioneering character of the socialist party's comprehensive program. There are also interesting sidelights on the election campaigns in which he participated, beginning in 1924 and including his six campaigns for the presidency of the United States. Mr. Thomas' political thought is put into capsule evaluations of F. D. R. , Upton Sinclair, Huey Long, Richard Nixon, H. S. Truman, Senator J. McCarthy, and D. D. Eisenhower. Using many modifying phrases his judgments appear to be very astute.

With regard to the career of politics he says: "Here I want to stand up a little for people who do go into politics and for their honesty... I do not think that I didn't accomplish anything because I wasn't elected. And I think I may have had more influence not being elected..."

I Can Hear It Now: David Ben Gurion[35] is an interview with Israel's Prime Minister, edited by Edward R. Murrow and Fred W. Friendly. The record is a reflection of the history and the religious and cultural aspirations of the Jewish people as expressed by David Ben Gurion. It is an excellent illustration of interview technique. The interview took place at the kibbutz of Sde Boker in the Negev Desert on February 3, 1956. Although unrehearsed, it effectively manages to give a large number of historic details, figures and interpretations of the development of modern Israel.

W. E. B. DuBois. A Recorded Autobiography[36] is the recording of the vexations and frustrations suffered by the Negro leader who eventually turned to Communism. This recording, in the distinguished speech of this Harvard graduate, was made in his eighty-third year.

Another kind of autobiography is found on the recorded testimony of Harry Howard, a psychopath. This is on the B. B. C. Radio Enterprises release, Born to Trouble.[37]

From the art front comes a recording of Frank Lloyd Wright on June 5, 1956, in New York City, shortly before his eighty-seventh birthday. Frank Lloyd Wright on Record,[38] with its economy and spinelike coherence is a model of knowing purposefulness in talk. Clarity might be expected of an architect but what really surprises is the mental agility and spontaneity of his delivery. One cannot but wish that it had also been possible to record the thinking aloud of the father of modern architecture, "Louis Sullivan, my old master."

Warren Forma, photographer's agent, editor and free-lance producer of documentaries, "... went to England in 1964 with a tape recorder and cameras to capture the ideas and thinking of five British sculptors." Each of the sculptors talks to us about what he seeks in his work, the way he goes about it, and the surroundings

in which he works, all without the seeming intermediation of an interviewer.   Mr. Forma explains: "I got to know each of the sculptors quite well and they were relaxed with me as I was with them
... In order to achieve the intimate quality which I seek in my work,
I worked entirely alone with each of the artists.   Reg Butler, in
fact, was so relaxed he did the entire interview lying on a day bed.
Henry Moore spoke comfortably on a soft couch in his den, and it
was much the same with the other three artists.   Some have visited
me in this country and I have visited them back in England."

       The result, Five British Sculptors Talk: Henry Moore, Bar-
bara Hepworth, Reg Butler, Kenneth Armitage, Lynn Chadwick,[39]
is a spoken art form of unusual naturalness.   The spoken words are
revelatory.   They follow the sculptors' designed way of thinking with
compression and economy of expression.   The listener is anyone in
the world who wishes to know and the givers are generous.

       Out of the experiences of his visit abroad, Warren Forma,
an artist himself, using various media in addition to the record, also produced an elegantly illustrated book published by Grossman,
Five British Sculptors Work and Talk; a documentary film distributed by Contemporary Films; and a traveling exhibit made up of
still photographs and recordings.   It is a project for the eyes and
ears of today.

       From a type of life not likely to be recorded again comes
the story of one of the last of the whalers out of New Bedford.   It
was about the time of his ninetieth birthday and the year before he
died that Captain Charles A. Chace told, on Road Recording III,[40]
something of the life of a whaleman as he knew it.   He first shipped
in 1879 as a cabin boy under his father as master.   Voyages for the
sperm whale took him as far off as Patagonia and along the coast of
Africa.   One voyage around the Cape took four years.

       Twice, as master himself, he was accompanied by his wife
and daughter.   Of his forty years in whaling that daughter could say
that as master "he lost only one man, who died at sea of beri beri,
and one who had to be left behind in port."

       The extraordinary experience of seeing the mating of the
whales which Captain Chace tells about on the record came to him

only once, to many whalers - never. In rhythms reminiscent of
W. B. Yeats, he recalls sighting one huge school of whales, and
then another of the cows lying still. With intense recall, approxi-
mating a song, he shares that moment in his long career as the
huge whales kept "... comin', comin', comin' ... comin' kept comin',
comin' ..."

Side two, by a younger man in his 50's, tells of sailing
closer to the New England coast in the early part of the century. It
is concerned with large scale fishing operations out of Gloucester
off the Grand Banks of Nova Scotia and Newfoundland, of prices at
the Fulton Fish Market, and of being wrecked in breakers fifteen
to twenty feet high on the shoals of Nantucket. The few sentences
about some dishonest practice towards whaling crews should be taken
as hearsay. According to the director of the New Bedford Whaling
Museum, they were of rare occurrence in the light of many existing records of paid accounts for crew members on whaling voyages.

Scattered bits of spoken documentary material occur on some
folksong albums. On The Elliots of Birtley, [41] a musical portrait in
song and talk of a Durham mining family, there is conversation a-
bout the terrible aftermath of an explosion, about the big strike in
1926, and about their lives: "... we used to work sixteen hours, no
overtime... Oh, yes, they were happy days for a 'tha' ..." Of
similar character is The Ritchie Family of Kentucky[42] on which
Jean Ritchie interviews her family and talks and sings with them of
their Kentucky lives.

On Blind Willie Johnson[43] his story is told, annotated and
documented by Samuel B. Charters. It is the fruit of the labors of
a musicologist who tried to find him in Texas. "Between 1927 and
1930 he (Willie Johnson) had recorded fifteen magnificent religious
records for Columbia Records."

Side 1 records the interviews with those who remembered
Blind Willie Johnson, together with the very poignant and moving account by his wife, Angeline Johnson, of their courtship and life together, and of the tragic death in 1949 of this major contributor to
jazz. They couldn't take care of him in the public hospital "because he was blind."

Side two contains a representative range of recordings by
Blind Willie Johnson. A small booklet on Blind Willie with notes on
the songs and recording data is an enriching accompaniment to this
record put out by Folkways. It is a most moving and impressive
recording.

The documentary has at last reached childhood where it
should have a long and fruitful life. The discoverer was Harold
Williamson, a B. B. C. radio interviewer who has a way of talking
with children as equals in completely spontaneous interviews with
them. Children Talking[44] is made up of interviews with children
in North Wales, Nottingham, London, Sunderland, Liverpool, North-
ern Ireland, etc. They answer questions all the way from "Where
do babies come from?" to questions about weddings, God and the
Bible, ambition, dreams, the world of grown-ups, etc. "Life in
Hospital" brings a comment on the food and one of the few observations from the narrator, that a child ought to be visited every day
by his parents. One child did not wish to belong to the Royal Family because they have blue blood and when they get cut they bleed to
death. Two wonderful gigglers discuss their state with more giggles
than words.

The interviewer's gift with children was finally discovered
by Michael Barton, Station Manager for B. B. C. Radio-Sheffield and
led to the partnership with Harold Williamson which produced a short
series of Children Talking. The record was released by arrangement with B. B. C. Radio Enterprises.

The record is more of an experience in listening than it is
entertainment. It is also of more than passing significance. It reflects the inner life of children from five to eleven years old, and
is greater than many record riches put together. Most people will
be so completely charmed by it that they will say, "Please sir,
more."

Public Speeches

There has been a large record output of public speeches.
On "Mr. President" from F. D. R. to Eisenhower,[45] the actual
voices of the presidents who made American history from 1933 to

1953 are heard.   Edited and narrated by James Fleming, N. B. C.
commentator, the interweaving of speeches by participants is lively
and instructive.

Side 1 of <u>Actual Speeches: Franklin D. Roosevelt and John</u>
<u>F. Kennedy</u>[46] gives the whole of the youngest President's Inaugural
Address with all the challenge and vocal reach of its outdoor delivery. It is in sharp contrast to the other side which contains
short excerpts from many of F. D. R. 's fireside chats.

The recording, <u>Adlai Stevenson: The Foreign Policy of the</u>
<u>United States</u>[47] also includes the introduction of Adlai Stevenson by
former Mayor Robert F. Wagner at a luncheon for the new U. S.
Ambassador to the U. N. on March 2, 1961. Stevenson spoke with
his usual clarity and humor concerning questions of independence and
intervention which must be faced by the U. N.   The end of the record gives some answers on American Vietnamese Policy in an interview with B. B. C. correspondent Thomas Barman shortly before
Stevenson died. There is the usual clear thinking of the man but no
humor.

Adlai Stevenson is also heard on <u>Adlai Stevenson Speaks,</u> [48]
edited and introduced by James Fleming.   These excerpts reflect the
philosophic bent, simplicity, flare for style and wit of the late
presidential candidate and U. N. representative. He decries "the vine-
yard of anxiety" and "legalized inferiority"; "There is no evil in the
atom, only in men's souls"; public servants often "serve you better
than your apathy and indifference deserve. "

Excerpts from the 1952 campaign speech before the American
Legion Convention in New York City and from the Salt Lake City
speech on "Tensions of the World Today" sparkle with his talent for
political debate.   A more extensive recording, which should include
the Harvard Commencement Address given shortly before his death,
would be of interest to many besides his political followers.   A
Columbia 2-record album, <u>Adlai Stevenson</u>, includes speeches and the
remembrance of friends.

What can be expected for the future of documentary recording is indicated in the recordings from the public life of the late
John F. Kennedy and the recording of the monumental memoirs and

speeches of Winston Churchill. A Winston Churchill Discography
(unpublished) prepared by Leonard Petts, the British discographer,
numbers close to two thousand items.

Three of the T. V. debates of the 1960 Presidential Campaign, September 26, October 7, and October 13, credited with turning the tide of that election, were put out in 1962. The material includes the answers to ten questions from a panel of reporters, longer speeches and rebuttals.

The reaction of everyone who witnessed the T. V. debates
rests in the context of his own decision-making at that time and in
that of the events which followed. For listeners in the future, the
recorded debates are a new form for political science study. The
picture of the handshakes of the two candidates on the outside of the
album, The Kennedy-Nixon Debates,[49] is the clue to the distinctive
vocal patterns of the two men: the Kennedy forward thrust and
Nixon's studied withholding.

Among speeches of the late President not widely known are
those made on his visit abroad in 1963. President Kennedy's European tour began with a visit to Germany. The album of his speech-
making on that occasion, June 23-26, 1963, Kennedy in Germany,[50]
narrated by Howard K. Smith, also records the waves of welcoming
cheers extended to him. In addition, there are six pages of photographs, five pages of the text of the speeches with Mr. Smith's
brief introductory descriptive notes, and a final two-page review of
the four days by W. Grant Parr of the Department of State.

J. F. K.'s warm response to the welcome accorded him as
President of the United States is expressed in his voice, as is the
strain of meeting the crowds during this tour. The now famous
speech at the City Hall in Berlin, his last day in Germany, was not
a prepared one. Its heartfelt spontaneity preceded his signing the
Golden Book of the city before the silent crowd as the freedom bell
tolled.

More folksy than official, the second side of President Kennedy in Ireland,[51] first published in 1964, carries his usual warmth
and wit and a "thank-you" for his four-day triumphal visit to Ireland. The first American President to visit Ireland during his term

of office, he fully realized the significance of a speech by him to
the "Joint Session of Dail Eireann and Seanad Eireann," June 28,
1963. It opens with a tribute to the Irish Brigade which fought at
Fredericksburg in 1862 and makes the presentation to Ireland of one
of the flags carried into that and other battles. Continuing in selective historic vein, the speech is a close woven structure of together-
ness and shared memories of national greatness. The speech has
charm and wit. With astute definition he threads his thought to the
peace-keeping role of small nations and especially of the one represented before him. In a final plea for no permanent enemies, he
renews his frequently expressed plea for the indivisibility of the
Children of God and a world of one human family.

By itself, the speech would have stood with the great orations
in Irish history. Its position as one of the last speeches in a tragic
calendar makes it a part of his last testament.

The tragedy of November 22, 1963, hovers over the many
records of President Kennedy which have come out since. Among
these the most representative is the Caedmon Memorial Album:
John F. Kennedy: A Self Portrait. The Gallant Warrior of the
Thousand Days. [52]

Most people will find the introduction on the record unnecessary. The album contains the whole of the inaugural address and
excerpts from many speeches drawn for the most part from the archives of N. B. C. News. Twenty-nine bands chronologically arranged bring back the late President's friendliness, his humor in
answering questions, and his habit of always speaking to his listeners, especially in the open air addresses.

The strong "defend" in the oath of office and the appeal for
support in the tired tense voice of November 29, 1962 and of October 26, 1963 tell the cost of the presidential office. The speech
on the Cuban crisis of October, 1962 is the strongest. The last
band is spoken by others in St. Matthew's Cathedral. The record
ends with salutes and taps.

That Was the Week That Was, John Fitzgerald Kennedy[53] is
the live B. B. C. television program transmitted November 23, 1963.
"When the news came through last night" focuses the words of the

panelists of the generally tough B. B. C. program the night after.
To Dame Sybil Thorndike came the summons to say the "amen" of
a shocked world: "May God give you good heart, little sister." A
few minutes later, the program from London closed. "It is a time
for private thoughts. Good night."

On two records produced by Goddard Lieberson, presented
with the illustrated book prepared by Atheneum Press, and with all
royalties donated to the John F. Kennedy Memorial Library, is
<u>John Fitzgerald Kennedy...As We Remember Him</u>.[54] This unique
biography, from childhood to the White House, is presented in the
written and spoken words of Rose Kennedy, Joseph P. Kennedy,
Jacqueline Bouvier Kennedy, Robert F. Kennedy, Eunice Kennedy
Shriver, his friends and close associates. Not all of these speak.
The foreword is by President Lyndon B. Johnson.

Memories, as they might have been expressed by those about
him as he moved in life, are shaped and cued together in the narrative written and spoken by Charles Kuralt. The gentle picture un-
folds at times without interruption for introduction of speakers, often
quietly named from the background as if to say, "Flow gently, sweet
Afton, disturb not his dreams."

The Duke of Wellington* and William Gladstone were accorded
state funerals. So also was Sir Winston Churchill. The night he
died the lights of Piccadilly Circus were unlit as they were during
World War II when he inspired the nation to fight on and win.

Of single Churchill records, the best is the pioneering one,
authorized by Sir Winston himself, released November 7, 1949 by
Columbia Masterworks on <u>I Can Hear It Now: Winston Churchill</u>.[55]
Edited by Edward R. Murrow and Fred W. Friendly, it includes por-
tions of the most important speeches with very little transitional narrative.

The recording is a compression of live oratory which conveys
the crises of the years, especially those of the war, and his determination and belief, even during the darkest times, in the eventual
outcome. It is a statement of courage, "Do not despair...," which

---

*One very old record gives an eye-witness account of his funeral.

seems to represent not one man but the people from whom the man
received it.   We hear the original speaker of such famous phrases
as "owed so much to so few," "their finest hour," and "blood, tears,
toil, and sweat."   An accompanying index of the first words of the
speeches, in the order in which they are heard, keeps them in context.   It is a record to return to.

About the time of his death, among the many released, were
a number of Churchill records with different approaches.   The first,
The Voice of Winston Churchill, [56] carries several items taken from
the war period section of the Decca twelve-record album.   A presentation of the successive steps toward final victory, it keeps to that
thematic thread.   The last band has the voice of President Kennedy
proclaiming Winston Churchill an honorary citizen of the United
States.   The weakness of the record is the use of too much connecting and background music; the cold facts of heroic valor are somewhat blurred by the patriotic musical comment.

Another memorial record, Winston Churchill--The Memory
of a Great Man, [57] is a short narrative of Churchill's life; early
education, military service, marriage, final career and destiny.
The material, written by William Alan Bales, N. B. C. newsman, and
narrated by N. B. C. news correspondent Chet Huntley, is well handled in the juxtaposition of passages.   A band near the close of the
record contains Churchill's speech on the correct use of the English
language.

Churchill, The Legend, The Man, His Great Speeches, His
Life, His Death, [58] has a commentary and reminiscences by James
Roosevelt, the son of the late President.   These last give the record a special historic value which one wishes had not been marred
by many noisy musical effects.

A Winston Churchill recording was prepared for the August
1965 issue of the National Geographic Magazine:

> The phonograph record opposite (pages 198 A-B) marks a
> publishing milestone; with it National Geographic now brings
> you the magnificent words of Winston Churchill. . . against
> the stirring background of his own funeral. . . The 4, 650, 000
> records distributed with this issue of the Geographic
> stand as a technical triumph in preserving high quality
> sound on durable vinyl flexible enough to bind into the

> magazine... This record... completes a truly three-dimen-
> sional portrait of Sir Winston Churchill...

Among the tributes accorded him towards the end of his life
was the publication, on his ninetieth birthday, November 30, 1964,
of the English Decca album on twenty-four sides: Winston Churchill: His Memoirs and His Speeches 1918 to 1945. [59] An extensive
recording of his thought and key speeches before and through the
war years, it is an historic spoken record of a kind never before
possible.   The first sides, mostly readings from his Memoirs of
the Second World War, were recorded by Mr. Churchill at his home
between 1948-49.   A passage on the 1918 Armistice, from his work
on The World Crisis, starts a stream of brooding prophecies, derived from his knowledge of what was happening across the Rhine,
which continued to pour from his pen and to thunder through his foreboding oratory.   The vigor of these memories pervades the beginning of the reading, but as he continues, the incapacitated seventy-
five year old man becomes labored in his reading.   Then, suddenly,
at the end of side five, in most intense recall, he speaks of "the
most terrible night" in his life, following the resignation of Anthony
Eden from the Foreign Office in February, 1938: "Sleep deserted
me." Not very long after, he speaks of being called to the Prime
Ministry and the first air raid with but one fourth of an hour's notice.   This was the beginning of events he describes in the words:
"I felt as if I was walking with destiny."

That destiny of leadership moves through the speeches and
broadcasts which are taken from radio transcriptions and introduced
with tightly worded non-intrusive briefings.   There is praise for the
Polish underground, the British pilots, the men who dropped with
fatigue at their lathes, and there is the continual spur: "This is the
time for everyone to stand together and hold firm... especially the
fire brigade." Following the radio speech, September 11, 1940, on
"The Crux of the Whole War," one crisis after another is met with
the steel of his undaunted courage.   "I expect the Battle of Britain is
about to begin." Henry V at Harfleur comes to mind as the wartime leader, not once but again and again, rallies support: before
the cheering crowd in Hyde Park, "London will not flinch!"; and in

world broadcasts such as the appeal on February 9, 1941, to "give
us the tools."

Some speeches bear scars of fatigue and in their mechanical
jerky rhythm the signs of what may have been prepared for the over-
burdened leader without time to make the speech his own. That
quality, also fatiguing to the listener, appears in several of the later
speeches. There is a very clear break from this monotony in the
midst of the speech to the United States Congress in Washington,
May 19, 1943. After the enthusiastic applause following his proud
observation that "our partnership has not done so badly," the old
fire returns, sparked first by the audience's reaction and then by his
outburst of deep gratitude: "I am proud that you have found us good
allies."

The October 28, 1943 speech on "Rebuilding the House of
Commons" is an illustration of Mr. Churchill's talent for succinct
analysis. The last side closes with the simple but dramatic May 8,
1945 broadcasts on Germany's unconditional surrender.

This album is a lesson of the undaunted last-ditch courage of
a people led by a man nourished by the lessons of history. In the
words of Arthur Bryant, who in the thirty-eight page brochure for
the album writes the appraisal of Churchill: "Britain... had as leader the man who of all others was fitted, as though by Providence,
for such a situation..." Ten hours of listening to this album vitalizes history in a way never before possible. But it must be said
that the listening throughout much of the memoirs is fatiguing because of Churchill's illness at the time of their recording. These
are better in print.

Abba Eban's Address Before United Nations Security Council,
June 6, 1967[60] also vitalizes history: "I have just come from Jeru-
salem to tell the Security Council that Israel, by its independent effort and sacrifice, has passed from serious danger to successful resistance..."

A second speech on the Middle East Crisis is to be found on
Abba Eban, Address Before United Nations General Assembly, June
19, 1967.[61] The speeches are delivered with vigor and cold logic
by the distinguished scholar, sometimes characterized as Israel's

golden-tongued foreign minister but, from these speeches, perhaps
better characterized as cold steel.

Up Ye Mighty Race [62] is a memorial to Marcus Garvey
with narration by the late Mrs. Amy Ashwood Garvey, first wife of
the co-founder of UNIA and the Marcus Garvey Foundation. Thelma
Massy is the vocalist. On one side Mrs. Garvey, with histrionic
effect, delivers the eulogy of the Negro leader. It is as though she
was speaking out of doors.

Malcolm X, His Wit and Wisdom [63] was excerpted from
speeches before very responsive audiences who were clearly in accord with the straight-from-the-shoulder hitting of the black leader:
"...I don't see an American dream, I see an American nightmare...
People who tell our people to be non-violent are almost agents of
Ku Klux Klan...we're anti-exploitation, we're anti-degradation, we're
anti-oppression, and if the white man doesn't want us to be anti-him
let him stop oppressing and exploiting and degrading us."

We Shall Overcome: The March on Washington, August 28,
1965 [64] is the authorized recording of the famous speech by Dr. Martin Luther King, Jr. One feels and at times hears the impact which
the speech must have had on the thousands gathered for that occasion in the shadow of the Lincoln Memorial in Washington. Also on
the record are messages by representatives from many groups:
Rabbi Joachim Prinz, Whitney M. Young, John L. Lewis, Roy Wilkins, Walter Reuther, together with Marian Anderson and others
from the entertainment world. The record is well planned and very
moving.

Another excellently planned recording is The Rev. Dr. Martin Luther King, Jr. in Search of Freedom. [65] Side one opens with
an excerpt from his speech in Memphis the day before he died:
"Well, I don't know what will happen...I've been to the mountain top
and I don't mind--like anybody I would like to live..." Side one also details his philosophy of nonviolence, his commitment to it and
to the national priority of social justice.

The recording makes good use of the possibilities through
stereo for capturing the audience's reactions. These are remarkable
on side two where Dr. King tells of his entrance into the civil rights

movement. This side also gives the eulogy he requested at his funeral. The side closes with a part of that powerful oration of modern times, "I Have a Dream."

There is an impact from this record. For some it will be an introduction to Dr. King and his beliefs and for others it will recall experiences of the civil rights movement to be relived. For content and efficiency in arrangement it is the best of the Dr. King records so far.

A Knock at Midnight[66] is a sermon by Dr. Martin Luther King, Jr., recorded as it was delivered at Mt. Zion Baptist Church, Cincinnati, Ohio, with occasional quiet responses from the congregation: "Oh yes," "Ah," "Yeah," "I know." These grew imperceptibly as the congregation warmed to the finishing paragraphs. At this point in the sermon Dr. King repeated, several times, "I feel discouraged." Each time was different in its expression and object: "I feel discouraged having to live every day under the threat of death."

But repetition was only one of the skills used in this sermon as it unfolded. King's belief in the underlying theme--persistence and prayer--and the carefully chosen supportive arguments and illustrations make this one of the great sermons of our time.

Recordings Discussed

1. Hark! The Years. A recorded scrapbook of famous personalities and historic events from two centuries, narrated by Frederic March, musical score by Nathaniel Shilkrit. Capitol (1-12") 2334.

2. Meeting of the James Joyce Society at the Gotham Book Mart, New York City, on October 23, 1951. Folkways (1-12") F19594. The original Orthological Society pressing, Cc17594-5, 78 RPM, was made by the Gramophone Co., Ltd., Hayes, Middlesex, England.

3. England Before the First Great War. Rococo (1-12") 4001.

4. The Russian Revolution. C. B. S. Legacy Collection (1-12") 32-A5-0005-1.

5. Edward R. Murrow, A Reporter Remembers. Vol. I, 1934-

    1948. Now issued as part of album <u>Old Time Radio,</u> Columbia (3-12")

6. <u>Edward R. Murrow, A Reporter Remembers.</u> Vol. II, 1948-1961. Columbia (2-12") 02L400.

7. <u>I Can Hear It Now.</u> Prepared by Edward R. Murrow and Fred W. Friendly. Columbia (2-12") ML 4095, 4261. Vol. I, 4095, 1933-1945; Vol. II, 4261, 1945-1949.

8. <u>The Sounds of Time 1934-1949.</u> C. B. S. Records (1-12") MG 20021. First issued in Nov. 1949 as Oriole St. 2001-5, 78 RPM. Reissued in March 1958 on L. P. as Oriole MG 20021 and later transferred to C. B. S. Oriole.

9. <u>Europe Since the War; The Story of Ten Years of European Co-operation.</u> Argo (1-12") RG 198.

10. <u>Report With Soundings.</u> A program prepared in 1959 to mark the centenary of the province of Marlborough in New Zealand. H. M. V. (1-12") MCLP 6130.

11. <u>Hitler's Inferno,</u> in words and music. Vol. I, 1932-1945. Audio Rarities (1-12") 2445. Vol. II, Audio Rarities (1-12") 2450.

12. <u>Harlem on My Mind.</u> A history in voices and music. Produced by Action Theatre in conjunction with the Metropolitan Museum of Art. Action Theatre (1-12") Action Theatre, Inc., 250 W. 57th St. , N. Y. C. 10019.

13. <u>The Coronation of Her Majesty Queen Elizabeth.</u> Recorded by "His Master's Voice" in collaboration with the B. B. C. The Official Recording of the Coronation Ceremony. His Master's Voice (3-12") ALP 1056, 7, 8.

14. <u>The Coronation to Commemorate the Crowning of Her Majesty Queen Elizabeth.</u> Allegro Elite (1-12") 3084.

15. <u>Behind the Lines; North Vietnam and the United States, with Harrison E. Salisbury.</u> C. M. S. (1-12") 104.

16. <u>Rome and Canterbury.</u> March 23, 1966. A B. B. C. Radio Enterprise, Mercer (1-12") Mer. 40A. The Mercer Press, Cork, Ireland.

17. <u>The Incredible Year, 1968.</u> A C. B. S. News production by Peter Wells and Joel Heller with Charles Kuralt as narrator. C. B. S. News (1-12") XSV 144898.

18. <u>A Review of '68.</u> How the world seemed and sounded through B. B. C. Radio Enterprises (1-12") RE 13 37 M.

19. The Hungarian Revolution. Narrated by the Commander-in-
    Chief of the Freedom Fighter Forces, Major General Bela
    R. Kiraly. H. Roach (1-12") Thr 1-4. H. Roach, Box
    4162, Grand Central P. O. Station, New York, N. Y. 10017.

20. The Promise of Education, Robert M. Hutchins. President,
    The Fund for the Republic. Former President, University of
    Chicago. Spoken Arts (1-12") SA 714.

21. Dr. Edward Teller. The Size and Nature of the Universe. The
    Theory of Relativity. Spoken Arts (1-12") 735.

22. The Art of Advocacy: Lord Birkett. Decca (1-12") LXT 6032.

23. Irish Tradition by Frank O'Connor. Folkways (1-12") FA 2316.

24. The Story of Jazz. Narrated by Langston Hughes. Folkways
    (1-12") FC 7312.

25. The Glory of Negro History. Written and narrated by Langston
    Hughes. Folkways (1-12") FC 7752.

26. Will Rogers Says. Columbia (1-12") ML 4604.

27. Invitation to Art by Brian O'Doherty. Research Fellow in Edu-
    cation. The Museum of Fine Arts, Boston. Spoken Arts
    (1-12") 763.

28. Edith Hamilton: Echoes of Greece. Spoken Arts (1-12").

29. Robert Edmond Jones: Towards a New Theatre. In Memoriam
    REJ, 1955. Vocarium (2-12") Vd. 1002. F. C. Packard,
    Jr., RFD #2, Brunswick, Maine.

30. Edward Gordon Craig. Radio Talks. Also extracts from a di-
    ary and some woodcuts. O. P. Discurio (3-12") EGC 1-3.
    Discuio, 9 Shepherd St., Shepherd Market, London W. 1,
    England.

31. This I Believe. Columbia (2-12") SL 192.

32. My Husband and I. Eleanor Roosevelt Recalls Her Years with
    F. D. R. Columbia (2-12") O2L314.

33. Human Rights. A documentary on the United Nations' Declara-
    tion of Human Rights featuring an interview with Mrs. Elea-
    nor Roosevelt. Written and produced by Howard Langer.
    Folkways (1-12") FH5524.

34. The Minority Party in America. Featuring an Interview with
    Norman Thomas. Produced by Howard Langer. A text ac-
    companies the record which is an edited version. Folkways
    (1-12") FH5512.

35. I Can Hear It Now: David Ben Gurion. An interview with
    Israel's late Prime Minister, edited by Edward R. Murrow
    and Fred W. Friendly. Columbia (1-12") ML5109.

36. W. E. B. DuBois. A Recorded Autobiography. Folkways (1-
    12") FH5511.

37. Born to Trouble. The recorded testimony of a psychopath.
    B. B. C. Radio Enterprises (1-12") REA 19M.

38. Frank Lloyd Wright on Record. Caedmon (1-12") TC1064.

39. Five British Sculptors Talk: Henry Moore, Barbara Hepworth,
    Reg Butler, Kenneth Armitage, Lynn Chadwick. Caedmon
    (1-12") TC1181.

40. Road Recordings, American Storyteller. Vol. III: Of Whaling
    and Shipwreck. Road Recordings (1-12") Vol. III 5009.
    Cook Laboratories, 101 Second St. , Stamford, Conn.

41. The Elliots of Birtley. Compiled and edited from material col-
    lected by Peggy Seeger and Ewan McColl. Folkways (1-12")
    FG3565

42. The Ritchie Family of Kentucky. Folkways (1-12") FA2316.

43. Blind Willie Johnson. His story told, annotated and documented
    by Samuel B. Charters. Folkways (1-12") FG3585.

44. Children Talking. From the famous B. B. C. series. EM (1-12").

45. "Mr. President" from F. D. R. to Eisenhower. RCA Victor
    (1-12") LM1753.

46. Actual Speeches; Franklin D. Roosevelt and John F. Kennedy.
    Library in Sound (1-12") U. S. P. I.

47. Adlai Stevenson: The Foreign Policy of the United States.
    Dover (1-12") 99406.

48. Adlai Stevenson Speaks. RCA Victor Red Seal Records (1-12")
    LM1769.

49. The Kennedy-Nixon Debates. Dover (4-12") Box K.

50. Kennedy in Germany. Narrated by Howard K. Smith. Philips
    (1-12") PCC 167-69.

51. President Kennedy in Ireland. EMI Ireland (1-12") (1)CLP 1732.

52. John F. Kennedy: A Self-Portrait. The Gallant Warrior of the
    Thousand Days. Caedmon (2-12") TC2021.

53. That Was the Week That Was, John Fitzgerald Kennedy. Decca
     (1-12"). D. 9116.

54. John Fitzgerald Kennedy... As We Remember Him.   A Columbia
     Heritage recording (1-12").

55. I Can Hear It Now: Winston Churchill.   Columbia (1-12") Vol.
     IV, ML5066.

56. The Voice of Winston Churchill.   London (1-12") RB100.

57. Winston Churchill.   The Memory of a Great Man.   An N. B. C.
     News Production.   RCA Victor (1-12") LM2723.

58. Churchill: The Legend, The Man, His Great Speeches, His
     Life, His Death.   With commentary and reminiscences by
     James Roosevelt.   Vee-Jay (1-12") VJ1130.

59. Winston Churchill: His Memoirs and His Speeches 1918 to
     1945.   London (12-12") XLI - 12.   Originally through English
     Decca WSC 1-12.

60. Abba Eban's Address Before United Nations Security Council,
     June 6, 1967.   Spoken Arts (1-12") 986.

61. Abba Eban, Address Before United Nations General Assembly,
     June 19, 1967.   Vol. II.   Spoken Arts (2-12") 987-988.

62. Up Ye Mighty Race.   Memorial to Marcus Garvey by Mrs.
     Amy Ashwood Garvey.   Garvey (1-12") 101.   Garvey Records,
     P. O. 776, Morningside Station, N. Y. C. 10026.   Speech by
     Hon. Marcus Garvey is found on Coleman (1-12") 1929,
     Newark, N. J. O. P. 78 RPM.

63. Malcolm X, His Wit and Wisdom.   Laurie Records (1-12")
     SD797.   Laurie Records, 165 W. 46th St. , N. Y. C. Malcolm
     X Talks to Young People.   Laurie Records (1-12") SD 795.

64. We Shall Overcome.   The March on Washington, August 28,
     1965.   Authorized recording produced by the Council for
     United Civil Rights Leadership (1-12") UCR 1A-1B.

65. The Rev. Dr. Martin Luther King, Jr. in Search of Freedom.
     Mercury (1-12") SR61170.

66. A Knock at Midnight.   A Sermon by Dr. Martin Luther King,
     Jr.   Creed (1-12") 3008.   Distributed by Nashboro Records.
     Nashville, Tenn.   Perhaps now through the Southern Chris-
     tian Leadership.

Chapter III
Authors' Readings

Listeners have the right to hope that when an author reads his own works he will convey what he meant in the way he meant it and that listening to such "informed" readings will bring them closer to the writer's work. But there are more uncommunicative, poorly read records by authors than by any other group. A striking example in this regard is the one known recording of Boris Pasternak[1] intoning his own Russian poems and others in French and German in the eccentric style of his time. The listener feels out of touch with the author.

In accommodating to the medium of recording, as with any new medium, preparation and practice are necessary. Without direction, writers, and especially those favorites of "recording for posterity," poets, frequently have come off poorly. One cannot place a neophyte before a microphone, tell him to relax and expect him to do much more than try to avoid making mistakes. What has often been recorded in the case of the poet has not been his poetry but the audible record of his struggle as a poor reader. In the struggle he usually tries to listen to it himself so as to be correct. In the process he sets up a cycle from mouth to ear which excludes other listeners. The person speaking for his own ear in this way adjusts the tone in terms of already present vibrations within his head, and produces a different sounding voice from the normal one of speech directed to another's ear. In addition, since the speaker to himself already knows the thought, meaningful speech to himself is not essential. What all too often reaches the snubbed listener's ear is a rise and fall of tone in mechanical accord with the rhythm of the speaker's breathing.

The self-addressed sing-song, with its regular downward intonation marking the end of the mechanical breath, if lugubrious

51

enough, is generally called "ministerial tone." Considered acceptable poetic chant by some, it is enemy number one to accurate accord with the often soaring wonder and true music of poetry. The
latter is exciting, whereas reading shared by the reader's own com-
pensating mind and ear and crippled by the dichotomy thus set up,
is boring, difficult to listen to, and even sleep-inducing. It is present on many of the early Library of Congress recordings and to a
degree on the T. S. Eliot records, where pedagogic watchfulness di-
vides the attention of the speech. Although Dylan Thomas has been
for many a source of illumination of the riches of spoken language,
his recording at times has a watchfulness over his own enthusiastic
elocution. Robert Frost is singularly free from self-listening. He
achieves excellent rapport with both material and audience and is a
delight to listen to. With careful listening one learns to discover
other poets and authors who have met the challenge of the medium.

Readings by Individual Poets

        In spite of occasional self-listening Dylan Thomas was a good
reader, an experienced one. He was the first poet to leave behind
an appreciable quantity of his poetry, prose writings and conversations on records, as well as readings of the works of other poets.
The "Dylan Thomas Discography" in the Journal of Recorded Sound
(Summer, 1961) filled fifteen pages.

        One of the freshest of his records, Dylan Thomas Reading, [2]
was the first one made by Caedmon in 1952. On it are the classic
"A Child's Christmas in Wales," and "Do Not Go Gentle Into That
Good Night." Four other Caedmon records by Thomas came out at
regular intervals until his death. More than ten years after the
first record in the Caedmon series, in November, 1963, the same
company issued, on two discs, Dylan Thomas Reading His Complete
Recorded Poetry. [3]

        There is no doubt that a great effort was made to include
"all of his own that Dylan recorded," for Caedmon, for educational
radio stations, for Library of Congress, for the B. B. C. etc. The
album provides a hearing of the full scope of Thomas readings, all
the way from masterpieces to the sententious performances of which

he was sometimes guilty.

He was capable of communicating strong, swift, vivid and
tender images in sound and movement.   Even some long sustained
"performances," especially evident on sides two and three, have
sections which completely escape the hypnotic dirge, for example,
"Do Not Go Gentle Into That Good Night" and "Ballad of the Long-
Legged Bait."   In the former is that most intense line, "Rage, rage
against the dying of the light..." and in the latter, a final crescendo
burst of which he was such a master.   "A Winter's Tale" also
breaks forth in powerfully realized words and sentences: "He wept,"
"May his hunger go howling," "Listen."

Side one spills over with illustrations of Thomas' capacity for
approaching a wide variety of material with the utmost accuracy
when he wanted to: with lusty relish in "If I Were Tickled by the
Rub of Love," tender compassion in "The Tombstone Told When She
Died," and intense closeness in "If My Head Hurt a Hair's Foot."

Changing aural images gloriously crowd side four in "Over
Sir John's Hill" and "The Poem on His Birthday."   Also on this side,
in the full pursuit of his reading art, he shapes the style and design
of "Lament" sharply in a comprehensive oral sharing of what he was
about: the changing touch and strength in each verse, the changing
rhythms, and the constant reason behind the repeated refrain: "the
old ramrod dying."   There is also a marvelously realized and terrible peek into "the soul from its foul mouse hole."   With vocal
sympathy the poet sings the elegy of his old ramrod.   In a way it is
his own.

On the Library of Congress recording of Robert Frost, [4] the
great American poet shows all the necessary gifts for translating
what he wrote into matching speech.   The "... speaking tone of voice,
somehow entangles in the words..." so that it would be difficult to
conceive of a better reader for his poetry.   When he says "He gives
his harness bells a shake," the spoken rhythm jerks and jiggles like
the little colt's harness.   This was rendered by Frost himself, a
reader with few gestures, with a happy accompanying jerking sweep
of the hand.

There are twenty-two poems on this record besides "Stopping

by Woods on a Snowy Evening," "The Witch of Coos," "An Old
Man's Winter Night," "Choose Something Like a Star," and "The
Gift Outright." In the phenomenal rendering of this last at the
Presidential Inaugural, the octogenarian so completely released to
the thunder of his poetic spirit that he sounded like a man of thirty-
five. No doubt, that unique reading will be available on a record at
some future time.

Such popular favorites as "Birches," "Mending Wall," and
"Death of the Hired Man," also well read, are to be found on some
other Frost records, notably Decca's Robert Frost Reads the Poems
of Robert Frost.[5] But the Library of Congress recording made in
1948 and a recording made at Yale in 1961, The Yale Series of Recorded Poets: Robert Frost,[6] have captured Frost at his best. They
make one glad that he lived when this was possible.

The recording made by Frost on May 18, 1961 at Yale was
before an obviously delighted audience of students and faculty. With
twinkling good humor and profundity the poet held them in the palm
of his hand. Frost and his college audience's reactions to the reading of twenty-five poems which span the years are caught perfectly.
There are poems never recorded before as well as one he refers to
as among his best: "Never Again Would Bird's Song Be the Same."
And there is "The Most Of It" too. His way with sound and rhythm
sings through lines, even becoming outright chant in "Desert Places."
The recording, made a year and a half before his death, was a magnificent last gift from the poet.

T. S. Eliot was recorded as early as 1931 through the pioneering project of Frederick Packard, Jr. at the Harvard Vocarium.
That early recording is not available but T. S. Eliot Reading His
Own Poems[7] for the Library of Congress was commercially processed early in the Library of Congress project to record living poets. In a typical reading, Eliot, like an orchestra maestro, con-
ducts the ear to significant movement, cadence, and recurring echo
in his poetry. Listening to the rhythm becomes an absorbing side
occupation for "A Game of Chess" and for the "Waste Land" motif
in "Ash Wednesday": "At the first turning of the second stair."
Throughout, the liturgical lines ring true. Swing is allowed in "New

Hampshire" and "Landscapes," and even a hopping rhythm in
"Sweeney Among the Nightingales."

    T. S. Eliot Reading Poems and Choruses[8] was made in London,
September, 1955.   The poems, all chosen by the poet, include:
"The Love Song of J. Alfred Prufrock," "Portrait of a Lady,"
"Preludes," "Mr. Eliot's Sunday Morning Service," "Ash Wednes-
day," "A Song for Simeon," "Marina," "Triumphal March from
Coriolan," "O Light Invisible from the Rock" and selections from
Murder In the Cathedral and The Family Reunion.

    These are the usual T. S. Eliot readings, careful of the pat-
terned form and language sound.   The tone for the most part turns
back on itself in a predictable downward cadence.   The habit is
lampooned in Dylan Thomas' reading of Henry Reed's "Mr. T. S.
Eliot's Sunday Evening Broadcast Postscript" on the Caedmon Dylan
Thomas IV.   The joy of "A Song for Simeon" breaks this gloomy
pattern as does the "Triumphal March of Coriolan" with its recur-
rent "stone" image.

    T. S. Eliot Reads His Four Quartets[9] is another recording in
which the reading shows too much guarding of vocal potential.   However, T. S. Eliot Reads Old Possum's Book of Practical Cats,[10]
one of his last records, tore through the ceiling to the sky.   In
"The Song of the Jellicoes," Eliot, on a spree with sounds and
rhymes, reads in the zestful spirit of W. S. Gilbert and Edward
Lear.   There is unprecedented gay humor in his sharing with us in
"Gus: The Theatre Cat," "Macavity: The Mystery Cat," and "The
Rum Tum Tugger."   Here at last is the delighted poet without spec-
tacles, outside his classroom as one wishes he had been recorded
before.

    Precious little of W. B. Yeats' reading has been preserved
because of the London bombings.   A small unit is to be heard on
The Poems of William Butler Yeats read by William Butler Yeats,
Siobhan McKenna and Micheal MacLiammoir.[11]   In spite of background noise, the ringing and at times incanting voice of Yeats, the
excerpts from talks and readings of his poetry between 1932 and
1937 are a treasure from early recording.   Lasting about fifteen
minutes, the material includes an extract from a talk on rhythm.

There are vigorous remarks about modern poetry and laudatory comments about Edith Sitwell's verse in the introduction to his reading of it.   Then follow readings from his own poetry with "The Lake Isle of Innisfree" done at two different times.   The second reading in 1934 has somewhat less emphasis upon incantation than the earlier one done in 1932.   It is concerned instead, as it should be, with memories.

W. H. Auden's tribute "In Memory of W. B. Yeats" on W. H. Auden Reading[12] is read with unusual release for this rigidly pedestrian reader.   "Five Lyrics" also unexpectedly sings out.   The poet's own brief summary notes on the formal structure of the poems are printed on the sleeve of the album.

Stephen Vincent Benét and Edwin Muir[13] were recorded at the Library of Congress, one in 1941 and the other in 1955, a short time before the death of each.   They are processed on the same record, one side carrying readings by Benét and the other those of Edwin Muir.   John Brown's Body (Book 7) is represented by the opening lines of the "Battle of Gettysburg."   "The Ballad of William Sycamore" (1790-1871) swings along in the poet's reading as a pioneer's proclamation, even when it says: "The eldest died at the Alamo, The youngest fell with Custer."   Side two contains a wide selection of Edwin Muir readings.   One of the best, and a gem in the reading, is "Horses," moving with taut control yet glorious ranging past such a line as: "And their great hulks were seraphim of gold."   The closing, "The Confirmation," is like a lover's seal upon the recording but in a Scots' way.

William Alfred Reading His Own Poems[14] was produced in a 200-record edition and is now out of print.   It is here noted because of its great lyric poetry and in the hope that it will be reissued at some future time.   It is a record singularly free from self-watched plodding, self-conscious discounting towards work-a-day speech, and protesting incantation.   It was made when the poet was twenty-eight, shortly after the writing of one of the poems recorded: "The Garden: To Archibald MacLeish."

The death of Atreus, the First Watchman's speech, and Clytemnestra's foreboding, all passages from the poet's free adapta-

tion of Agamemnon, have the narrative excitement, horror and foreboding of the writing.   There is fine speech precision when Aegis-
thus discovers that the man he had been sent to kill "... spoke pure
palace Greek ..."   And there is fitful movement in Clytemnestra's
"All night on shuttered streets, half-lit with stars."   The larklike
lyricism comes in "An Office of St. Francis of Assisi," one of the
long poems on the record.

The spontaneity and rare sharing of poetic personality of
The Poems of James Stephens Read by the Author[15] may have come
from his wide lecture experience with audiences, meeting their expectations and delightfully answering their questions.   "... First they
are not, and very suddenly there they are...," he says of poems.

The introductions to the poems he reads recall with whimsi-
cal, philosophic, and humorous touches something about how each
came into being.   "Simple to read, but not simple to write..." he
says of "Cadence."   Then he sings the poem.   And one hears the
last line, "See the mother running to her child..." change from a
song of nature into a quiet human song.

"Goat Paths" has the jerky movement of the goats' "... stare
and turn and bound."   "Main-deep" sings out the sounds as he
heard them, "... chill rushing, hush hushing, hush hushing..."

The recording has what one hopes for on poets' recordings:
realized insights and remarkable beauties.   Stephens' choice of
which poems to sing and which to read is the answer to moot questions about poetic chant.   The record can be enjoyed again and a-
gain.   It should be required listening for poets.

The combination of material and readers on Lynn Fontanne,
The White Cliffs of Dover, Edna St. Vincent Millay Poems[16] make
this 1941 recording exceptionally valuable today.   There is the fine
reading by Lynn Fontanne of Alice Duer Miller's verse narrative on
war and Edna St. Vincent Millay reciting at her best such mile-
stones in her career as "The Ballad of the Harp Weaver," "Recuerdo," and "Renaissance."   Although an early work, "Renaissance" is interestingly and rightly placed last.   It is the poem which
epitomizes the fiery release and dramatic power beneath much of
what was written later.

An Informal Hour with Dorothy Parker[17] is one of the best
author recordings. Dorothy Parker begins with her short story
"Horsie," a tight, illuminating piece of writing with a final twist.
Side two contains twenty-four of her short poems in an excellent
reading. When the time comes for rediscovering Dorothy Parker,
this record will play a role in locating her true niche. Conceived,
planned and directed by Arthur Luce Klein, the recording is a tribute to his pioneering acumen.

John Masefield can be heard on a number of records. One
concurs with relish in the comment by H. J. Usill of Argo on the
sleeve of John Masefield, O. M. Reads a Fox's Day: A Special
Adaptation of Reynard the Fox:[18] "... Masefield brings to this recording a special quality, a personal touch that no other reader
would have achieved." The poet even interrupts his tale to tell us:
"... when I had written to this point... I saw a fox crouched at the
pond's edge... from that time I had a deeper sympathy..." The
story is told with vivid recall by the author in his eighties. A
Fox's Day is a listening experience for anyone. On the other hand,
The Story of Ossian[19] read by Masefield is a monotonous, watched
attempt at bardlike reading.

Masefield sings his love for the sea, its men and ships, and
their service in the national life on John Masefield O. M. Reads the
Fortune of the Sea, The Wanderer's Image.[20] "... It was my fortune to be among ships with sailors. These have been much in my
memory and my work. ... I touch my country's mind... thinking of
these ships."

The recording, although occasionally indistinct, is a culminat-
ing success for the Masefield series directed by Harley J. Usill.
Here Masefield's love for the sea poured forth in a wide range of
excerpts from his poetry and spilled over to his own painting of a
sailing ship for the record sleeve.

A similar enjoyment awaits the listener to John Masefield
Reads "Seafever," "Cargoes," and Other Poems.[21] The sleeve,
with its wind, waves and seas of the "stately Spanish galleons," fit-
tingly predicts Masefield's spoken "wind's kick" and his "must" toward the sea. He is also that rare poet who has immediacy; he

hears and can incorporate immediate responses to sensual images
as he reads: "fire!" "the beetle droning," and the warning tone of
"I who was Pompey."

Ezra Pound Reading his Poetry[22] does not communicate easily on the first volume of this two-volume set. But the reading of
Cantos XLV, LI, LXXVI on volume two is alive and worth much time
in listening.

On _Carl Sandburg Reading Fog and Other Poems_,[23] Sandburg
reads in a flagwaving pattern, intrusive for those wishing to hear
the poetry. Only "Fog" escapes.

J. R. R. Tolkien: Poems, Songs of Middle Earth[24] can be a wonderful discovery of what poetry is for the bright older child. It will
of course delight scholars and students of Anglo-Saxon. Mostly
translations into lovely poetry, there are also a few short passages
in Elvish. With the exception of a few tightly mouthed lines, it is
a gay and vivid recording. "The Hoard" pours forth in riches so
ecstatically described one can only say with others that this experience is "something enchanting."

_Words for the Wind: Selections from the Poetry of Theodore
Roethke, Read by Theodore Roethke_[25] is an enthusiastically shared
reading by the poet. The material is grouped into Poems for Children, Love poems, Praise to the End, and Shorter Poems. They
illustrate the range of his experiments with rhythm, even to nursery
rhyme repetition and song. Like Dylan Thomas, the poet uses
sounds and rhythms with complete abandon to the needs of the material. Among the poems read are: "A Rouse for Stevens,"
"Praise to the End," "My Poppa's Waltz," "Reply to a Lady Editor," and the lovely "Elegy for Jane." This well prepared reading
of his representative works was recorded shortly before the poet's
death.

The Rubaiyat of Omar Khayyam[26] has the translation by Edward Fitzgerald on one side and the recent translation by Robert
Graves and Omar Ali-Shah on the other. The translation by Fitzgerald is read in alternating verses by Robert Speaight and Maxine
Audley. It is intelligent, easily following the form of the quatrains,
and distinguished in rendering the music of the lines. The read-

ers bring to the task their rich experience in reading poetry and the
result is a delight for devotees of the Rubaiyat.

At the end of side one the director, Peter Orr, has skillfully
fitted Omar Ali-Shah's spoken introduction to the translation prepared
by Robert Graves and Mr. Ali-Shah. For those who might like to
familiarize themselves with the poetic cadence, Mr. Ali-Shah also
reads verses 1 and 11 from the original of the manuscript of 1153
A. D. This manuscript, which had been presented to one of his an-
cestors by the Sultan, is the one used as the basis for the 1967
Graves, Ali-Shah translation. Robert Graves alone reads on side
two. He is a more metronomic reader than the two found on side
one, which sometimes makes it difficult for the listener to grasp the
meaning. But anyone familiar with Fitzgerald will find himself making comparisons between the two translations. Graves does give a
great moment in the reading of the last line of his translation. It
is too bad this talent was not exercised oftener.

Lolita and Poems Read by Vladimir Nabokov[27] has passages
from Part 2, Chapter 35 of Lolita on Side 1 and seven poems on
Side 2. The author's reading has the musical movement and design
of his writing. The bizarre surroundings are created, as is the
lunatic excitement which overtakes incitement when the two men con-
front each other. The readings of the poems, labored as they are,
stretch us towards Nabokov's discoveries about the loom of English
words which those born to the language are inclined to take for
granted. "The Ballad of Longwood Glen," "The Swift" and "The
Discovery," concerned with one of his lepidopterous discoveries, are
for those kindred spirits who also enjoy discovering.

On Antiworlds: The Poetry of Andrei Voznesensky,[28] poems
by Andrei Voznesensky are read in Russian by the poet and in English by his translators, W. H. Auden, Stanley Kunitz, William Jay
Smith, Richard Wilbur. Each poem is read in English by a translator, immediately followed by the poet's reading of the original.
Stanley Kunitz readings in English of "Goya" and "Fire in the Archi-
tectural Institute" come through well.

Listening to the poet one notices long pauses, which are not
heard in the readings of the translations, making one realize how

much this poet turns to silences to speak. One also hears the poet's daring to let what he has written grow, laying early fires for
eventual eruptions. The contrast between the fiery reading of the
originals by the poet and some of the tame translation reading on
this record pinpoints the need for more reading release by English-
speaking readers.

Two stories and ten poems are to be found on <u>Padraic Colum</u>
<u>Reading His Irish Tales and Poems.</u> [29] They sketch in simple form
what the Irish poet had to tell about Blarney Castle, the "Wiz and
the Earl," and the "Old Woman of the Roads." The listening experience is authentic for Irish folklore and fantasy.

e. e. cummings: <u>six nonlectures</u>[30] were given in lecture
periods by the poet alumnus in Sanders Theatre at Harvard, 1952-
53. The question, "Who as a writer, am I?" was answered impres-
sionistically on (1) I and my parents, (2) I and their son, (3) I and
discovery, (4) I and you is, (5) I and now and him, (6) I and am
and Santa Claus.

Usually, towards the end of a "nonlecture," Cummings read
poetry in the original from a wide range of poets: Sappho, Horace,
Dante and Goethe, as well as Shakespeare, Wordsworth and himself.
The selection of ideas and of poems is unexpected, yet one realizes
afterwards how they fit. Cummings' vocal way, an exaggerated slow
repetition of a little inflected pattern, is most difficult to listen to
for any length of time.

Another recent release also combines the Russian with a
translation: <u>Yevgeny Yevtushenko: Babi Yar and Other Poems Read</u>
<u>by the Author in Russian and in English by Alan Bates.</u> [31] Respond-
ing to the exaltation of Yevtushenko's reading, an enthusiastic audience's applause often breaks in on the recording. Yevtushenko
reads nine poems with characteristic joie de vivre. The dramatic
poems "Babi Yar" and "The Woman and The Sea" are vigorously assertive. But a poem like "The Woman Looks Into White Trees" just
as truly reflects the woman's delicate loveliness, gentle as the softly falling snow described in the poem.

A text in Russian and English accompanies the record. The
English version of the poems, read by Alan Bates, gives neither the

spirit nor the imagery of the originals. Indeed, the reading is an
illustration of a poorly spoken translation. Nor can the failure in
this case be attributed to the admittedly inadequate translation of the
poetry.

Readings by Several Poets

Pleasure Dome[32] by Lloyd Frankenberg, now out of print, is
an early listenable anthology of modern poetry read by the authors:
T. S. Eliot, Marianne Moore, e. e. cummings, William Carlos Williams, Ogden Nash, W. H. Auden, Dylan Thomas, and Elizabeth
Bishop.

The sleeve of Pleasure Dome gives the saga of the search in
the late nineteen forties for a way to bring about a collection of
readings by poets for commercial distribution. It is a milestone in
that history and a sensible effort to acquire a wider audience of listeners for the poetry of our time. The good selection and the brevity of the readings eliminate the danger of dullness. It is attractive
in the humor, as well as in the gloomy, jazzed section of T. S.
Eliot's "Wasteland," the wheeling rhythm of W. H. Auden's "Ballad,"
and the sight images of Elizabeth Bishop's "The Fish. "

In 1941 the Library of Congress began its recordings of living poets. An important release in this program is the anthology of
poets' readings, An Album of Modern Poetry, [33] with Oscar Williams
as editor. The forty-six poets chosen for inclusion will not satisfy
everyone, nor will all the selections of individual poems. In some
cases a much desired poet is missing, e. g. , Dylan Thomas, for
whose recording necessary permission was not granted. The readings by Robert Frost, Wallace Stevens, T. S. Eliot, Robert Lowell,
W. H. Auden, Edwin Muir, Allen Tate and Robert Graves are generally well shared with the listener. Richard Eberhart and e. e.
cummings, however, are discouragingly monotonous. The less well
known Roy Fuller produces a good reading of "Meditation. " Theodore Roethke's warmth and energy support three well chosen poems:
"Elegy for Jane," "I Knew a Woman" and "The Shimmer of Evil. "
The final line of the latter gives an interesting idea through the author's phrasing and pause: "There was no light; /There was no

light/ at all."

W. R. Rodgers' reading is characterized by its intellectual
clarity and its concentration on telling just what to "beware" in
"Directions to a Rebel":

>Who offers you his watertight word
>Backed by his wickerwork art...

Henry Reed's reading of "Naming of Parts" makes interesting
comparative listening with the reading of this poem by Dylan Thomas on the Caedmon <u>Dylan Thomas, IV.</u>

The <u>Caedmon Treasure of Modern Poets Reading Their Own</u>
<u>Poetry</u>[34] is carefully mined and programmed. "Some of the best of
the Twentieth Century is gathered here": a precious part of Yeats
himself, W. H. Auden in one of the best readings by him, "In Memory of W. B. Yeats," a distinguished Wallace Stevens thinking "Key
West" through quietly, Robert Frost swinging his thought from the
tops of trees, Elizabeth Bishop and Conrad Aiken, both in good form,
and a tired T. S. Eliot in "The Wasteland." There are also others,
some with and some without elocutionary heresies. A few of the
readers remain fixed in the pattern of childhood recitation or in stiff
poetic posture.

Mention has already been made of the Robert Frost recording in the <u>Yale Series of Recorded Poets.</u>[35] Among other good
readings in the series are those by Louis MacNeice, Marianne
Moore, Allen Tate, Robert Lowell, R. P. Blackmur and Dudley
Fitts. The series was an attempt by Lee Anderson to secure good
readings by poets. They are not evenly successful but there is com-
mendable conversational directness and sometimes dark whispering
in Robert Lowell's "Beyond the Alps" and "Memories of West Street
and Lepke." Louis MacNeice reads with exact accommodation to
rhythms and sounds in "Brandy Glass," "Bagpipe Music," and "Nuts
in May." There is also controlled sympathy and noble form in the
structured vistas of "The Death of a Cat."

Marianne Moore's oral gifts are not remarkable. But her
readings, it may be emphasized, have always communicated her
meaning through phrasing and rare urgency. On this Yale recording she has an easier rapport with the listener than heretofore.

Side two on this record is better in this respect than side one.   It
also caries her reading of "Pangolin."

Here Today,[36] poems by 45 contemporary authors, mostly
spoken by themselves, presents "a cross-section of present day
Britains." It was released by Juptier Recordings on two discs in
the spring of 1963, simultaneously with the book Here Today published by Hutchinson Educational, Ltd.   Spoken Arts has issued the
two records in America.   The recordings give an unsparing impression through poets' voices of these none too cheerful times.   It is
indeed a sociological document and one of the first of its kind among
poetry recordings.

The two records are a milestone for poets' recordings because for the first time a large group of poets has been recorded
with exceptional attention to their reading.   These poets, who have
been coached, compare favorably with a supporting group of stand-
in professional readers who take the absentee parts.   With no more
than three to four seconds between, each poem moves in smartly
and with successful clarity.

The director, V. C. Clinton-Baddeley, brought devotion and
professional competence to the direction: "One should be able to
hear the end of a line by the gentle emphasis which rightly belongs
to the last and the first words of a line..."; "Keep to the lines and
the sense will take care of itself." The readers follow that dictum,
ringing lines with sensitive rhythm and word value, especially the
last lines which so often clinch the sense.

The accomplishment on these records was the result of many
more than the number of studio rehearsals usually assigned for recordings.   At times there were as many as twelve or fifteen takes.
Such care paid off in Charles Causley's fervent reading of the first
poem, "Timothy Winters." Its last line heart crack ranks with the
mighty moments of the best on records.   Two other poems by this
Cornish school teacher, "My Friend Maloney" and the lovely "Nursery Rhyme of Innocence and Experience," are read with compassion
and insight yet with "no comment" artistic distance.

Another poet, Michell Raper, experienced B. B. C. broadcaster,
achieves the same level.   An extraordinary performance is that by

John Heath-Stubbs for "The History of the Flood." From the first hard "Bang, bang, bang," to the final harsher bangs, he leaves no doubt of his intent. Between rolls from side to side, the leisurely procession of the animals goes "two by two." There is the best humming line on record for: "A queen bee, a king bee."

Vernon Scannell's "First Fight" moves with vocal adroitness through six pages which recount the surface battle as well as the many levels of conflict within the boxer's mind. And the poet's reading makes eminently clear the reason for the change in line length at the beginning of the third verse. The hard battle for professionalism is won at last: in this case by both boxer and poet-reader.

Anthony Thwaite reads two poems. The sense of one of these, "Disturbances," is clinched in the last line with a lowered voice and strong stress: "An owl/calls/from a tree."

C. Day Lewis is in best reading form in "Sheep Dog Trials in Hyde Park." Bernard Kops plays with the fun of sounds in "Peach, Plum or Apricot." The Yorkshire poet, Ted Hughes, really "thumped" his line in "View of a Pig." D. J. Enright, in Midland accent, makes a strong assertion for the quality of "The 'Black' Country," and John Wain's reading of "Au Jardin des Plantes" succeeds in confronting the listener with a plea for a sense of responsibility.

Perhaps when the values in Here Today have been discovered by enough listeners, there will be greater insistence upon high level poets' recordings. A Here Today of American poets coached to read their best is greatly to be desired.

Another well prepared anthology stemming from the same English Jupiter source has also been issued in America by Folkways: Contemporary English Literature, Vol. I, Poetry,[37] read by Robert Graves, Elizabeth Jennings, Edith Sitwell, and C. Day Lewis; and Contemporary English Literature, Vol. II, Prose and Poetry[38] read by Laurie Lee, Christopher Logue and Professor C. Northcote Parkinson. The prose on the record is an analysis of the pursuit of progress by Professor C. Northcote Parkinson, discoverer of Parkinson's Law. In fifteen minutes of scenes with characters at

several levels in the interview situation, he proves the best way to
get things done.   This is clever playwrighting and skillful directing
of delightful scenes.   It would make an amusing interlude for a busi-
nessmen's luncheon.

Poets read and discuss their works in another series edited
by Peter Orr.   It is called The Poet Speaks. [39]   On this recent undertaking of Argo, the poets were recorded in association with the
British Council and the Poetry Room in the Lamont Library of Harvard University.   It is a useful undertaking, with more than ten
volumes released so far.   Some idea of the range can be gathered
from Volume IV, which records Tony Connor, Thomas Kinsella,
Elizabeth Jennings and Peter Redgrave.   The "volumes" (each one
a record) are distributed in the U.S.A. by the McGraw-Hill Book
Company.

Other Readings by Authors

William Faulkner Reads from his Works [40] has the Mississip-
pi novelist reading selections from the "Dilsey" section of The
Sound and the Fury, and the "Lena Grove" and "Joe Christmas" sections of Light in August.   He reads his stories with ongoing urgency.
The Dilsey section ends with the sermon by the visiting preacher.
Giving the preacher's psalm-like song and the congregation's anti-
phon, a two syllable "m-wh," Faulkner tells, with regional intonation and evangelic rapture, his remembrance of that incident.   The
director of the record, Jean Stein, has guided Faulkner to his sharing best.

Sean O'Casey Reading from his Works [41] has the opening and
final scenes from Juno and the Paycock, and The Death of Mrs.
Cassidy from "Inishfallen, Fare Thee Well."   In his introduction
Sean O'Casey describes Captain Boyle: "He's full of himself and
wishes the world was full of him too... he walks with a slow conse-
quential strut... Here then is my Juno and the Paycock, a tale of
the Dublin tenements--the time of the trouble, the time of the Civil
War in Ireland. "

The playwright time and again lifts the lines off the page as
he sings out the lines in musical repetition.   We find this kind of

emphatic intensity in Captain Boyle's talk to Joxer at the end of
Act I: "... them was the days, Joxer, them was the days... what is
the stars... what is the moon." The last passage on the record
swings the stolen jaunting car "along the roads... the cart swagging
..." Poignantly beautiful is the moment O'Casey wrote about so
well and tells lovingly: "... he remembered he'd left a lovely bunch
of crimson and golden berries he'd plucked for his mother, and his
heart felt a little sad again."

Lawrence Durrell's record for La Voix de l'Auteur series,
Lawrence Durrell Reading from Grecian Echoes, Bitter Lemons, [42]
etc., was ready to be heard when the time came for it to be recorded. Like the working of minstrels of old, it had been perfected
through frequent tellings before it was written down. Nowhere else
on a record does Durrell sustain for so long a period the spontaneous confluence of language choice and speech sound as in the recital
from Bitter Lemons of how the house was purchased. One hears
the rememberd "reptilian concentration... silence." He sees "The
glint of the sea...," "the view... indescribable," and hears as "the
wind moaned." There is no waste, no feeling of energy expended,
no detail missing in the excitement of the tale of bargaining with
the woman: "her sigh of rapture... before so much edible money...
the bangs and counter bangs until... it was a matter of time before
we started winding her in..."

The world of the Odyssey is the inspiration for the wonderful matching of images and spoken words in readings from his poetry. They pour out the wonders of the Isles of Greece and, with
ecstatic beauty, his "Reflections On a Marine Venus." Part of an
enterprise to get living authors of many languages on record, the
record brings to the ear Homeric narrative of lasting value.

Frank O'Connor Reading My Oedipus Complex and the Drunkard, [43] is hilarious story telling by the writer. Among other author
story tellers of the same vintage reviewed in previous editions are
Katherine Anne Porter, Eudora Welty and Carson McCullers.

Evelyn Waugh[44] recorded for Verve, April 9, 1960. The
material comes from two extremes in his writing: Vile Bodies and
Helena. The tight style and timing in Waugh's seemingly casual nar-

ration makes this a record for study by young writers as well as
readers, especially in the account of the death of Fausta.   Waugh
does an especially fine reading of the description of Constantine's
Court.

Goddard Lieberson's wish to perpetuate the sound of a writer's
voice and therefore a dimension of his personality led to the album
of twelve records called The Columbia Literary Series. [45] Why
many things were written and what they meant to their authors is
permanently recorded through this series.   It is most interesting to
listen to John Steinbeck telling how he came to write the two sinis-
ter tales, which he also tells–"The Snake" and "Johnny Bear."   A-
mong the other tellers are W. Somerset Maugham, Aldous Huxley,
Katherine Anne Porter, and all three of the Sitwells.   The full list
of authors with their selections is to be found in the Appendix.

Prix de Rome, National Book and Rosenthal Awards, publication in The New Yorker, etc. , figure in the accomplishments of
young Turk novelists of the late 50's and early 60's recorded by the
now defunct Calliope Records.   Mostly young men in their thirties
who have become the New Literary Establishment, each one of the
eight authors recorded a fifteen- to seventeen-minute reading of
some significance from one of his works.   Some of these readings
are now to be found on the CMS releases of James Baldwin, Bernard Malamud, Philip Roth, William Styron and John Updike.

CMS has also released Peter Ustinov Reads His Own Works.[46]
It shows what acting talent can contribute to the creation of characters in a reading.   The material is chosen from "The Loser" and
"The Aftertaste. "   The Painted Bird Read by the Author, Jerzy
Kosinski is another recording in the CMS group of recordings by
authors.   The five selected episodes illustrate well the author's
writing range in his descriptions of stupidity and the cruelty of ignorance.   His oral reading follows the jerky, mechanical phrasing
of one not at home with the language.   The impact is there nonethe-
less.

During January of 1954, at the time of her farewell New
York engagement, Ruth Draper recorded some of the most memorable of her original monologues.   This was after 40 years of ap-

pearances before cosmopolitan audiences around the world. Varied
and warmly human, her unique one-woman show of old favorites as
well as new creations was always eagerly anticipated by her ad-
mirers.

Arthur Luce Klein, director of Spoken Arts, writes: "The
Ruth Draper albums... were made several weeks prior to her death
in 1954 before Spoken Arts was even begun... the germ of Spoken
Arts came about through a conversation with Miss Draper when I
was teaching at the Royal Academy of Dramatic Art in London, in
fact soon after making a series of recordings with Miss Draper for
the British Drama League on dialects. She mentioned that it was a
pity that the works of literature and the theatre were not recorded
systematically.   During the decade we have been functioning, our release list of recordings, now more than 250, attests to our feelings
about this. " So also does the handsome boxed edition of all five
Ruth Draper records that his company produced.

With pathos, humor and exactness in dialect and intonation
pattern, right rhythm, and the created listeners conjured up with un-
believable presence, she moved through an evening's performance
with ever unfolding warmth and understanding for the women she por-
trayed.

On Side one of The Art of Ruth Draper, Vol. I, [47] "The Italian Lesson" goes briefly on through the interruptions of a hectic so-
cialite's household duties and telephone conversations.   Then there
is the last call. With hitherto unused vocal color and tittering inter-
jections, the woman surprisingly changes, presaging possible tragedy.

On Side two are "Three Generations in a Court of Domestic
Relations" and "The Scottish Immigrant. " This last concerns an
immigrant, a bride-to-be, young and vibrant. With a sudden movement, it bursts into her paean of thanks:

> ... You helped me wie my luggage
> and ye gave me books to read,
> and ye told me many things about
> America so I won't feel strange...

Final confirmation of the deep realization in the art of Ruth Draper,
were any needed, comes in the intensity of "... My Sandy, I'm
here!" It ranks with another kind of intensity, with Gielgud's Angelo

on Ages of Man.

The last of the Ruth Draper series, Doctors and Diets. The
Actress, is a compact manifesto of her prodigious range and famili-
arity with languages, dialects, feminine foibles and passions played
with a comprehending heart. It is a record of genius in our time,
which thanks to the perfection of sound recording can now be preserved.

Just as poets and prose writers reading their own works are
an object of interest to the listener in the new world of sound recording, so too are playwrights, reasoned Arthur Luce Klein when
he undertook The Distinguished Playwright Series. On Arthur Miller, Speaking On and Reading from The Crucible, Death of a Salesman, [48] Miller discusses the two approaches which he has used in
his plays: that of men in public life and that of men in private life.
Paul Green Discussing and Reading From In Abraham's Bosom and
Roll Sweet Chariot[49] is another record in this series bringing the
play and its author closer to us.

Recordings Discussed

1. Pasternak Speaks. Discurio (1-7").

2. Dylan Thomas Reading. Caedmon (5-12") Vol. I, TC 1002;
   Vol. II, TC1018; Vol. III, TC 1043; Vol. IV, TC 1061; Vol.
   V, TC 1132.

3. Dylan Thomas Reading His Complete Recorded Poetry. Caedmon (2-12") TC 2014, First Edition, First Printing; November, 1963.

4. Robert Frost: Twentieth Century Poetry in English. Library
   of Congress (1-12") PL 6.

5. Robert Frost Reads the Poems of Robert Frost. Decca (1-12")
   D. 9033.

6. The Yale Series of Recorded Poets: Robert Frost. Carillon
   (1-12") YP 320. Reissued by Decca (1-12") D. 9127.

7. T. S. Eliot Reading His Own Poems. Library of Congress (1-
   12") PL 3.

8. T. S. Eliot Reading Poems and Choruses. Caedmon (1-12")
   TC 1045.

9. T. S. Eliot Reads His "Four Quartets." Angel (1-12") 45012.

10. T. S. Eliot Reads "Old Possum's Book of Practical Cats."
    Spoken Arts (1-12") 758.

11. The Poems of William Butler Yeats Read by William Butler
    Yeats, Siobhan McKenna and Micheal MacLiammoir. Spoken
    Arts (1-12") 753.

12. W. H. Auden Reading. Caedmon (1-12") TC 1019.

13. Stephen Vincent Benét and Edwin Muir. Library of Congress
    (1-12") P. 23.

14. William Alfred, Reading His Own Poems. (O. P.) Vocarium (1-
    12") 78 RPM, SP 45083.

15. The Poems of James Stephens Read by the Author. Spoken
    Arts (1-12") 744.

16. Lynn Fontanne. The White Cliffs of Dover, Edna St. Vincent
    Millay Poems. RCA Victor (1-12") LCT 1147.

17. An Informal Hour With Dorothy Parker. Spoken Arts (1-12")
    726.

18. John Masefield, O. M. Reads a Fox's Day. A special adapta-
    tion of Reynard the Fox. Argo (1-12") RG 224.

19. John Masefield: The Story of Ossian. Spoken Arts (1-12")
    755.

20. John Masefield, O. M. Reads the Fortune of the Sea. The
    Wanderers Image. Argo (1-12") RG 230.

21. John Masefield Reads "Seafever," "Cargoes" and Other Poems.
    Caedmon (1-12") TC 1147.

22. Ezra Pound Reading His Poetry. Caedmon (2-12" Vol. I,
    TC 1122, Vol. II, TC 1155.

23. Carl Sandburg Reading Fog and Other Poems. Caedmon (1-
    12") TC 1253.

24. J. R. R. Tolkien: Poems, Songs of Middle Earth. Caedmon
    (1-12") TC 1231.

25. Words for the Wind: Selections From the Poetry of Theodore
    Roethke, Read by Theodore Roethke. Folkways (1-12") FL
    9736.

26. The Rubaiyat of Omar Khayyam. Translation by Edward Fitz-
    gerald, Side I; Translation by Robert Graves and Omar Ali-

Shah, Side II.   Spoken Arts (1-12") SA 965.

27. Lolita and Poems Read by Vladimir Nabokov.   Spoken Arts
    (1-12") 902.

28. Antiworlds: The Poetry of Andrei Voznesensky.   Columbia (1-
    12") OL 6590.

29. Padraic Colum Reading His Irish Tales and Poems.   Folkways
    (1-12") FL 9737.

30. e. e. cummings: six nonlectures.   Caedmon (6-12") TC 1186-
    91.

31. Yevgeny Yevtushenko: Babi Yar and Other Poems Read by the
    Author in Russian and in English by Alan Bates.   Caedmon
    (1-12") TC 1153.

32. Pleasure Dome (O. P.) By Lloyd Frankenburg.   Columbia (1-
    12") ML 4259.

33. An Album of Modern Poetry.   An anthology read by the poets
    and prepared by Oscar Williams.   Library of Congress (3-
    12") P 20-22.

34. The Caedmon Treasury of Modern Poets Reading Their Own
    Poetry.   Caedmon (2-12") TC 2006.

35. Yale Series of Recorded Poets.   Decca (22-12")

36. Here Today.   Poems of 45 contemporary authors.   Jupiter (2-
    12") Jur 00A 6-7.   American distributor, Spoken Arts (2-
    12") 943, 944.

37. Contemporary English Literature, Vol. I, Poetry.   Read by
    Robert Graves, Elizabeth Jennings, Edith Sitwell, C. Day
    Lewis.   Folkways (1-12") FL 9888.

38. Contemporary English Literature, Vol. II, Prose and Poetry.
    Read by Laurie Lee, Christopher Logue, Professor C.
    Northcote Parkinson.   Folkways (1-12") FL 9889.

39. The Poet Speaks.   Vols. I-X, Argo (10-12").   (1) RG 451, (2)
    RG 452, (3) RG 453, (4) RG 454, (5) RG 455, (6) RG 456,
    (7) RG 517, (8) RG 518, (9) RG 519, (10) RG 520.   Dis-
    tributed in the U. S. A. by McGraw-Hill Book Company.

40. William Faulkner Reads from His Works.   MGM (1-12") E
    3617 ARC.

41. Sean O'Casey Reading from His Works.   Caedmon (1-12")
    TC 1012.

42. Lawrence Durrell Reading From Grecian Echoes, Bitter Lemons, Prospero's Cell and Reflections on a Marine Venus. LaVoix de L'Auteur (2-12") LVA 1003-4.

43. Frank O'Connor Reading My Oedipus Complex and The Drunkard. Caedmon (1-12") TC 1036.

44. Evelyn Waugh Reading from His Works. Verve (1-12") MG 1508.

45. The Columbia Literary Series. Distinguished Authors. Goddard Lieberson, Editor. Columbia (12-12") ML 4752-63.

46. Peter Ustinov Reads His Own Works. CMS (1-12") CMS 524.

47. The Art of Ruth Draper. Vols. I-V. Spoken Arts (5-12") Vol. I, 779; Vol. II, 793; Vol. III, 799; Vol. IV, 800; Vol. V, 805; all five albums available as R.D. 5.

48. Arthur Miller, Speaking on and Reading from The Crucible, Death of a Salesman. Spoken Arts (1-12") 704.

49. Paul Green Discussing and Reading from In Abraham's Bosom and Roll Sweet Chariot. Spoken Arts (1-12") 719.

Chapter IV

Readings by Other Than Authors

While the sense of much poetry has been lost on records because poets themselves read poorly, some non-poet readers also contribute to the failures of poetry on records. With the painter of Browning's "Andrea Del Sarto," the poets might exclaim:

> ... You don't understand
> Nor care to understand about my art,
> . . .
> I do what many dream of all their lives,
> - Dream? Strive to do, and agonize to do,
> And fail in doing. I could count twenty such
> On twice your fingers, and not leave this town,
> Who strive - you don't know how the others strive
> To paint a little thing like that you smeared
> Carelessly passing, with your robes afloat,

Contributing to its sense, many resounding echoes and near echoes may be found within the framework of verse and, for that matter, of much prose, especially folk drama. They are some of those melodic elements through which the writer, sometimes obviously and at other times most unobtrusively, conveys and orders his concepts for the listeners' conscious and subconscious tyings together.

Robert Frost, in a letter to his favorite pupil, John T. Bartlett, wrote:

> The sentence-sounds are very definite entities...
>
> They are apprehended by the ear. They are gathered by the ear from the vernacular and brought into books. Many of them are already familiar to us in books. I think no writer invents them. The most original writer only catches them fresh from talk, where they grow spontaneously.
>
> A man is all a writer if all his words are strung on definite recognizable sentence sounds. The voice of the imagination, the speaking voice must know certainly how to behave, how to posture in every sentence he offers.

74

> A man is a marked writer if his words are largely strung
> on the more striking sentence sounds...
>
> The ear does it. The ear is the only true writer and the
> only true reader. I have known people who could read
> without hearing the sentence sounds and they were the
> fastest readers. Eye readers we call them. They can
> get the meaning by glances. But they are bad readers be-
> cause they miss the best part of what a good writer puts
> into his work.
>
> Remember that the sentence sound often says more than
> the words. It may even as in irony convey a meaning op-
> posite to the words. *

Their creation is an aspect of oral art. When this element of the
oral art is silenced in the failure to grasp and share what is written, there is uninformed, insensitive reading which results in dull
listening.

There are some spoken records on which the sentence sounds
live, where the sound and sense relationships mesh. They are an
enjoyable listening experience. It is appropriate that a sampling of
some of these works, written to be heard, begin this discussion of
recordings of literature read by other than their authors.

A Sampling from Modern Literature

James Joyce: Portrait of the Artist as a Young Man[1] was
the first in a group of Joyce recordings brought out by Caedmon.
The reader, Cyril Cusack, is an Irish actor sensitive to the Dublin
of Joyce's time and with vocal qualities comparable to those of
Joyce himself. With maturity and wonder, he fluidly develops
Stephen's memories of childhood, especially the Christmas dinner
and that later moment of "the first noiseless sundering of their
lives" as the grown Stephen felt the "new wild life in his veins."
In the deep engagement with the liberated oral expression of this
timeless work, memories also involve the listener.

The recurring sounds flow on with the river Liffey in the
soliloquies of Molly and Leopold Bloom in the excerpts of James

---

* Selected Letters of Robert Frost edited by Lawrence Thompson.
Portion of a letter from Robert Frost, Feb. 22, 1914 to John T.
Bartlett.

Joyce: Ulysses[2] as read by Siobhan McKenna and E. F. Marshall.
Like the sea, never the same, pulsing from depths beneath with
infinite variety of formation, rhythm and pause, thoughts arrive on
the shores of consciousness. The "yes" of this Molly Bloom will
long be remembered; so also will the intimate memories of this
Leopold.

Miss McKenna also reads "Anna Livia Plurabelle" and Cyril
Cusack "Shem the Penman" on another recording, James Joyce:
Finnegans Wake.[3] The director, Howard Sackler, says on the
sleeve-notes: "... The reading aloud is not one more tool to help
penetrate the jungle, but a part of the text... both performance and
score are provided..." It took especially equipped artists for the
difficult language, vocal movement, touch of irony and innuendo,
loveliness and harshness of this allegoric symphony.

The Poetry of Yeats[4] is another of the group of readings
of modern Irish literature essayed by the same director. Included
are "The Lake Isle of Innisfree," "The Wild Swans at Coole," "The
Second Coming," "Sailing to Byzantium," "Leda and the Swan,"
"Crazy Jane and the Bishop" and other Crazy Jane poems, "Lapis
Lazuli," "The Three Bushes," "The Wild Old Wicked Man," "Why
Should Not Old Men be Mad?," "Cuchulain Comforted," and other
poems.

Cyril Cusack begins "The Song of Wandering Angus" with the
images of delicate "White moths on the wing" and moves on to the
even more delicate "little silver trout." From the first words by
Cusack, speech texture and cadence are let loose to the song of the
line. It is as though the sound had aged with the first stirrings of
the words to conjure up their rich beauty later. With accurate distinctions, he ends the last two lines:

> The silver apples of the moon,
> The golden apples of the sun.

By way of contrast, there is swift, barbaric movement and
fierce touch in "The Second Coming": "Turning and turning in the
the widening gyre."

Siobhan McKenna, attuned like Cusack to the music of the

sounds, with aged-in-the-word tone and without occasional untoward
extension or lengthening of sound, sometimes a distracting quality in
this actress' work in the theatre, believably creates the Crazy Jane
poems in all their varying moods. In "The Lady's Three Songs,"
she has a right "contrapuntal serpent hiss" and stress. On the evidence of these and other spoken records stemming from modern Ireland, there is hope beyond Yeats' fear that ". . . the tongue may lose
that part of its function which is related to sound."

     An event of some magnitude for poetry took place in 1937
when the B. B. C. invited W. B. Yeats to arrange four broadcasts of
poetry chosen and directed by himself. V. C. Clinton-Baddeley, a
frequent broadcaster of poetry readings was a reader on the first
three of these programs.

     In 1958, Baddeley, assisted by Jill Balcon and Marjorie West-
bury, prepared for a Jupiter recording, Poems by W. B. Yeats.[5]
All these poems Baddeley had rehearsed and broadcast with Yeats,
closely following the latter's directions. The poems, which take
fourteen minutes and one side of a ten-inch record, are: "An Irish
Airman Foresees His Death"; "I Am of Ireland"; "The Rose Tree";
"Imitated From the Japanese"; "Sailing to Byzantium"; "Sweet
Dancer"; "The Curse of Cromwell"; "O, But I Saw A Solemn Night"
and "Mad as the Mist and Snow."

     In his prefatory remarks on the sleeve of the record, Clinton
Baddeley says of Yeats: ". . . All that he really wanted was what
any poet ought to want, an expert understanding of the rhythm and
an exact observance of the line-endings. . ." Elsewhere, Baddeley
wrote, "Yeats was a master of hidden rhythms. . . he longed for a
tongue to declare these perfections. . . and his best hope of conveying
them to future generations lay in the establishment of an oral tradition. . ."

     The observation is often made that W. B. Yeats had a perfect
sense of rhythm but no sense of pitch. The monotonous pitch in existing stentorian pieces by him bears this out. The hieratic approach, line endings, timing and pause are also there.

     Many specifics gathered from the meetings and friendship
with Yeats have been translated by Baddeley into the readings. Thus,

the greatest poet of our time, physically limited himself, had his
poems brought to life by an artist in the unique situation of being
able to follow his exact directions.   One can hear the vocal approach Yeats wanted in all Baddeley's readings, the unmistakable
rhythmic movement in Jill Balcon's "Sweet Dancer," the faithful observance of line endings, especially telling in "Mad as the Mist and
Snow," the timing and pause in "Can make/ a right/ rose tree."
There is Yeats' bitterness towards old age in the biting sounds of
"a tattered coat upon a stick." There are hidden rhythms in "Sailing to Byzantium" and the authoritative thunder of the poet in the
"Curse of Cromwell."

The second side of the Yeats record contains recordings of
"Conversation Pieces" and "Poems for Several Voices," with eight
of them speaking up from under tombstones and through the bells of
two ingeniously conceived readings of Hardy poems.   Other poems
are done in duet or with three voices.

On Lennox Robinson Presents William Butler Yeats: Poems
and Memories[6] are reminiscences and readings of Yeats' poetry
which one suspects are read as the friend remembered Yeats himself reading, in a monopitch with high priest incantation.   Among
the poems are "The Lake Isle of Innisfree," "The Stolen Child,"
"Ballad of Father Gilligan," "Ballad of Moll Magee," "Cap and
Bells," "The Fiddler of Dooney," and the last chorus from Yeats'
adaptation of Oedipus at Colonus.   There is also a group of patriotic poems, including "Easter 1916" when "a terrible beauty is born."
The final poem is appropriately "Under Ben Bulben."

Summarizing Yeats' views on good verse speaking on Plays
and Memories of William Butler Yeats,[7] Robinson says "Good verse-
drama speakers are not chanters or crooners but speakers... rich
and varied in voice, with a sense of acting and the necessary practice which makes verse come as naturally from the lips of the player as prose..."

The thoughts of another poet on verse-reading are packed into nearly fifteen minutes of vastly amusing, alliterated comment on
poets, poetry, visiting poets, ponderables and imponderables on
Dylan Thomas Reading, IV.[8]   Here, speaking of his reading of other

poets, he says "...I try to make them alive from inside...to get across what I feel to be the original impetus of the poem... But in my own poems, I've had my say...I'm only saying it again."

The absence of "alive from the inside" was at times unfortunately true of Thomas for the reading of his own work. When, with thundered vocal glory, an appropriate quality for his bardic writing, he continued in the superficial "sounding" of one of his poems, he was unfair to that work. But, when he let other poets' minds sing under their words, the brilliant virtuosity of his reading talent and his important contribution to public verse reading was manifest. In this mood it is wonderful to hear him read, on the above mentioned record, Walter de la Mare's "The Bards," poems by W. H. Auden, an absolutely unforgettable burlesque, "Mr. T. S. Eliot's Sunday Evening Broadcast Postscript" by Henry Reed, and three Thomas Hardy poems which we are not likely to hear better done.

A like enjoyment is to be heard on An Evening with Dylan Thomas[9] reading his own and other poems. Fresh, dedicated, and hitting the mark each time, Thomas here read for poetry with the volcanic power and talent which he could muster when he wanted to. Only in one case does an apologetic attitude towards the Irish dialect interfere.

This record was made on April 10, 1950 at the University of California before a live audience. With all the provocation for relaxing play which that meant for Thomas, he never loses concentration or lapses into tonal fatigue. The record is an intense experience in listening. It is one of the finest portraits one can have of Dylan Thomas, for it communicates him at his best. He even did well with his own "Poem in October" with its echoes and wind-swept images. Sudden rhythms are also discovered in his reading, especially of Yeats. They make one wish for an accompanying text so that the eye could help one, along with the ear, to read poems better.

Recordings of Early English Literature

From the foregoing illustrations it is evident that there has

been a responsible, commercial interest in spoken recordings of the
greatest in modern English literature.   But this interest encom-
passes all worthwhile literature.   Recording efforts have reached far
into the past, even to oral reconstruction of the sound of language of
an older time.   An example of this is the Harvard Vocarium record
by Francis P. Magoun, Jr., Reading from Old English Prose and
Verse. [10]   This out-of-print record deserves to be reissued.

The vocal quality of the scholar's reading, with its anchored,
earthy strength, conveys to the listener Professor Magoun's sense
of the texture of the old language.   He is so steeped in that time
that we believe he could just as expertly have yoked the West-Saxon's
oxen, ploughed his field or followed the church bell's call.

There are eight selections on each side of the Old English
record.   The first opens with a strong voice telling of the parable
of the sower according to St. Mark.   Other passages include parts
of The Wanderer and The Seafarer.   Then, at the end of side one,
is an excerpt from The Dream of the Rood.   The second side has
eight passages from Beowulf, starting with a section of the poem
preceding Beowulf's funeral obsequies.

The introduction to Beowulf Read in Old English by Norman
Davis and Nevill Coghill[11] is given by Norman Davis.   He discusses
the original Beowulf, written on parchment about the year 1,000,
its pronunciation and metre:

> ... Old English had a system of short and long vowels.
> The alliteration is nearly always easily heard making the
> parts of the long line perform a strong pattern of rhyth-
> mic sound that is capable of a range of great effects.

Side two contains readings by Nevill Coghill of such key passages as the "Speech to Hrothgar," "The Dragon Fight" and "The
Funeral of Beowulf" with noble resolution and stately movement.
Those without a knowledge of the original would do well to follow
with a modern version as well as with the text which is provided.

Gawain and The Green Knight and The Pearl, [12] examples of
the poetry of courtly love and heavenly love, are read by New York
University Professor J. B. Bessinger and Yale Professor Marie Boroff.   The alliterative verse, verbal repetition, interlaced end and

initial rhyme are all respected. Both readers are vocally and dramatically equipped to communicate the rugged and delicate qualities required by the material. Especially thrilling is the vigorous and sure tonal quality of Marie Boroff who reads the woman's lines. Le Morte D'Arthur[13] with Harry Andrews, William Squire, Joan Hart, Tony White and supporting cast, is adapted from Sir Thomas Malory and produced by John Barton. It resurrects the art of story-telling in ancestral halls.

The condensation of the last part of the Arthurian Legend was prepared and directed by John Barton who is also the voice of Malory in reflection. Music connecting the parts of the story was compiled from medieval sources and directed by Thurston Dart.

The record contains many helpful illustrations for student readers. There is the comment by John Barton in a style accustomed to the hall and to commanding the attention of listeners. Another lesson comes in the recital of the long list of knights who sought to cure Sir Urre, read by Tony White. This is an excellent illustration for Bible readers who must plow through many lines of "begats." The album will certainly be enjoyed by those of cultivated taste with the leisure for troubadours.

The Canterbury Tales of Geoffrey Chaucer,[14] on four records, is presented in modern translation by Nevill Coghill. The tales were originally dramatized for the B. B. C. 's Third Program. Told in the spirit of the original tellers they may lead some listeners back to the originals. A few short passages are read by Nevill Coghill in the original, as it would have sounded in Chaucer's time. The modern version is juxtaposed. For those who want more such beautiful readings of the original Chaucerian English, The Prologue to the Canterbury Tales[15] is available, read in Middle English by Nevill Coghill, Norman Davis and John Burrow.

The Jupiter Book of Ballads[16] is also in keeping with the spirit and beauty of old material as literature for hall and hearth. It is a record careful in the choice of readers whose experience in poetry reading should be passed on. The program is balanced in its sung and spoken parts and in use of men's and women's voices.

The oldest group of ballads starts with an assertive dialect telling by John Laurie of "The Wife of Usher's Well." "Lord Randall" is sung by Isla Cameron. Then Clinton-Baddeley, the director, in stolid belief and with wonder, recreates the ancient story of "Saint Stephen and King Herod." John Laurie is heard again in a heavy dialect recital of the tale of "Mary Hamilton." For this, Isla Cameron, in a fine stroke of casting, sings Mary's final song. The spirit of "High Barbaree" by the same singer will be contagious for most listeners. In "Shameful Death" come the contrasting "Glad to think of the moment when/ I took his life away" and the final asking for prayers for himself and Alice his wife.

"The Watercresses," with Osian Ellis' singing and harp accompaniment, has a rhythmic stay in the last two lines not readily relinquished by the ear. Then one is suddenly absorbed in Thomas Hardy's "A Trampwoman's Tragedy" in Jill Balcon's finished recitation. There is especially beautiful vocal depth and shading for: "Then in a voice I had never heard."

The news of William McGongall's "The Taybridge Disaster" returns the record to John Laurie's very homely dialect and pertinent rhythms for the awful summary of the Taybridge disaster "which will be remembered for a very long time." The record is rounded to a finish by Isla Cameron, accompanied by her guitar, with the plaintive singing of "The House of the Rising Sun."

The metaphysical poets are not included on <u>Elizabethan Love Poems,</u>[17] read by Robert Speaight and Maxine Audley. (Lyric readings of flowing beauty take care of some of this material on <u>Anthony Quayle Reading Sonnets from Shakespeare and Other Elizabethan Lyrics.</u>[18]) The contents come from Elizabethan and early Jacobean verse. Like many of the poems, serious and cerebral in the treatment of love, Robert Speaight's reading follows a strong intellectual bent, businesslike without surplus, and unyielding even to the appeal in the women's lines, read by Maxine Audley. The two make a delightful team for the sequence of poems by Thomas Campion. At the close of the first of these Speaight breaks to a deep: "Then tell, then tell how thou didst murder me." It is shocking and profound at that moment because of the tight rein maintained for the rest of the poem.

The dialogue "Ulysses and the Siren" by Samuel Daniel inches on in a losing argument. In the nymph's reply to the Shepherd by Sir Walter Raleigh, the woman's last word is final. Robert Greene's "The Shepherd's Wife's Song" sings with warm conviction of the joy of that life. A lovely delicacy permeates Miss Audley's reading of "Rosalind's Madrigal" by Thomas Lodge and both readers share the slowing verses of Edmund Spenser's "Prothalamion" with its halting refrain: "Sweet Thames, run softly till I end my song."

On Sir Cedric Hardwicke and Robert Newton read XVII Century Metaphysical and Love Lyrics[19] of Herbert, Marvell, Vaughan, Traherne, Herrick and others, one finds the new appreciative intellectuality emerging in Cowley's "Ode upon Doctor Harvey." The Metaphysical Poets,[20] Record 2, Secular, has some excellent readings by John Stride of Suckling, Stanley and Waller.

A Poetry Reading by Sybil Thorndike and Lewis Casson[21] is the recording for their Golden Wedding Anniversary by a royal pair of the theatre. It is spread out and brimming over with resourceful variety. Each reading has accurate touch and right rhythm: "A Toccata of Galuppi's" by Robert Browning, Gerard Manley Hopkins' "In the Valley of the Elwy," and "A Ditty, in Praise of Eliza, Queen of the Shepherds" by Edmund Spenser. In the steel-like "all smiles stopped together" of "My Last Duchess" one knows thoroughly the rare no-smile of the most famous of dramatic monologues. They play beautifully together the answer to Sydney Dobell's "How's My Boy?"

Very interesting listening comes from A Personal Choice, Alec Guinness.[22] "There may be rhyme in this choice of poems but there is very little reason," writes Alec Guinness for the sleeve notes on what he has chosen to share. It is a record from the mind of a lover of poetry who has the skill to share it with others. To the anonymous "Clerk Saunders" as well as to Shakespeare he brings all the vocal difference and variety of pitch and volume needed. Besides being a thoroughly enjoyable record it is very interesting for those who are trying to master skills in reading, e.g., the tonal difference between King John and Father Abbot, or a last line of Browning. If the record should lead to a desire for more, there is

the delightful <u>Alec</u> Guinness: A Leaden Treasury of Poesie,[23] a
delightful piece of lachrymose clowning.

Anthologies: General, Scotch, Irish

The London Library of Recorded English[24] (Book I: Lyric
Poetry; Book II: Lyric Poetry; Book III: Narrative Poetry; Book
IV: Shakespearean Dramatic Poetry; Book V: 16th and 17th Century
Poetry; Book VI: 18th and 19th Century Poetry) is the first planned
recorded anthology of English literature. Begun in 1947 on 78 RPM
discs, it is now available on six 33 1/3 RPM discs. The record-
ings are edited and directed by V. C. Clinton-Baddeley, actor, au-
thor, and a director of Jupiter Recordings, with the assistance of
Joseph Compton, at one time director of the English Festival of
Spoken Poetry.

There is an abundance of aesthetic pleasure on these records.
The poems go all the way from such comparatively simple fare as
Marlowe's "The Passionate Shepherd to His Love," Wordsworth's
"She Dwelt Among the Untrodden Ways," Thomas Hardy's "Weathers,"
Walter de la Mare's "Sam," and Alice Meynell's "Shepherdess" to
the wonderful excitement of the chase in John Masefield's "The Fox"
and the barbaric zest of "The War Song of Dinas Vwar." The bold
abandon of Dylan Thomas' rendering of this last is a masterpiece.
Another delight is James Stephens' reading from his own poetry and
soaring into the ecstatic song of "Peg has an egg, egg..." John
Laurie's authentic Border Scot accent and spirit contribute to the
beautiful delivery of several old ballads, including our best hearing
of "My Love is Like a Red, Red Rose." Perhaps the peak of
Laurie's power comes at the close of "Pibroch of Donuil Dhu!"

Passages from eight of Shakespeare's plays open up a varied
picture of the Bard's range in writing, characterization, and por-
trayal of diverse moments in life. Beginning with the stalwart prologue from <u>Henry V</u>, this section closes with the stabbed last lines
of <u>Othello.</u> Readers and passages vary widely yet fit together.
Such favorites as "My Gentle Puck" and "Methinks I am a prophet
new inspired" mix with the less often heard "Farewell, a long farewell to all my greatness" in a great reading by the late Sir Lewis

Casson with his swift "Vain Pomp and Glory of this world, I hate thee. " Comparisons with sections of Gielgud's Ages of Man pop into one's listening memory, though not necessarily to the disadvantage of either record. One of the most beautifully read sections of Shakespeare to be heard anywhere is at the end of Act I, Scene I when Marcellus and his friends speak, with awe, of the crowing of the cock. This side, which takes under 25 minutes, could delight a large audience. It should certainly be heard by young students of Shakespeare.

The recordings as a whole are a project bound to bring back the taste for reading in the home. Here is a cultural wealth of many vocal textures to be happily shared. It is also an ideal experience in spoken language for the young. The London Library albums should not be confused with the less well done albums of Cambridge Library.

The Jupiter Junior Anthology of English Verse, Part III, [25] also directed by Clinton-Baddeley, has a sobering post-war personality of its own. Here is no casual selection of content. One finds a designed intent, beginning with such knowing sorrow-anonymities as "Bonnie Boy" and "My Little Wee Croodin' Doo. " Lord Randall is also retold, with the victim a child and the poisoner his stepmother. Laurie Lee reads his own "April Rise" and "Apples. " And the whole ends with Jean Ingelow's "The High Tide on the Coast of Lincolnshire" read by Dame Sybil Thorndike, a Lincolnshire woman herself whose reading knows the tradition of tragedy for that coast and its kind of mourning.

Readings from Scottish and Irish Literature

Frederick Worlock and C. R. B. Brookes, an ancient Scots border man, read the best-loved poems of Burns and Scottish border ballads on The Poetry of Robert Burns and Scottish Border Ballads.[26] At times, it is difficult for the non-Scot to understand the authentic accent but vigorous sounds give an idea of how much vitality the language has lost in time. Of Mr. Brookes, Tyrone Guthrie wrote: "... I have never heard any man, or woman, who could come near him as a speaker of poetry. I think his interpretation of Scots ballads may never be excelled... "

An interesting complement to the Worlock and Brookes readings is <u>Robert Burns Read by Jean Taylor Smith,</u> [27] a lassie with
spunk and tenderness.   Here are the woman's poems: "Tom Glen,"
"Ye Banks and Braes," "Auld Lang Syne," "Last May a Braw
Wover," "John Anderson" and "There's a Youth in this City."
A few weeks before the death of Harold Weightman in February 1963 he made <u>A Recorded Anthology of Scottish Verse. Part
One, Poems of Robert Burns.</u> [28] As a stand-in for Robert Burns,
his reading reminds one of Dylan Thomas when he read the poetry
of others: versatile, vocally rich and always fresh in the approach
to a poem.   A native of Ayrshire, brought up on Burns, Weightman
had the background for reading him.   His remarkable breath control throughout the narrative detail in the fast driving lines at the
end of "Tam O'Shanter" is well described in the sleeve notes by
George Bruce.   Those unacquainted with the Scots dialect will need
a footnoted copy of Burns' poetry.

In forty-five minutes of listening to the thirty-three poems
on <u>Poetry of Ireland,</u> [29] now out-of-print, one can receive a pene-
trating understanding of the modern Irish spirit, its culture and values, better than from hours of study.   Richard Hayward, himself a
poet, has chosen 25 poets from two centuries, opening with "The
Dead of Clonmacnoise" from the Irish by T. T. Rolleston (1857-
1920).

The readings are by Hayward, John Hewitt, whose poems are
also included, and a remarkable woman reader, Eithne Dunne. She
reads with notable sense of line length and meaning: "The Rose-
tree" by W. B. Yeats, "The Hungray Grass" and "The Day Set For
Our Wedding" by Donagh MacDonaugh (b. 1912), "Youth of the Bound
Black Hair" by Douglas Hyde (1862-1946), and Hayward's "The
Stranger."   Rolled out with charm is "When I was A Little Girl"
by Alice Milligan (1866-1953), with a nice dialect patch from the
old nanny.   Another dialect piece, pathetically "longing for the Wex-
ford shore," is "In Service" by Winifred Letts (b. 1882).

John Hewitt, more solemn-toned than Eithne Dunne, does
very sympathetic, if lugubrious, readings of Louis MacNeice's "Car-
rickfergus" and "Dust," "Outcast" by AE (1867-1935), and "Arm-

agh" by W. R. Rodgers (b. 1909). In this last he does not miss,
as a stranger might, the import of the "graves of the garrulous
kings." Hewitt also reads his own "The Little Lough" with nostalgic
recall.

Delighted with speaking the rhythms for which he holds so
much warmth, Hayward's readings are very catchy. His own "Love
in Ulster" is a quizzical, humorous commentary. In similar dialect
is "The Whins" by Florence L. Wilson (1892-1946). Like a Van
Gogh of the fields, it is blown through with love. "Dear Dark
Head," from the Irish by Sir Samuel Ferguson (1810-1886), is one
of the most intense on the record. Hayward's handling of James
Stephens' (1882-1952) "The Goat Paths" and "Little Things" is not
sufficiently close to the images or as rhythmically strong as Stephens'
own reading of these poems. However, his reading of "The Lover
and Birds" by William Allingham (1824-1889), an achievement in
bird calls which is in a class by itself, has an unexpected "lark" at
the end.

One finishes the record ready to hear it again. The com-
piler and his readers, knowing the function of poetry, competently
take a high road of hominess in a world of lofty spirits, sensing
the movement and sound of the material. It is a valuable and useful record for the meditative exploration of a culture. Out of print
too long, it should be revived.

Complimenting the anthology just discussed, Siobhan McKenna
reads Irish Verse and Ballads. [30] "The Ballad of Moll Magee," essentially women's meat, is a most sympathetic reading. Of the fifteen other Yeats poems on side one, several favorites might be
singled out for their brisk pointedness: "The Song of Wandering
Angus," "The Mermaid" and "The Drinking Song."

Brief comments introduce and tie together the Irish ballads,
folksongs and lyrics on side two. Several among these, "I Am
Raftery," "Walk With Me, My Beloved," etc., are read in Gaelic
as well as in English translation.

Of particular interest is Miss McKenna's change in textural
touch in a new voice for James Joyce, which she maintains with
stride and twanging nasals. This most interesting choice and ar-

rangement of Irish poetry closes with Padraic Colum's "A Cradle
Song."

An eighteenth century Gaelic poem translated into English by
Frank O'Connor is read by Siobhan McKenna on Brian Merriman:
The Midnight Court. [31] Using the genre appropriate to the text, the
recording is a good example of the once popular art of declamation.

Ireland Free: Micheal MacLiammoir in Revolutionary
Speeches and Poems of Ireland [32] is worthy of study both for content
and artistic achievement. The record includes Robert Emmet's
speech before his execution (Sept. 19, 1803), Patrick H. Pearse's
oration over the grave of O'Donovan Rossa, Proclamation of the
Irish Republic, and poems by Patrick H. Pearse and William Butler
Yeats.

Readings of American Literature

On A Golden Treasury of American Verse, [33] Bryant, Long-
fellow, Whittier, Holmes, Poe, Dickinson and Whitman are represented. Nancy Wickwire reads two Emily Dickinson poems, "I'm
Nobody, Who Are You?" and "The Bustle in a House," creating
well the atmosphere of the morning after a death.

Alexander Scourby, who reads most of the poems on the record, does so with the directness he brings to his reading for the
blind. Greater yielding to the lyricism and delicate whisper of
some of the lines would have added enjoyment. When he plays with
the dialect of Lowell's "The Courtin' " the result is charming.
There is also a very simple and touching reading of Whitman's
"Come Up From the Fields, Mother." The arrangement of poems is
easy to follow and the timing good. The occasional use of music
for transitions and background is carefully limited.

There is so much dubious "poetry" on An Historical Anthology of American Poetry from Its Inception to Poets Born Before
1900 (Argo) and on American Poetry to 1900 (Lexington) that the
production of these albums is questionable. The many mannered
and mechanical readings contribute to the boredom. Nancy Mar-
chand's very beautiful readings from Emily Dickinson on the last
named album are an exception.

Concentrating upon the poetry of a fellow American, two professors have created a program, <u>Lucyle Hook Reads Poems of Emily Dickinson</u>.[34] Henry Wells, author of <u>Introduction to Emily Dickinson</u>, gives a brief comment before each of the eighteen subject groupings into which the program is divided. Lucyle Hook is the experienced reader. She has long been a student of the poetry of Emily Dickinson, the exactness of whose writing is matched in the disarmingly barren vocal quality of her reading. Long acquaintance with the poetry has allowed Miss Hook to assimilate a sense of the polish, shape and structure of the Dickinson way of thought and feeling.

The dedication is whole-hearted. Throughout, Miss Hook's control produces a rightly solid vocal quality. Like life stirring within granite come the lines on death: "Now feet within my garden go..." For "no brigadier throughout the years," there is the suggestion of military jauntiness, there is flashing perception in "the sky is low, the clouds are mean," and uncompromising assertion in "Tell all the truth/But tell it slant." The one poem under the classification <u>Flowers</u> is a warm "South Winds Jostle Them." Train movement trickily fits "I like to see it lap the miles," and the reader does not hesitate to release loud oo's to help the satire of: "Some tremendous tomb/ Proclaiming to the gloom..."

Julie Harris and Nancy Wickwire, in two professional attempts at a program of Emily Dickinson poetry, showed mediocre results, while the art of Miss Hook, involved with the peculiar taste and accuracy of word in Dickinson poetry, is first rate. Her phrasing leaves no doubt of the poet's meaning; her chiseled words permit no escape from her purpose, which is underlined by her granite stance.

One might expect that the academic world would by now have made many lasting contributions to the recording of poetry, but this has not been the case. There have been attempts, but knowledge, without the skills of disciplined spoken language, make only for amateurism on a recording.

<u>Emily Dickinson's Letters</u>[35] are read by Samuel Charters. Here one finds knowledgeable comment and very sensitive reading.

Side one of Treasury of Walt Whitman: Leaves of Grass
Read by Alexander Scourby[36] is a good example of approximate
reading with such missed images as "lilac," "coffin," "sing on,"
and "the night in silence." It is a self-watched recording. However, side two moves into the accuracy of more artistic reading.
There is an absorbed attention to the recall of the look of the red
squaw, for example. There are also excellent readings of "The
Sleepers" and the "Wound-Dresser." The lines, "poor boy I never
knew you" and "yet deep in my heart is a fire" are Scourby at his
best.

Professor Howard Mumford Jones, on Walden by Henry David
Thoreau,[37] is another right reader. In no time, one is at Walden
Pond becoming closely involved in Thoreau's experience of the loon's
call, the water, the ax, his mouse, the woodchuck with her young,
and the war between the ants. In seculsion we listen to the philosopher promising that one "... will meet with success undreamed
... in proportion as he simplifies his life..."

Another right person, the one for telling the range traditions
in the American Southwest, is to be found on An Informal Hour with
J. Frank Dobie,[38] recorded a few years before Dobie's death.

Born in 1888, J. Frank Dobie, folklorist, historian and lit-
erator of the Southwest, tells the yarns with resonant Texas accent.
Adults and children will enjoy the Trail-Drivers' Song taught to
Dobie by his grandfather, and can also enjoy hearing together the
hickory-nut spoof and the guessing about the "Mezela" man.

One story told in dialect is that of the old camp cook in the
cornfield when they'd "... been playing green corn for dinner without any banjo." He saw a bear gathering the ears "... as smart
as any corn-crib thief that ever took off his shoes... I was telling
my eyes not to click too loud." The bear carried the corn ears to
a tree stump where a hog the cook was fattening ground them between his jaws "as happy as a banjo talkin' to little brown jug."

On Bret Harte Read by David Kurlan[39] the two tales of frontier life and death, "The Luck of Roaring Camp" and "The Outcasts
of Poker Flat," are recreated with the language style and philosophic toughness of the characters of Bret Harte's Rogues' Gallery.

Once David Kurlan starts with his rugged Western "r" one thinks
no longer of the teller but of these taciturn tales threading to the
end of very strange lives.

Readings of Individual Poets

Among recordings of individual poets Milton's Paradise Lost,
Read by Anthony Quayle[40] and The Treasury of George Gordon,
Lord Byron, Read by Peter Orr[41] rank very high on the list.
The joint labors of an experienced reader and director a-
chieved the glorious sound of Milton's verse on the Caedmon recording of parts of Milton's Paradise Lost Read by Anthony Quayle.
Having once established the heroic stance of the poem, the reading
sings with unchecked boldness, delicate lyricism and horrible devas-
tation. The Fall, with sweeping vocal action through the magic of
imagination, covers a limitless space. But this is not mere wild
enthusiasm; the magnificent lines are controlled preparation for such
tremendous concepts as: "Him the Almighty hurled headlong...,"
"All the hollow deep of Hell resounded." "He rears... his mighty
stature," "What there thou seest fair creature is thyself," and, in
the confrontation between Gabriel and the scornful Satan, "his stature reached the sky... But fled murmuring and with him fled the
shades of night." Another recording by the same reader, The Poetry of Milton, misses the greatness of his reading of Paradise
Lost. It perhaps did not receive the same good direction.

The Treasury of George Gordon, Lord Byron Read by Peter
Orr is also an excellent recording. This reader's empathy ranges
from "Don Juan" to "The Prisoner of Chillon." In the latter there
is such closeness and supporting tonality for the life in Chillon's
dungeon that it is made real. Don Juan adroitly begins with the
first sense of touch and moves suavely into the temptation of night.
Elsewhere, "the sound of revelry by night," "whispering with white
lips," and "the sweetest song ever heard" are heard in the fine
rendering of the lines. The passages from Childe Harold's Pilgrimage include the apostrophe to the ocean with all of Byron's passionate love for the majestic sea. For choice of passages, skilled execution, and sensitive grasp of the meaning and sound in the writing,

this is a record worthy of study by those who want to learn how to
read. It is also a fine example of good direction.

Besides such majestic works as those just discussed, there
are able readings of such relatively homespun material as The
Georgics of Virgil, [42] translated and read by C. Day Lewis. The
thoughts from the Latin of a gentleman farmer and poet have a bear-
ing on husbandry today, especially the last section on bee-keeping
where Lewis is at his best as a reader.

Caedmon's The Poetry of John Dryden Read by Paul Scofield[43] is a carefully communicated work with concise point-convey-
ing readings. "Absalom and Achitophel" reaches heights in the outburst of anger in the last section of the great political satire.

On The Poetry of Coleridge,[44] read by Sir Ralph Richardson,
the reading of "Kubla Khan" has grandeur but lacks the mystery of
"deep ancestral caverns." It is side two of this record which deserves attention. It probes the lonely tragedy of the Ancient Mar-
iner. There is great skill in characterization and dialogue with
moments of intensity, as in the terrible confession of the killing of
the albatross. Throughout there is a sense of beauty, of eeriness.
The oral rendering is responsive to image, form and sound, as the
poet must have intended. The whole is a fine example of skillful
cutting and sustained control in the reading of a narrative of unusual length. It makes circles around a reading of the same work by
Richard Burton.

On The Poetry of Browning Read by James Mason,[45] "The
Bishop Orders His Tomb," "Andrea del Sarto" and "Fra Lippo
Lippi" are read with implication and suave interpretation. Treasury
of Robert Browning Read by Robert Speaight[46] also brings the poet
to life with great competence. The dramatic gifts of the reader con-
tribute to the varied characterizations in the poems. One side
moves through the believable tight conflict in "Fra Lippo Lippi."
"And I choose never to stoop" takes over in the excellent "My Last
Duchess." One believes and hears the hypocrisy as "The Bishop
Orders His Tomb at Saint Praxede's" and then the quality changes
radically for "Meeting at Night," "Parting at Morning," "Home
Thoughts From Abroad" and "Oh, Soul of My Soul" from "Prospice."

For those who have heard too little of Browning, the record will be
an unusual delight.

The Poems of William Blake and Gerard Manley Hopkins, [47]
by the same reader, begins with a well read Introduction to Blake's
"Songs of Innocence" and a forceful rendering of a section from "The
French Revolution." The reading of "The Tyger" misses its fierce-
ness but there is a rare and tender reading of "The Little Black
Boy."

Gerard Manley Hopkins Read by Cyril Cusack[48] is an inspired choice for poetry of fire and purged imagery. "Shook foil"
well describes Cusack's reading. The first poems, "Windhover" and
"God's Grandeur," are almost inaudible, but "Starlight" comes
through more strongly, placing the reader in magnificent stride for
the storm and range of "Wrack of the Deutschland." Instinctive with
the rhythms and intent of Hopkins' frequent repetitions, Cusack gives
us one of those very great moments in listening in his reading of
"I Wake and Feel the Fell of Dark."

Poems by Gerard Manley Hopkins and John Keats Read by
Margaret Rawlings[49] makes fine use of her talent for verse speaking. "Heaven-Haven," a woman's poem, emerges in the simplicity
of her reading as the rare work of art it is. Like a dancer, right
for the music, she attacks the hurtling, catapulting lines of "Starlight Night" and "Spring" and "Pied Beauty" and then reins in "...
to keep beauty back" in "The Leaden Echo." Her accuracy is accompanied by intimate warmth in such closings as: "... send my
roots rain," ("Thou Art Indeed Just"), "... yonder, yonder," ("The
Leaden Echo"), and "Help me Sir, and so I will" ("Thee, God, I
Came From").

Listening to A. E. Housman: A Shropshire Lad and Other
Poetry Read by James Mason,[50] one is aware of a cloud of restraint hanging over the reading. This characteristic seems to be
true for Housman's poetry. The listener often wishes for a break-
out to the joy which is being held back. It is a tension which only
occasionally permits an upsurge, all the more powerful because of
its rarity. Among the many beautifully read poems are "Brendan
Hill," "Is My Team Plowing," "The New Mistress," "Fancy's

Knell, " "When First My May to Fair I Took, " "The Culprit, "
"Stones, " "Steel, " and "Dominions Pass. "

T. S. Eliot: The Wasteland and Other Poems[51] is read by
Robert Speaight. Besides "The Wasteland" there is also "The Love
Song of J. Alfred Prufrock, " "The Hollow Men" and "Ash Wednes-
day. "

The reading is true to the generally low ceilinged personal
gloom of Eliot's poems. Always accommodating to the structured
movements and pauses of the material and echoing sounds, it is a
good record for those learning to read--provided that the limiting
idiosyncrasy of the poet's gloom is understood as uniquely his. It
is a valuable recording because Speaight had become the world lecturer and definitive reader of Eliot's poetry before the latter's death.

Rubaiyat of Omar Khayyam, Omar Repentant, Ballad of Reading Gaol[52] is a record from Australia. The reader of the Rubaiyat,
Frank Semple, is not as close to the material or to belief in it as
is Mayne Linton in his reading of Richard Le Gallienne's Omar Repentant. The latter is believably in violent protest against the vine.
So also is he believable in the high level account of Oscar Wilde's
Ballad of Reading Gaol.

Robinson Jeffers: Roan Stallions, Read by Marion Seldes[53]
is a beautiful reading. This had previously been presented in concert performance as "An Evening of the Poetry of Robinson Jeffers. " It has easy at-homeness with material and audience and is
tongued by a reader of impressive skill.

Homer: The Iliad (Books 15, 16, 18) Read by Anthony
Quayle[54] and Homer: The Odyssey (Books 9, 10, 11, 12) Read by
Anthony Quayle[55] come from the modern translation by Richard Lattimore. The second makes possible an experience close to that of
the ancient audience which heard the great epics as the author intended. The vocal resources and dramatic power of the ancient
bards and rhapsodists must have been somewhat akin to that of Anthony Quayle. Towards the close of the Iliad excerpts he gives
magnificent readings of such widely contrasting descriptions as
Hector's triumph, the death of Patroklos, and the making of the
shield of Achilleus. Similar examples of Quayle's artistry are also

found throughout the Odyssey. It is great exciting storytelling, an
assignment any actor might covet. Listening to it is a wondrous
experience.

The Poetry of Langston Hughes Read by Ruby Dee and
Ossie Davis[56] is the Harlem Langston Hughes in unrelieved social protest. The touch on each short verse is different: fed-up,
threatening, pert, militant, frustrated, with some self-pity but always on the line and with feet on the ground. The rhythms change,
sometimes in fast rushes as in "Dream Boogie," or in question and
answer as in "Mother in Wartime." The readers never miss a
point. They take on a poem together like the "Ode to Dinah" but
most of the reading is solo and always from deep conviction. Ruby
Dee is especially declarative and in fine release in "Final Call."

Two Major Literature Recording Projects, 1963-64

Great as the activity in recording literature had been before
1963-64, even greater impetus came at that time through the an-
nouncement of major projects being initiated by two companies.
"From Chaucer to Yeats" was the plan for 60 discs by Argo in association with the British Council, Oxford University, and the Lamont Library at Harvard University. Distribution in the United
States is through McGraw-Hill who also now handle the Argo Marlowe Society recordings of Shakespeare. "From Middle English to
Eliot" on 70 discs, the second major project, is an undertaking of
Spoken Arts.

The ambition of many recording projects has been a mark
of enthusiasm not always matched with competent execution. A few
recordings from these projects are included in previous reviews.
It is, however, fitting at this time, five years later, to assess
some of the achievement. A few examples of the trend of work
from the two projects follow.

An early release in the Spoken Arts series was The Treasury
of John Milton Read by Robert Speaight and Robert Eddison.[57] The
two readers, with command, stance, and an instinct for how the
music of this sacred river runs, divide their work; "L'Allegro" and
"Lycidas," for example, read by Robert Speaight, and "Il Pense-

roso" and "On the Morning of Christ's Nativity" by Robert Eddison.
Often missed images of "L'Allegro" and "Il Penseroso" are made
very clear.   Extraordinarily beautiful is the "Nativity of Christ."
Speaight's fond reading of "On Shakespeare: 1630" will be a boon to
many college professors.   The reader also remarkably communicates the "loss" in his reading of the lines from Paradise Lost:
"At last, words interwove with sighs/ Found out their way."

The same two readers are responsible for The Treasury of
Keats. [58] "Ode to a Nightingale," "La Belle Dame Sans Merci" and
"On First Looking Into Chapman's Homer" are among the most fully
realized of Robert Speaight's readings.   "The Eve of Saint Agnes,"
read by Robert Eddison, occupies the whole of side two.   It is a
work of art worthy of study.   The structured whole is never lost,
although such details in the poem as the description of the feast of
dainties are rendered with fastidious detail.   Eddison's concentration as he threads his way to the end of the tale unifies the experience, and it is over before one thinks of time.   The qualities of
the poetic design are responded to in the reading.   The common elements at the beginning and end of the poem unobtrusively frame it.
The "escape" is negotiated in the reading with the suspense and ease
that is present in the writing.

Another recording of Keats by the pair of Argo readers does
not come up to the one on Spoken Arts.   The concentration is too
often on performance.   Intellectual skimming on the part of some
readers and a tendency towards mechanical expression limit the
realization of meaning, rhythmic movement and imagery.

The material covered on Treasury of William Wordsworth
Read by Robert Speaight[59] also in the Spoken Arts program is an
especially good orientation to Wordsworth and his influence on English poetry.   "Intimations of Immortality from Recollections of Early
Childhood" and "Lines Composed Above Tintern Abbey" have the intimate conversational character for which Wordsworth strove.   Occasionally the reader only approximates images as he engages in
some critical watchfulness.   But on most of the record, Speaight is
right, for example, in the reading of "To Toussaint L'Ouverture,"
"To Sleep," and the "Milton! Thou Shouldst be Living at This Hour."

He is also intensely close in catching the beauty and emotional power of "She Was a Phantom of Delight" and "The Solitary Reaper. "

To the reading of the Poems of Gerard Manley Hopkins, [60] Speaight, like a lover, brings all his accumulated knowledge and practice of rhyme and rhythm of sound and sense in the reading of poetry. It is a learned work, calculated to send listeners back to these and other Hopkins poems. Meeting the heavy demands of "God's Grandeur," Speaight moves into easy command of the catapulting inner rhymes and rhythms of "The Windhover," "To Christ Our Lord," "Pied Beauty" and "The Leaden Echo" and "The Golden Echo. " The readings are religiously sensitive to Hopkins: "I wake and feel the fell of dark. "

The Pre-Raphaelites: Christina Rossetti, Dante Gabriel Rossetti, Charles Swinburne, William Morris[59] is directed by George Rylands and read by Peter Orr, Gary Watson and Flora Robson. It is part of the Argo project, "From Chaucer to Yeats. "

The second side of this record is eminently worthwhile but side one is not good. "The Blessed Damosel" is recited with heavy voiced rhetorical assertion by Gary Watson instead of with the lyricism and imagination of this delicate work. This is a good illustration of a mechanical reading. The same wooden reading is to be found for Rossetti's "Three Sonnets: The Choice. " Here the progression of images is missed because the reader is not imaginatively behind the meaning of the words or the images which should be created. By way of illustration, three missed ideas are here underlined.

> Nay come up hither. From this
>   wave-washed mound
> Unto the furthest flood-brim look with me;
> Then reach on with thy thought till
>   it be drowned.
> Miles and miles distant though the last line be,
> And though thy soul sail leagues and leagues beyond, --
> Still, leagues beyond those leagues, there is more sea.

Flora Robson reads the poetry of Christina Rossetti with insights true to its religious as well as bitter philosophic song from the heart. She reads with all the senses alive to visual and heard beauty, with sadness, intensity and leaping hope.

Peter Orr reads from Swinburne's "Hymn to Proserpine" and
"The Garden of Proserpine" with fast Swinburnian exultation in a
song of language, with delight in the cadence, in the echo of rhymes
and in the leap of lines. It is superior reading of Swinburne. Although the same reader is more absorbed in the activity of reading
than in what is there in the Rossetti poems on side one, he turns out
a superior job for both Swinburne and the poetry of William Morris
which closes the work.

Prose Recordings

Jonathan Swift: Gulliver's Travels[62] as read by Michael Redgrave fits the detached style of Swift's barefaced telling the truth
outrageously. The section about abolishing words in "The Voyage
to Laputa" is brazen farce. Continuous wonder permeates the narration of the "Houyhnyms" up to the final preference for the stable,
all the more tragic for being told in human speech.

Only a few of the same selections from Swift are read on
Alec Guinness Reads from Gulliver's Travels, The Modest Proposal,
Epitaph, and Other Writings by Jonathan Swift.[63] With urbane rel-
ish Guinness talks this most caustic of English satire.

Treasury of Jonathan Swift, Gulliver's Travels[64] is read by
Denis Johnston and directed by Arthur Luce Klein. The reader,
Dublin born, is author of nine plays including The Old Lady Says
No, at one time was a member of the Abbey, and was a pioneer in
early television work. He is author of In Search of Swift and a
choice reader for Swift. The storytelling is in a casual mood as
the reader moves with great immediacy through interestingly selected material: side one, "A Voyage to Lilliput" Chapter I: side
two, Chapters II and V, concluding with the fire in the Empress'
apartment.

On another front, an adapted section of Boswell's London
Journal[65] read by Anthony Quayle makes brilliant use of recording
technology for passages of profound social significance.

Daniel Defoe's Moll Flanders,[66] read by Siobhan McKenna,
is ably cut and narrated and is one of the most distinguished por-

traits of a woman on records. The reading is true to the target:
Defoe's ongoing story. The linguistic expert will have to decide on
Moll's Cockney accent.

The Autobiography of Frederick Douglass,[67] edited by Dr.
Philip Fouer, is read by Ossie Davis with appropriate simplicity for
the account of the slave who escaped to freedom. There is an easy
intimacy throughout this unfolding saga of Douglass' escape and rise
to leadership in the early nineteenth century anti-slavery agitation.
There is also an accompanying text. Among black culture records
this one is of lasting value, both for its contents and its fine execution.

Silas Marner (abridged) as Read by Judith Anderson[68] is an
excellent job of cutting yet holding to the main thread of George
Eliot's story. Judith Anderson carries the burden of narrating the
story. It is one of the most competent, self-effacing pieces of narration to be found on records. Effortless, leaving all to the listener, she meticulously follows the structure, writing style and imagery of the author.

Very beautiful in their simplicity are many lines:

...he moaned very long, not as one who seeks to be heard...

... he sat in his robbed home...

... the little one toddled... in perfect contentment...

There are such beautifully read passages as the rearing of
Effie, teaching her seeing and listening, and the description of the
wedding couple. There is a fine supporting cast, particularly in
the scene where Effie, holding the hand of the weaver, makes her
choice. This record in its excellence is one of the rich contributions of modern recording to the oral study and appreciation of the
classics.

Dickens Recordings

There have been more readings from the works of Charles
Dickens than from any other prose writer. In his later life Dickens
successfully toured with "Readings" from his works. In America,

he was lionized. His cool reaction is recorded on the pages of contemporary American diaries and in the acidulous account of the experience which he set down himself upon his return to England. His continuing popularity is attested by the large number of Dickens recordings which have been produced.

One hundred years after Dickens' travels, the bite of the sharp observer and vivisectionist of humankind is again heard on Emlyn Williams as Charles Dickens. [69] Giving a solo performance of scenes from his novel, dressed as Charles Dickens, and using an old fashioned reading stand with upholstered arm rest, Williams also scored with audiences as he brought them the Dickens scenes. Poignant, eerie, harsh, aware of the powers of dialect, of repetition, of the "click" of words and the sly scratch through gloved hand, Williams' oral performances dramatically underscore and illuminate the many passages he reads from: Our Mutual Friend, Dombey and Son, Pickwick Papers, Christmas Stories and A Tale of Two Cities.

Less dramatic and formal but for enjoyment at the hearth is Readings From English Literature: Dickens read by V. C. Clinton-Baddeley for B. B. C. , English by Radio. The passages are from A Christmas Carol, Pickwick Papers, Nicholas Nickleby and Great Expectations. [70]

As the cold penetrated to the marrow of Mr. Pickwick's bones when he fell through the ice, so does the sharpness in these readings gradually penetrate to the inmost bone of the listener. It is sophisticated, smooth reading, in the oldest tradition of oral literature in the home.

Lines in Mr. Pickwick are given with easy grace:

> Mr. Winkle expressed exquisite delight and looked exquisitely uncomfortable. . .

> . . The males turned pale and the females fainted. . .

> . . . With an accuracy which no degree of dexterity or practice could have insured. . .

Humor wisps through Nicholas Nickleby. As he tried his hand at theatre:

> ... the orchestra playing a variety of popular airs,
> with involuntary variations...
>
> ... There was a gorgeous banquet ready spread for the
> third act consisting of two pasteboard vases, one plate
> of biscuits, a black bottle and a vinegar cruet; and in
> short everything was on a scale of the utmost splendour
> and preparation...

A rare listening experience, because of its intensity, comes in the passage from Great Expectations where the terrified Pip and the fearful Man meet in the graveyard. "He tilted me again." And for the student who would study phrasing there is the effortless reading of a sentence of several lines describing how the play finally "came out."

On Dickens' Duets Presented by Frank Pettingell,[71] Uriah Heap, Mr. Peggotty, Sam Weller, Pip and Joe are among the vignettes in duet from Pettingell's repertoire of a lifetime playing Dickens. The habit of phrase, unique vocal quality and special rhythm for each of the several characters on this record, give the neophyte listener interesting tips about some things which go into making the printed line breathe.

The two readers on Charles Dickens: The Pickwick Papers,[72] Sir Lewis Casson reading "Mr. Pickwick's Christmas" and Boris Karloff telling us about "The Goblins and the Sexton," make it fine Christmas entertainment. Sir Lewis Casson participates in the gay coach-and-four Christmas party with proper elderly relish for the telling, especially when Mr. Pickwick is caught under the mistletoe. Gabriel Grub's experience with the goblins keeps an even keel with the neat tension in Boris Karloff's spinning of the tale of the gloomy sexton whose grim joke about "grave lodgings for one" is interrupted by unearthly grave doings.

Horror Stories

Among the horror stories on records are several from Robert Louis Stevenson. Sir Lawrence Olivier in a Robert Louis Stevenson Album[73] (O. P.) chooses "The Suicide Club" and passages from The Strange Case of Dr. Jekyll and Mr. Hyde. The reader follows the writer's cool, tight-reined style, never succumbing to the temptation to horriplate, although the subjects are a suicide club and Mr. Hyde. The calling out of the cards at the Club comes off suspensefully with effortless economy.

"The Imp of the Perverse Shadow" and "Lionizing" by Edgar Allan Poe are also on James Mason Reads Herman Melville's Bartleby the Scrivener. [74] Nice clarity for the two characters marks the dogged steps of Bartleby. The tales have concentrated horror impact, especially "The Shadow."

It is a terrifying experience when Roddy McDowall Reads the Horror Stories of H. P. Lovecraft. [75] "The Outsider" and "The Hound" are two macabre tales in the best tradition of horror stories. Most remarkable in the recording is the design of Roddy McDowall's storytelling. Prepared, constrained and selfless, he pours belief, horror and living images into the design of each tale. With a discipline to fit the structure yet also with immediacy, he recalls "nothing... could compare in terror with what I now saw," and "horror reached a culmination." At the other extreme, he recalls his "fantastic wonder" and "the purest ecstasy I have ever known." The connoisseur will cherish this record. It is not an easy piece to read aloud.

On The Treasury of Nathaniel Hawthorne, The Minister's Black Veil Read by Robert S. Breen [76] New England cold hangs over the story as its cold outlines unfold. There is brief relief in Professor Breen's account of the comments of the congregation on the first appearance of the minister's black veil and in his farewell to the woman he loved. The rest moves on to the fearful climax of his deathbed and the final words following his burial.

The Tales of Horror and Suspense by Ambrose Bierce Read by Ugo Toppo [77] are: Vol. 1, "An Occurrence at Owl Creek Bridge" and "The Man and the Snake." Vol. 2, "The Boarded Window" and "The Affair at Coulter's Notch." These stories convey the horror, suspense and surprise endings of Bierce without intrusive give-away by the teller.

Among the Selections from the Marquis de Sade Read by Patrick McGee [78] are an excerpt from Justine, a letter from prison

written to de Sade's wife, and an abridgment of the story of "The
Mystified Magistrate." Patrick McGee, the de Sade of the Marat-
Sade stage production, reads in the characterization he created
there. Close listening is necessary because of the peculiar speech
quality used for the unbalanced de Sade.

Some Modern Prose Writers

In Frank Pettingell Presents Oscar Wilde,[79] the reader turns
to the different world of: "The Selfish Giant," "The Remarkable
Rocket," "A Group of Witticisms," "A Scene from the Trial of
Oscar Wilde" and "A Talk with Mr. Oscar Wilde." The record has
sparkle as Wilde's interpreter pursues the writer's idea of himself.
At the same time, Pettingell is given a chance to create a range of
characters from giant to duck. The witticism and meat of Wilde is
in a one-sided dialogue from the trial which is sandwiched between
the stories.

When Sir Michael Redgrave Reads Chekhov[80] the woes of
average man are told. In a different style for each Chekhov piece
he gets to the heart of the matter, whether it be "On the Harmful-
ness of Tobacco," "The First-Class Passenger" or "A Transgres-
sion." In this last especially Redgrave's skill in exposition emerges
with structural sensitivity and delicate perception.

Little on Spoken Records can equal, much less surpass, the
easy coherence of "Swann in Love" read by Sir Ralph Richardson on
Proust, Remembrance of Things Past.[81] Far beyond noticed craftsmanship, yet with superb craft, are the outbursts of Odette, the
philosophic observations of "my grandfather" and the felicitous description of the elegant trivia of the meeting in the bus with Madame
Cotter. The climax of the dream sequence clarifies and sharpens
both Swann's wisdom and our own. The dream flows in and out with
something akin to the reader's own ease with words.

The Painted Bird Read by the Author, Jerzy Kosinski[82] is
valuable for the impact of the five selected episodes which exemplify
the author's range in dealing with the cruelty of ignorance. The author's reading follows the jerky mechanical phrasing of one not at
home with the rhythm of the English language.

Langston Hughes' Simple, [83] read by Ossie Davis, is Langston Hughes "explaining and illuminating the Negro condition in America." The character is a simple "Harlem Everyman" in commonsense rock-bottom talk. The selection encourages one to further reading of Langston Hughes. "The Banquet in Honor" is a modern chapter in the history of rhetoric. The banquet opens with the conventional introduction by Mrs. Sadie Maxwell Reeves, the toast mistress. Then the rigid battlements of a hide-bound system of conventional public speaking are blasted open. The truth spoken by the old man "being honored" at the banquet made sense to Simple: "This is not a banquet in my honor." The description of Simple's appreciation of that truth makes for a memorable moment in literature.

For those who like to be read to, Hubert Gregg as Jerome K. Jerome [84] is satisfying listening. "The Tandem, or How Harris Lost His Wife" is uproarious after-dinner company. It brings to mind another entertaining British record, a delightful "best" to have around for visitors. This is the dramatization of P. G. Wodehouse's Jeeves [85] starring Terry Thomas and Roger Livesey and directed by Howard Sackler. "Indian Summer of an Uncle" and "Jeeves Takes Charge" are sure to please. The speech is "nice" British with a Cockney surprise in the offing. The reading team is a good one. This perfect butler of a record is ready for long service in giving enjoyment.

Concert Programs

Mention has already been made of the tour of Emlyn Williams as Charles Dickens. Micheal MacLiammoir in The Importance of Being Oscar [86] was the vehicle for the Irish actor's concert tour based on the life and works of Oscar Wilde. With vocal ostentation, he describes, as Wilde might have, the lecture in 1880 to the brawny miners of Leadville. He reads from letters the sharp pointed wit in his subjects' many encounters with an antagonized world, the permeating evil and horror of Dorian Gray, the parts of the ladies as well as the gentlemen of The Importance of Being Earnest, and Wilde's words from his inmost being as death approached: "Robbie, I don't know what to do."

Micheal MacLiammoir also successfully toured with <u>I Must Be Talking to my Friends,</u> [87] introducing Ireland's poets, wits and revolutionaries. The recording benefits from fine programming and execution and is of great historic as well as artistic interest.

MacLiammoir sweeps through the historic and literary life of Ireland in forty minutes. It seems like a few minutes of delight, charm, humor, pathos and love to the listener who is as out of breath as the actor at the conclusion. One hears, among many others, Cormac on women, St. Patrick, Robert Emmet, The Galway Woman, W. B. Yeats, including "Easter 1916," and, what has now become legend, MacLiammoir's reading from Joyce as the lustful Leopold ogles the crippled girl. It is an effective vignette of Irish history.

Another concert reader in our times is recorded on <u>Hal Holbrook in Mark Twain Tonight</u>[88] and <u>More Mark Twain Tonight</u>[89] and presents material Mark Twain used on his lecture tours and passages from his writings. In England, Max Adrian has scored a similar success with <u>An Evening with G. B. Shaw.</u> [90]

The first Mark Twain record includes the audience's response to expert "milking" for laughs. Side one especially illustrates the effective use of comic timing: Holbrook lets the laugh subside before making the second and third onslaughts. There are several crescendos of humor similar to "... she'd neglected her habits / she was a sinking ship... / I guess one or two bad habits... /"

Margaret Webster toured the United States and England with a dramatic reading of <u>The Brontes.</u> [91] Their lives are reconstructed through extracts from diaries, poems, Mrs. Gaskell's Life and passages from <u>Jane Eyre,</u> <u>Wuthering Heights</u> and <u>Agnes Grey.</u> Beautifully restrained, letting the listener sentimentalize, it is an easy album to listen to, facile in transition and skilled in the delivery. It is executed in the best tradition of theater and polished by many confrontations with audiences.

<u>A Lovely Light. Edna St. Vincent Millay,</u> [92] a dramatization by Dorothy Stickney of the poems and letters of Edna St. Vincent Millay, was presented at the Hudson Theatre in New York City in 1960 and again in a return engagement in 1964. Among biographi-

cal albums this is one of the most fulsome and tightly planned.
Dorothy Stickney has dug well into the many letters and poems of
her subject.   A poem as early as "Renaissance" and one as late
as the poem unfinished at her death are read in a voice very like
the famous poet's own.   The poetry is gay like "Recuerdo," brave
as in "Well, I Have Lost You," and matured in "The Courage That
My Mother Had" and "The Room Is Full of You."   The reader
meets every whispering mood of her subject in the letters which tie
together the life.   Although they were contemporaries, the poetess
and the actress never met.   But there is such a matching of spirit
in the reading that one would believe they had.

Group Concert Readings

        Group concert readings gained recognition through the enter-
prise of Paul Gregory in the long run tour of Bernard Shaw's Don
Juan in Hell[93] starring Charles Boyer, Charles Laughton, Cedric
Hardwicke and Agnes Moorehead.   On the disc, no dull moment is
permitted by the players who debate this usually omitted central
scene from Man and Superman.   Fast to catch and call each point,
they meet with a crescendo of hoot, laugh and snort the Commander's: "It was this sincerity that made me successful!"

        In the middle of the last act, Charles Boyer, as Don Juan,
with brilliant conservatoire-schooled technique, builds with increasing intensity the long succession of accurately realized distinctions:
". . . They are not moral. . . only conventional. . . not kind. . . only sentimental. . . " so that Satan admiringly wishes that he could talk like
that to his soldiers.   Even the down-to-earth listener is caught by
the deep emotion of Boyer's heroic style and finds acceptable the
dramatic vibrato of ". . . past the colossal mechanism. . . " and ". . . by
which I grasp the sword. . . ," to mention only two examples.
Boyer's technical design for the longer speeches and the variants in
emotional color on word and phrase, such as those quoted, are
worthy of study by younger artists.

        Another commercial as well as artistic success was Stephen
Vincent Benét: John Brown's Body[94] adapted for dramatic reading
by Charles Laughton, Tyrone Power, Judith Anderson and Raymond

Massey. The long American Civil War epic poem is an achievement in editing, arrangement, musical transition and casting. The
four star performers share the narration and create, as needed, the
medley of characters who appear in the poem. The à capella chorus, together with well-planned musical and sound effects, supply the
background of war or peace, crowd voices and fitting songs all the
way from joyous, lilting "Like Moses ridin' on a bumble bee" to
the stirring finale, "It is here!"

In movement and song its language speaks: "The fill of the
possum, fall of the coon, / And a lop-eared hound dog baying at the
moon." When there seems to be danger of lingering on the sentimental, the lines forge on to some such hard reality as the proud
Southern lady's resistance: "They won't drive me from ma home!"

The Hollow Crown, [95] devised and produced by John Barton,
is an entertainment on the theme of monarchy. Anglo-Saxon Chronicles, Shakespeare, and letters (one by Jane Austen) yielded material for the album. Songs are sung between readings and impersona-
tions, and piano as well as harpsichord supply accompaniment.
Cast support comes from Dorothy Tutin, Max Adrian, Richard Johnson, John Johnson and Tony Church.

The Death of Patroclus [96] is not at all Homer (as is
claimed), but as a free adaptation by Christopher Logue from Book
XVI of Homer's Iliad, it is a new work and should be judged and
valued as such. As directed by Douglas Cleverdon, it is a great
recording achievement.

The commander Achilles is cast with a contrasting voiced
Patroclus and with gods and goddesses speaking from Olympian dis-
tances as effectively as do the warriors and fallen men: "Greek,
get back where you belong!" Every dimension, every new slanting
light on the story has been followed in the phrasing and assignment
of voices for the narrative.

In beautiful design, the five readers take turns picking up
the story and passing it on, sometimes for only a swirling moment
of vivid detail. Most perceptive and with great purity of line is the
clear-voiced reading of Vanessa Redgrave. It ranges from descriptions of moments in nature to such a line as: "Saying these things,

Patroclus died..."

Christopher Logue, the poet-adapter, reads part of the narrative. In spite of a distractingly delicate vocal quality, he reads with an urgent stride and authority good to hear. The record is a concert reading of unusual aesthetic appeal.

Another concert performance which achieved Broadway success was the Spoon River Anthology, [97] originally produced by a West Coast group. For the director, Charles Aidman, it began with an early interest in Edgar Lee Masters. Years later this interest continued through many months of hard work on the text and with a cooperative group of young actors: Betty Garrett, Robert Elkston and Joyce Van Patten. This group meets one of the tests of the isolated world of sound recording by never sounding like themselves. Each character impersonated, and several are taken on by each member of the cast, has its distinctive vocal quality, touch, rhythm and style. Band one on side two illustrates these qualities. It is also a good example of the director's skill in effecting the facile flow of many presences. Edgar Lee Master's work is a gloomy, unhopeful one. But this excellent rendition by a group of young actors is full of promise for American Theater.

Reconstructed Documentaries

John Dos Passos: U. S. A. , Selections from The 42nd Parallel[98] is read by Ed Begley, George Grizzard, Rip Torn and John Dos Passos, the author. This is a reconstructed documentary covering the story of radical and labor movements in the U. S. A. for some thirty years before World War I. It has portrayals of many of the leading agitators and of such public figures as Bryan, Edison and La Follette. There is considerable bite to the seamy sided material with occasional breakthrough of music or newscasts interrupting and fused into the thread of happenings. It is all skillfully managed with the author himself carrying the ball for the Camera Eye, the evolving revolutionary.

What Passing Bell, [99] a commemoration in prose and poetry of the fiftieth anniversary of the outbreak of the First World War, is a bitter piece. It has British bite to the end.

The Sinking of the Bismarck[100] is a reconstructed documentary of a crucial sea engagement in World War I. It is a model of
restrained, non-intrusive theatrical skill. It is also worthy of imi-
tation by script writers because of the strict commitment to original documentary sources and the economically structured arrangement of very exciting war operations.

Official records are allowed to tell of the crucial battle to
protect the British supply line. British Naval records, documents
in the archives of the German navy, and accounts of eye-witnesses
who survived are arranged like a game of chess with brief pinpoint-
ing of such determinants as weather, radar, and oil supplies. This
inspired account of bravery and Naval sagacity, now out of print,
should be reissued.

The Mormon Pioneers[101] is the seventh release in the Columbia Records Legacy Collection produced by Goddard Lieberson.
This one is reconstructed from excerpts from letters, journals and
memoirs between 1846 and 1853. The readings are dignified and in
appropriate homespun speech. Adding to the mood are choruses and
folk songs sung between the documentary materials by a Chorus with
solos by Jack Elliott, Ed McCurdy, Clayton Kreibel and Oscar
Brand. The world famous Mormon Tabernacle Choir closes the recording. A handsome 48-page history in words and pictures accompanies the record. The album is an interesting experience. It
vivifies the history of the American frontier through scholarly research and the dramatization by Charles Burr.

Homage to Dylan Thomas and T. S. Eliot

Under Milk Wood by Dylan Thomas[102] carries the premiere
performance recorded in New York on May 14, 1953. It had the advantage of the poet's coaching as well as his narration and will always be valuable for study and comparison.

Homage to Dylan Thomas[103] is a recording of the memorial
meeting held at the Globe Theatre in London on January 24, 1954,
sponsored by the Sunday Times and staged by the Group Theatre.
"The Requiem Canto" by Louis MacNeice opened the program of

Thomas' poems including several excerpts from "Return Journey:
What Has Become of Him Now?" These were read by Hugh Griffith, followed by Richard Burton's readings of "A Hunchback in the
Park" and "Poem in October." A third Welshman, Emlyn Williams,
read "A Visit to Grandpa's," drawing the full measure of laughter
from the audience. The closing poem, "Fern Hill," read by Richard Burton, may be better than Thomas' own recorded reading.

Although not on the record, it is reported that this solemn
meeting closed with Dylan Thomas' recording of "And Death Shall
Have No Dominion."

On January 25, 1954 there was a concert broadcast of Under
Milk Wood[104] by a distinguished Welsh cast and children of Laugh-
arne School. The direction by Douglas Cleverdon and the national
spirit behind this recorded performance of Homage to Dylan Thomas
are the record of a public lament.

While not a group reading, the fitting postscript to these
memorials was a fellow Welshman's concert tour: Emlyn Williams
as Dylan Thomas. A Boy Growing Up.[105]   It is now on an Argo
Record.

The Memorial Record of Homage to T. S. Eliot[106] has among
the readers of Eliot's poetry: Laurence Olivier, Paul Scofield,
George Devine, Ian Richardson, Alec McCowan and Groucho Marx.
The place was the Globe Theatre in London, June 19, 1965. The
audience honored the silent pauses and applauded appreciatively after
each reading. Perhaps it was the solemnity of the occasion which
made some of these able actors take themselves rather seriously
although Paul Scofield came through with fine readings from "The
Wasteland" and "Ash Wednesday."

Following the intermission, formality ceased and Groucho
Marx, after an introduction, plunged into the reading of "Gus the
Theatre Cat." The delight of the audience was matched only by
Groucho's delight in letting the cat steal the show. The final enter-
tainment was a lusty last scene (unpublished) of "Sweeney Agonistes."
The excellent cast was directed by Peter Wood.

Biblical Recording

While churchmen might be expected to be good Bible readers,
they often take themselves too seriously.   Like some poets they also
become mechanical readers or self-listeners before a microphone.
The lugubrious "ministerial" tone one sometimes hears is really
self-listened-to speech and is no holier than any other form of self-
watching.   Anti-ministerial attempts to be "natural" are often just
as self-watched.

Old Testament Psalms and The Tale of David, [107] a good
reading by Judith Anderson, has meaningful accuracy and an unclut-
tered response to the spirit of prayer.   It is sensitive to the quality
and structure of the language.   The One-hundred and Twenty-third
Psalm is an example of reading stemming from an accurate center,
in this case David's deep sorrow reaching out to ". . . Jonathan my
brother. . ."   and to God, in ". . . Unto Thee I lift up my eyes. . ."
Similarly, in the story of "David and Goliath" the center is that of
the storyteller.   It follows the design of the ongoing narrative in its
gentle building to "So David prevailed. . . and. . . the Philistines. . .
fled."   Listening to a record as well done as this can be helpful
to any student of reading.

There have been many other Bible recordings.   But it is not
within the compass of the present work to review them.   Suffice it
to say that many Bible readers tend to give themselves rather than
the scriptural texts.   It takes knowledge about how to work, and
then work to read the Bible well.

Children's Records

Many noisy recordings are to be found on the children's market.   Mechanically read and overlaid with artificial vocal and other
sound effects, they are deadening to sensitive listening and may do
more harm than is realized.   While it is not within the scope here
to enter into an extensive discussion of children's records, it may
be useful to mention a few of the good ones.   The next two reviewed could top any list.

Miracles, Poems Written by Children[108] is a collection by
Richard Lewis, who undertook a search for poems written by chil-

dren all over the world.   The poems were chosen for inclusion in
the book, Miracles, for their childlike quality and the adult implications in perspective.   Throughout, the two readers, Roddy McDowall
and Julie Harris, fulfill the assignment of reading with respect for
the material and absolute self-effacement.   The child's urge towards
wonder, warm feelings, movement, play with sounds, use of repetition, etc., are very simply conveyed.   An adult does not say
things the way a child does: "I just know I'm sad."   "It's my
house."   "I wonder why."

Sophisticated Roddy McDowall and Julie Harris permit one to
sense such child experiences as "a breath of wind," "the castle of
the fairies," the child's consideration of a tadpole, the little fish
and the scared child.   Children will find themselves in much of
what is read and the grown-up will be grateful for the recall to his
own childhood.

Among very important British productions in this area are
A World of Searching Eyes, an original collection of verse and prose
written, read by children (the verse is chosen by John Betjeman).
Abbey (2-12") Abbey VP 631-32; and The Searching Years '68--
Abbey (3-12") MVP 635-6-7.   The last three records, covering ages
8, 11 and 14 plus, are devoted to poetry and prose written and
read by children and to music composed and performed by children.
Regional accents are used in the readings which are introduced by
Robert Gittings the poet.   All these Abbey productions are available
through Discourses.

The Jungle Books by Rudyard Kipling Read by Christopher
Casson and Eve Watkinson, [109] a Spoken Arts production directed by
Christopher Casson, is on two records: (1) "Mowgli's Brothers,"
"Rikki-Tikki Tavi" and (2) "Tiger Tiger" and "Toomai of the Ele-
phants."   Indian music for introductions and backgrounds is performed by Mr. T. S. Banga of the Indian Embassy in Dublin and
his two young daughters.   "Animal sounds come through the cooperation of the inmates of the Dublin Zoo."

The son of Dame Sybil Thorndike and the late Sir Lewis Casson has brought the cooperative plenty of the Dublin community, his
own talents and those of Eve Watkinson to the Kipling stories.   Like

the magical stage lighting of the late Jean Rosenthal, his artistry
with sound conjures up the atmosphere of the jungle. The records
are a gift for childhood and age as well. Besides the exciting story
thread, there is depth and range of wonder in such lines as: "Take
me with you," "Alone on the back of the seventy year elephant,"
"The terrible charge of the buffalos," "The shock of meeting of the
herds." The riches of the world of sound so sensitively assembled
here are a milestone in children's recordings. It is one of the
works of art of recording which should not be missed.

The gently gay Jupiter Poems and Songs for Younger Children[110] has the "Three Little Kittens" off to a bright start with a
stroke of the harp strings. A young and fresh-as-spring "Who
Killed Cock Robin?" yields the variously imagined responses with
beetle, owl, and Michael Hordern as clerk far out in front. Some
of the other readings are uneven but there is plenty to satisfy.

The arrangement of the poems and songs and the gentle
touch in the reading make this a record for genteel parlor entertainment and fun for the sick child too. Copies of the poems and songs
are included in The Jupiter Book of Verse.

This same English Jupiter also produced Play Songs[111] and
The Mulberry Bush. [112] Designed with good taste, they will intrigue and delight very young children with their engaging rhythms,
sounds of words, instruments and tunes. The recording of many of
the songs is by school children.

Accompanied by a Gaelic harp Christopher Casson sings and
reads Treasury of Nursery Rhymes. [113] If anyone becomes tired
before the fifty-third rhyme he can go to sleep to the song of the
harp.

Because of the unusual bumptious spirit on Mother Goose[114]
featuring Cyril Ritchard, Celeste Holm and Boris Karloff, it may be
thought by some to be out of place in a highly disciplined classroom. But a houseful of young Alcotts, to their cultural gain, will
thrive on the soundful language play and the variant dramatic suggestions. It happened when three gifted old hands were let loose to
"take stage" by the exuberant director, Howard Sackler, who also
knows how to use music in this recital of the poems.

Much is told with wonder and playful sound:

    If all the seas were one sea...
    What a splish-splash that would be!

Some verses are sung, as would be expected for "London Bridge."
Some are lilted, as is "The House That Jack Built." Then the three
readers, on a gay spree, flit in and out of the characters who did
not kill Cock Robin. They appear to be able to incite any party of
competitive youngsters or suppressed adults (except in the case of
the chief mourner for Cock Robin) to try to outdo them.

A great love for childhood has gone into this record. It is
the stuff of which poetry is made and through which budding young
poets may be led to it. The blurb on the sleeve of the record
closes a justifiable paean with "...a very small monument to us
will do! Thank you..." "Yes," say we, "It must be a very small
monument but just right too! Thank you." One should be warned
that this is really a record for nostalgic oldsters and for the very
bright older child. It is too swinging fast for the very young.

Knowledgeable and loving appreciation went into the selection
and arrangement of the choices from Robert Louis Stevenson's A
Child's Garden of Verses.[115] It is contagious, read for the most
part by Basil Langton who brings to each poem wonder, manly remembrance and the sense of fresh believing. Adults, from whose
viewpoint Stevenson wrote, will respond to the exceptional reading of
"The Lamplighter" and recognize the tender discovery in the last
line. The recitations will appeal because of their freshness. Lessons about poetry planning can be learned from the repeated lines,
e. g. , "I Saw You Toss Your Kites On High," and from movement and
sounds in "The Pirate Story," "Travel," and "Marching Song."
The last line to foreign children: "Don't you wish you were me"
will intrigue anyone. Nancy Wickwire's "Foreign Lands," "The
Swing" and "North-West Passage" are well done.

Planned for older children and giving them credit for dis-
criminating taste and interest in good poetry is The Golden Treasury
of Children's Verse.[116] Read by Jill Balcon and Robert Speaight,
it sounds as though as the children they must have been glad to hear

not only Edward Lear and Lewis Carroll but Shakespeare, Milton
("On His Blindness"), Keats and Emily Bronte as well.

The pithy meat of Aesop's Fables Read by Boris Karloff[117]
is given time for relaxed digestion by the ingenious device of a
shepherd's piping the separation between the forty-two tales. Sometimes the piper's phrase is a sigh. Easily and simply, without unction or scolding, Boris Karloff lets the tales tell themselves.

The CMS label has several recordings of fairy tales told by
Anne Pellowski. At one time, as Group-Work specialist at the New
York Public Library, Miss Pellowski visited the libraries and public parks telling these stories in the traditional manner. It is simple storytelling, easily at home with materials and children. American Indian Tales for Children[118] (2 Vols.), English Folk and Fairy
Tales[119] and The Seventh Princess and Other Fairy Tales[120] are a
few of the tales already recorded.

Asian Folk and Fairy Tales[121] told by Christine Price is
rich-voiced storytelling. The tales on this record are "The Valiant
Chattee Maker" (India), "The Boy Who Drew Cats" (Japanese), and
"The Great Stone Fire Eater" (Korea). One looks forward to recordings of folk-tales from other parts of the world by the same
teller.

Folk Tales of the Tribes of Africa[122] are read by Eartha
Kitt. The selections come from the collection made by Paul Radin
for African Folktales and Sculpture. There are not always happy
endings. The truth is down to earth. The tribes represented are
Hottentot, Efiko-Ibibio, Masai, Bakongo, Ashanti, Baila, and Ba-
venda, if some child wants to know.

In April, 1955, Michael Redgrave, on the occasion of the
150th anniversary of Hans Andersen's birth, gave the first televised
readings at Hans Andersen's desk before their Majesties, the King
and Queen of Denmark. On Hans Christian Andersen Read by Michael Redgrave[123] he reads "The Tinder Box," "The Emperor's
New Clothes," "The Steadfast Tin Soldier" and "The Emperor's
Nightingale." All are well done. "The Emperor's New Clothes,"
with the child's sudden exclamation, "He hasn't got anything on,"
and the beautiful "Emperor's Nightingale" are especially well done.

Several fairy tales have been recorded by Boris Karloff on
two records: Hans Christian Andersen: The Little Match Girl and
Other Fairy Tales[124] and Boris Karloff Reads The Ugly Duckling
and Other Tales by Hans Christian Andersen.[125]

"The Little Match Girl" can always take her prize for sad
appeal, but the masterpiece is the creation of the exquisite world of
"Thumbelina." She is discovered by Boris Karloff inside a walnut
shell. With minute and unsuspected delicacy, he presents the portrait of her: "taking her sash, she tied one end to the butterfly
and the other to the leaf."

Children could listen to Boris Karloff a long, long time in
this mood because he never seems to grow tired, never forces, and
is always fresh for the next story. On the second record the
"Tally-ho" of "Clod-Poll" is fun, and "The Collar" is also cunningly
done. All the tales are very human in sorrow and joy.

Boris Karloff reads from another old favorite, The Just So
Stories:[126] "How the Whale Got His Throat," "How the Camel Got
His Hump" and "How the Rhinoceros Got His Skin"; and on side two
of the record, an abridgement of "Mowgli's Brothers" from The Jungle Book. The record turns out to be a "find" in simple storytelling. The right kind of wondrous believability goes along with the
language playfulness the author intended in "... Change here for the
Fitchberg line...," in the djin's real whistle and the camel's
"humph."

The second side takes the unprepared listener most by surprise. "Mowgli's Brothers" is moving in the tender and fierce pro-
tectiveness of the mother wolf for the man's cub who "... came
naked by night... and yet was not afraid." There are powerful moments of climax and of silence when Mowgli is admitted to the pack,
when Bakira asks Mowgli to "... save Arcala from the death..." and
finally and poignantly when "... something began to hurt Mowgli."
It is storytelling for children of all ages.

The age that can accommodate a dialect will enjoy Animal
Tales Told in the Gullah Dialect by Albert H. Stoddard of Savannah,
Georgia.[127] Accompanying textual transcriptions as well as a glos-
sary by Mr. Stoddard add to the pleasure and understanding of the

stories. Told by an old-timer, born and brought up on one of the
Gullah dialect islands off the South Carolina coast, the storytelling
is an example of folktale recording by a last survivor. Some of
these are versions of the Joel Chandler Harris Uncle Remus stories,
e. g. , "The Tar Baby. " The telling is the ongoing deadpan of simple human insight, leaving all comment to the listener. At times
one senses a kinship with William Faulkner. Mostly concerned with
the crafty doings of Br'er Rabbit, the stories also tell of his down-
to-earth usefulness and final comeuppance.

Kenneth Grahame's The Wind in the Willows[128] survived
many broadcasts before it was pressed on a record. Richard Gold-
en's Mole makes his lovable way under the skin of even those for
whom moles have heretofore spelled only trouble. In the course of
listening, all is forgotten and forgiven for the inhabitants of this
animal wonder world, interesting because they sympathetically reflect so much of our own. There is remarkable understandability
of the speech of the "animals" supported by glorious sound effects.

Charles Dickens: A Christmas Carol, [129] with Sir Ralph
Richardson, Paul Scofield and a cast directed by Howard Sackler,
was conceived solely as a recording and not as a radio program or
stage play. From the first "Bah, humbug" of Scrooge to his chuck-
ling ". . . Delightful boy! Its a pleasure to talk to him. . . ", Sir
Ralph Richardson's characterization moves on in believable trans-
formation. Once the ghost arrives, there is the mouse-like plan to
get it over with "Couldn't I take them all at once?", the emotional
heaving of "Oh dear, oh dear, oh dear, oh dear, bless me!", the
anguished "Take me back, haunt me no longer!" and then the courageous, "Lead on, lead on, spirit" and the climatic soul cry, "Spirit, I see, I see!"

Ghosts speak through transparent bodies, crowds merge and
make merry, chattering phantoms fly in the dark night, and
Scrooge's nephew laughs to the contagion of all who hear. What
sounds! There are bells, chains, clocks, and even the voice of
one calling out the opened window in the cold night air. It is an
enjoyable production, with many nuances made possible by stereo-
phonic recording.

Lewis Carroll's <u>Alice in Wonderland</u>[130] is told by Margaretta Scott and Jane Asher in a production adapted by Douglas Cleverdon. The adventures are simply told, without exaggeration but with great delight. The Alice has absorbed the essential qualities of the writing. This holds true for the Frog Footman, the Duck, the Queen and all the others. And that includes the baby sounds and the cook's noises. It may be one of the best Alices available. Young people will enjoy the <u>Poems of Rudyard Kipling</u>,[131] especially those read by an old friend, Boris Karloff, on side one. The side two dialect readings of "Gunga Din," "The Ladies," "Fuzzy-Wuzzy," "Mandalay," "Tommy," and "Danny Deever" have an "Empire" feeling.

<u>Tales from Shakespeare by Charles and Mary Lamb: The Taming of the Shrew and Macbeth</u>,[132] will continue to orient the very young and stimulate their interest in Shakespeare. On this well spoken record with some parts presented as in the original play, the value of the "Tales" is increased. This is especially true for <u>The Shrew</u> with much of the quarrel dialogue between Catherine and Petruchio. <u>Macbeth</u> is almost entirely as in the Lamb abbreviated narrative. Only the final confrontation scene between Macbeth and Macduff is enacted. The record is a creative educational aid for the introduction of Shakespeare to the young.

<u>Black Pioneers in American History</u>,[133] Vol. 1, read by Eartha Kitt and Moses Gunn, has well selected parts of the autobiographies of four nineteenth century black Americans: Frederick Douglass, ex-slave and early leader in the anti-slavery movement; Charlotte Forten, a school teacher; Susan King Taylor, a teacher and nurse with the Union regiment of ex-slaves; and Nat Love, a Negro cowboy who won the championship of the West for riding, roping and shooting and the title of "Deadwood Dick." Charlotte Forten recalled meeting Harriet Tubman and hearing her tell of one slave's escape to Canada and how he reacted when she told him "now we are in Canada." The readings are shared by the two well equipped artists. The sampling will send some adults and bright children to the longer autobiographies. The descriptions of the

slaves' struggles for an education and to learn the mystery of reading will inspire the young to learn to read.

The Man Without a Country[134] by Edward Everett Hale, read
by Edward G. Robinson, is good listening for older children. Robinson's empathy with the character keeps this from being the maud-
lin tale it might become through a different reader. The author's
structuring of subordinate and major incidents is carefully followed.

The descriptions move through Nolan's life on shipboard with
the deepest engagement when he took command of the cannon and
when the "heart-wounded man" read from Scott's Lay of the Last
Minstrel. The record may introduce children to what books have
to offer.

A Gathering of Great Poetry for Children[135] is not to
be missed. Material was selected and edited by Richard Lewis,
poet, teacher and editor of books for children, among them Miracles.
The four records planned for kindergarten, second grade and fourth
grade and up are read by Julie Harris, Cyril Ritchard, David Wayne,
with readings by poets themselves when these were available and good.
Fortunately Caedmon had many of them on records.

Some notion of the content can be gained from the following:
on Vol. I, Robert Frost's "The Pasture" (Robert Frost), William
Blake's "Spring" (Julie Harris), Langston Hughes' "Sea Calm" (David Wayne), Carl Sandburg's "Doors" (Carl Sandburg), and Walter de
la Mare's "The Window" (David Wayne); on Vol. II, T. S. Eliot's
lines about the yellow fog from "The Love Song of J. Alfred Prufrock" (T. S. Eliot), e. e. cumming's "o by the by" (e. e. cummings), Theodore Roethke's "The Lady and the Bear" (Julie Harris,
David Wayne), "The Waggle Taggle Gypsies" (David Wayne) and A.
C. Swinburne's "Envoi" (Julie Harris); on Vol. III, William Blake's
"The Tyger" (David Wayne), W. B. Yeats' "The Lake Isle of Innis-
free" (Cyril Ritchard), Gerard Manley Hopkins' "Pied Beauty" (Cyril
Ritchard), William Shakespeare's "You Spotted Snakes" (Cyril Ritch-
ard), and Stephen Spender's "My Parents Kept Me from Children
Who Were Rough" (Stephen Spender); on Vol. IV, Dylan Thomas'
"Fern Hill" (Dylan Thomas), Gertrude Stein's "I Like What I Like
When I Do Not Worry" (Poem V) (Julie Harris), Elizabeth Bishop's

"The Fish" (Elizabeth Bishop), Robert Graves' "Warning to Children" (Robert Graves), and Hal Summers' "The Rescue" (David Wayne).

The editor says, "One of the expectations we have for those who hear this record is that it will be a beginning as well as a continuation towards a lifetime of exploring the richness of poetry and that by hearing poems of value a new dimension will be added to the experience of being alive."

Recordings Discussed

1. James Joyce: Portrait of the Artist as a Young Man. Caedmon (1-12") TC1110.

2. James Joyce: Ulysses. Caedmon (1-12") TC 1063.

3. James Joyce: Finnegans Wake. Caedmon (1-12") Tc 1086.

4. The Poetry of Yeats. Caedmon (1-12") 1080.

5. Poems by W. B. Yeats. Spoken according to his own directions. Side two, Conversation Pieces from other poets. Jupiter (1-10" 00B 2. Conversation Pieces only, Folkways (1-12") FL 9880. The Yeats material is scheduled for a to-be-released Asche-Folkways record.

6. Lennox Robinson Presents William Butler Yeats: Poems and Memories. Spoken Arts (1-12") 752.

7. Plays and Memories of William Butler Yeats. Spoken Arts (1-12") 751.

8. Dylan Thomas Reading (I-V). Caedmon (5-12") Vol. I, TC 1002; Vol. II, TC 1018; Vol. III, TC 1043; Vol. IV, TC 1061; Vol. V, TC 1132.

9. An Evening with Dylan Thomas. Caedmon (1-12") TC 1157.

10. Francis P. Magoun, Jr. Reading from Old English Prose and Verse (O. P.) Harvard Vocarium (1-12") L 6000-01.

11. Beowulf Read in Old English by Norman Davis and Nevill Coghill. Spoken Arts (1-12") 918.

12. Gawain and The Green Knight and The Pearl. Dialogues in Middle English read by J. B. Bessinger and Marie Boroff. Caedmon (1-12") TC 1192.

13. Le Morte d'Arthur. Adapted from Sir Thomas Malory and pro-

duced by John Barton. Argo (3-12") RG 227-9, London
A 4369.

14. The Canterbury Tales of Geoffrey Chaucer. Spoken Word (4-
12") SW - A1.

15. The Prologue to the Canterbury Tales. Read in Middle English.
Argo (1-12") RG 401.

16. The Jupiter Book of Ballads. Jupiter (1-12") jur oo a 3. Folkways (1-12") 9890.

17. Elizabethan Love Poems. Read by Robert Speaight and Maxine
Audley. Spoken Arts (1-12") 896.

18. Anthony Quayle Reading Sonnets from Shakespeare and Other
Elizabethan Lyrics. Spoken Arts (1-12") 729.

19. Sir Cedric Hardwicke and Robert Newton Read XVII Century
Metaphysical and Love Lyrics. Caedmon (1-12") TC 1049.

20. Metaphysical Secular Poets. Argo (1-12") RG 427.

21. A Poetry Reading by Sybil Thorndike and Lewis Casson. Jupiter (1-7") 45 RPM jep oo c 3.

22. A Personal Choice, Alec Guinness. Victor (1-12") VDM 102.

23. Alec Guinness: A Leaden Treasury of Poesie. Jupiter (1-7")
45 RPM jep oo 24.

24. The London Library of Recorded English (I-VI) Britam (6-12")
XTV 23862, 64, 66, 68, and XTV 91157, 59.

25. The Jupiter Anthology of English Verse, Part III. Jupiter (1-
10") 00 B5.

26. The Poetry of Robert Burns and Scottish Border Ballads.
Caedmon (1-12") TC 1103.

27. Robert Burns Read by Jean Taylor Smith. Scottish Records
(1-12") 78 RPM SR 1252.

28. A Recorded Anthology of Scottish Verse. Part One: Poems
of Robert Burns. Read by Harold Weightman. Scottish
Records (1-12") SR 124.

29. Poetry of Ireland (O. P.). Beltona (1-12") LBE 29.

30. Irish Verse and Ballads. Read by Siobhan McKenna. Spoken
Arts (1-12") SA 707.

31. Brian Merriman: The Midnight Court. Spoken Arts (1-12") 742.

32. Ireland Free: Michael MacLiammoir in Revolutionary Speeches and Poems of Ireland. Spoken Arts (1-12") SA749.

33. A Golden Treasury of American Verse. Read by Nancy Wickwire and Alexander Scourby. Spoken Arts (1-12") 772.

34. Lucyle Hook Reads Poems of Emily Dickinson. National Council of Teachers of English (1-12") RL 20-5.

35. Emily Dickinson's Letters. Read with a critical introduction by Samuel Charters. Folkways (1-12") FL 9753.

36. Walt Whitman: Leaves of Grass Read by Alexander Scourby. Spoken Arts (1-12") SA 946.

37. Walden by Henry David Thoreau. Read by Howard Mumford Jones. Spoken Arts (1-12") 832.

38. An Informal Hour with J. Frank Dobie. Spoken Arts (1-12") 722.

39. Bret Harte Read by David Kurlan. Folkways (1-12") FL 9740.

40. Milton's Paradise Lost Read by Anthony Quayle. Caedmon (2-12") TC 2008.

41. The Treasury of George Gordon, Lord Byron, Read by Peter Orr. Spoken Arts (1-12") SA 908.

42. The Georgics of Virgil. Spoken Arts (1-12") 733.

43. The Poetry of John Dryden Read by Paul Scofield. Caedmon (1-12") TC 1125.

44. The Poetry of Coleridge Read by Sir Ralph Richardson. Caedmon (1-12") 1092.

45. The Poetry of Browning Read by James Mason. Caedmon (1-12") TC 1048.

46. Treasury of Robert Browning Read by Robert Speaight. Spoken Arts (1-12") 861.

47. The Poems of William Blake and Gerard Manley Hopkins. Read by Robert Speaight. Spoken Arts (1-12") 814.

48. Gerard Manley Hopkins Read by Cyril Cusack. Caedmon (1-12") TC 1111.

49. Poems by Gerard Manley Hopkins and John Keats Read by Margaret Rawlings. Argo (1-12") RG 13.

50. A. E. Housman: A Shropshire Lad and Other Poetry Read by

James Mason. Caedmon (1-12") TC 1203.

51. T. S. Eliot: The Wasteland and Other Poems. Read by Robert
     Speaight. Spoken Arts (1-12") 734.

52. Rubaiyat of Omar Khayyam, Omar Repentant, Ballad of Reading
     Gaol. Read by Frank Semple and Mayne Linton. Rex (Aus-
     tralia) (1-12") RA 2012.

53. Robinson Jeffers: Roan Stallion Read by Marion Seldes. Folk-
     ways (1-12") FL 97766.

54. Homer: The Iliad. Caedmon (1-12") TC 1196.

55. Homer: The Odyssey. Caedmon (3-12") TC 3001.

56. The Poetry of Langston Hughes Read by Ruby Dee and Ossie
     Davis. Caedmon (1-12") TC 1272.

57. The Treasury of John Milton Read by Robert Speaight and
     Robert Eddison. Spoken Arts (1-12") 867.

58. The Treasury of John Keats Read by Robert Speaight and
     Robert Eddison. Spoken Arts (1-12") 868.

59. Treasury of William Wordsworth Read by Robert Speaight.
     Spoken Arts (1-12") 860.

60. Poems of Gerard Manley Hopkins Read by Robert Speaight.
     Spoken Arts (1-12") 814.

61. The Pre-Raphaelites: Christina Rossetti, Dante Gabriel Ros-
     setti, Charles Swinburne, William Morris. Argo (1-12")
     RG 534.

62. Jonathan Swift: Gulliver's Travels. Read by Michael Redgrave.
     Caedmon (1-12") TC 1099.

63. Alec Guinness Reads from Gulliver's Travels, The Modest Pro-
     posal, Epitaph and Other Writings by Jonathan Swift. MGM
     (1-12") E 3620 ARC.

64. Treasury of Jonathan Swift, Gulliver's Travels. Read by Denis
     Johnston. Spoken Arts (1-12") 856.

65. Boswell's London Journal. Read by Anthony Quayle. Caedmon
     (1-12") TC 1093.

66. Daniel Defoe's Moll Flanders. Read by Siobhan McKenna.
     Caedmon (1-12") TC 1090.

67. The Autobiography of Frederick Douglass. Edited by Dr. Philip
     Fouer. Folkways (1-12") FH 5522.

68. Silas Marner (abridged) as Read by Judith Anderson.   Caedmon
    (2-12") TC 2024.

69. Emlyn Williams as Charles Dickens.   Argo (1-12") RG 231.

70. Readings from English Literature: Dickens.   A Christmas Carol,
    Pickwick Papers, Nicholas Nickleby and Great Expectations.
    B. B. C. English by Radio Gramophone Course (2-10") II, III.

71. Dicken's Duets Presented by Frank Pettingell.   Argo (1-12")
    RG 157.   Spoken Arts (1-12") 741.

72. Charles Dickens: The Pickwick Papers.   (Caedmon (1-12")
    TC 1121.

73. Sir Laurence Olivier in a Robert Louis Stevenson Album.
    London (1-12") 5425.

74. James Mason Reads Herman Melville's Bartleby the Scrivener.
    Prestige (1-12") 3000-7.

75. Roddy McDowall Reads the Horror Stories of H. P. Lovecraft.
    Prestige (1-12") 30003.

76. The Treasury of Nathaniel Hawthorne: The Minister's Black
    Veil Read by Robert S. Breen.   Spoken Arts (1-12") 940.

77. The Tales of Horror and Suspense by Ambrose Bierce Read by
    Ugo Toppo.   CMS (1-12") 513.

78. Selections from the Marquis de Sade Read by Patrick McGee.
    Caedmon (1-12") TC 1214.

79. Frank Pettingell Presents Oscar Wilde.   Spoken Arts (1-12")
    724.

80. Sir Michael Redgrave Reads Chekhov.   Spoken Arts (1-12")
    SA 828.

81. Proust: Remembrance of Things Past.   Swann in Love.   Read
    by Sir Ralph Richardson.   Caedmon.   (2-12") TC 2017.

82. The Painted Bird Read by the Author, Jerzy Kosinski.   CMS
    (1-12") 516.

83. Langston Hughes' Simple.   Caedmon (1-12") TC 1222.

84. Hubert Gregg as Jerome K. Jerome.   Argo (1-12") RG 319-
    320.

85. Jeeves.   Caedmon (1-12") TC 1137.

86. Michael MacLiammoir in the Importance of Being Oscar.

Columbia (1-12") OL 5690, OB 2090.

87. <u>I Must Be Talking to My Friends.</u> Michael MacLiammoir introducing Ireland's Poets, Wits and Revolutionaries in an entertainment. Argo (1-12") RG 493.

88. <u>Hal Holbrook in Mark Twain Tonight.</u> Columbia (1-12") OS 3080.

89. <u>Hal Holbrook in More Mark Twain Tonight.</u> Columbia (1-12") OS 2030.

90. <u>Max Adrian: An Evening with G. B. Shaw.</u> EMI Music for Pleasure (2-12") MFP 2120-1.

91. <u>The Brontes.</u> Vanguard (2-12") VRS 9176-7.

92. <u>A Lovely Light: Edna St. Vincent Millay.</u> Vanguard (2-12") VRS 9201-2.

93. <u>Bernard Shaw's Don Juan in Hell.</u> Starring Charles Boyer. Columbia (2-12") 8L 166.

94. <u>Stephen Vincent Benét: John Brown's Body.</u> Columbia (2-12")

95. <u>The Hollow Crown. The Fall and Fables of the Kings and Queens of England.</u> Argo (2-12") ZRG 5287-8, RG 287-8, London (2-12") OSA 1253.

96. <u>The Death of Patroclus.</u> Originally presented by "77" Records. Now reissued by Discourses (1-12") LT 12-1.

97. <u>Spoon River Anthology.</u> Columbia (1-12") OL 6010, OS 2410.

98. <u>John Dos Passos: U. S. A. , Selections from The 42nd Parallel.</u> Caedmon (3-12") 3002.

99. <u>What Passing Bell.</u> Argo (1-12") RG 385.

100. <u>The Sinking of the Bismarck.</u> (O. P.) CBS Records (1-12") MG 20056.

101. <u>The Mormon Pioneers.</u> Columbia Records Legacy Collection (1-12") LS 1024.

102. <u>Under Milk Wood by Dylan Thomas.</u> Directed by Dylan Thomas with Dylan Thomas and the original cast. Caedmon (2-12") TC 2005.

103. <u>Homage to Dylan Thomas.</u> Angel (1-12") RG 29.

104. <u>Under Milk Wood.</u> Directed by Douglas Cleverdon. Argo

(2-12") RG 21-2.

105. Emlyn Williams as Dylan Thomas: A Boy Growing Up. Argo
     (1-12") RG 547.

106. Memorial Record of Homage to T. S. Eliot. Odeon (1-12")
     PCLP 1924.

107. Old Testament Psalms and The Tale of David Read by Judith
     Anderson. Caedmon (1-12") TC 1053.

108. Miracles, Poems Written by Children. Collected by Richard
     Lewis and Read by Julie Harris and Roddy McDowall. Caed-
     mon (1-12") TC 1227.

109. The Jungle Books by Rudyard Kipling. Read by Christopher
     Casson and Eve Watkinson. Spoken Arts (2-12") Vol. I,
     SA 933; Vol. II, SA 929.

110. Poems and Songs for Younger Children. Jupiter (1-7') 45
     RPM jep oc 11.

111. Play Songs. Jupiter (1-7') 45 RPM jep oc 40.

112. The Mulberry Bush. Jupiter (1-7") 45 RPM jep oc 42.

113. Treasury of Nursery Rhymes. Read by Christopher Casson
     accompanied by a Gaelic harp. Spoken Arts (1-12") 304.

114. Mother Goose. Featuring Cyril Ritchard, Celeste Holm and
     Boris Karloff. Caedmon (1-12") TC 1091.

115. A Child's Garden of Verses. Read by Basil Langton.
     Spoken Arts (1-12").

116. The Golden Treasury of Children's Verse, Vol. I. Read by
     Jill Balcon and Robert Speaight. Spoken Arts (1-12") 820.

117. Aesop's Fables Read by Boris Karloff. Caedmon (1-12")
     TC 1221.

118. American Indian Tales for Children. Told by Anne Pellowski.
     CMS (2-12") CMS 500-1.

119. English Folk and Fairy Tales. Told by Anne Pellowski.
     CMS (1-12") CMS 504.

120. The Seventh Princess and Other Fairy Tales. Told by Anne
     Pellowski. CMS (1-12") CMS (1-12") CMS 502.

121. Asian Folk and Fairy Tales. Told by Christine Price. CMS
     (1-12") CMS 508

122. Folk Tales of the Tribes of Africa. Told by Eartha Kitt.
     Caedmon (1-12") TC 1267.

123. Hans Christian Andersen Read by Michael Redgrave. Trans-
     lated by R. P. Kaigwin. Caedmon (1-12") TC 1267.

124. Hans Christian Andersen: The Little Match Girl and Other
     Fairy Tales. Told by Boris Karloff. Caedmon (1-12") TC
     1117.

125. Boris Karloff Reads the Ugly Duckling and Other Tales by Hans
     Christian Andersen. Caedmon (1-12") TC 1109.

126. The Just So Stories. Read by Boris Karloff. Caedmon (1-
     12") TC 1038.

127. Animal Tales Told in the Gullah Dialect by Albert H. Stoddard
     of Savannah, Georgia. Library of Congress (3-12") AAFSL
     44-6.

128. The Wind in the Willows. Argo (2-12") RG 221-222.

129. Charles Dickens: A Christmas Carol. With Sir Ralph Rich-
     ardson and Paul Scofield. Caedmon (1-12") TCS 50001.

130. Alice in Wonderland. With Margaretta Scott and Jane Asher.
     Argo (1-12") 145-6.

131. Poems of Rudyard Kipling. Caedmon (1-12") TC 1193

132. Tales from Shakespeare by Charles and Mary Lamb: The
     Taming of the Shrew and Macbeth. Spoken Arts (1-12")
     SA 976.

133. Black Pioneers in American History, Vol. I, 19th Century.
     Read by Eartha Kitt and Moses Gunn. Caedmon (1-12")
     TC 1252.

134. The Man Without a Country. Read by Edward G. Robinson.
     Caedmon (1-12") TC 1178.

135. A Gathering of Great Poetry for Children. Edited by Richard
     Lewis and Read by Julie Harris, Cyril Ritchard, David
     Wayne, and the poets themselves. Caedmon (4-12") TC
     1235-8.

Chapter V

Plays

Wellsprings of Drama

More plays have been put on records in the past ten years
than in all previous years taken together. As a result, it is now
possible to study drama from its beginnings to the present. And
accompanying texts are more and more frequently supplied with albums. Accounting for some of the output has been the recording
of all Shakespeare in unabridged and in shortened form by several
companies. The large production of Shakespeare recordings will be
discussed at the end of the chapter.

The First Stage[1] is a chronicle of the development of English
drama from its beginnings to the 1580's, prepared by John Barton
for the B. B. C. 's Third Program. It was originally issued in four
albums by Spoken Word. It is a monumental work executed with superior direction and musical planning.

John Barton gives the introduction describing the scope of the
programs with extracts illustrating the beginnings of drama in Eng-
land from the tenth to the fourteenth century. Mysteries, Miracles,
Moralities, Moral Interludes, Mere Interludes, Late Moralities,
Drama in the Schools, Drama at the Universities and Inns of Court,
and The Popular Drama are major headings. The Creation and
Fall, the "Nativity Extract" from Mary Magdalene, Fulgens and
Lucres, Calisto and Melibaea, Nice Wanton, Ralph Roister Doister,
Gammer Gurton's Needle, and The Spanish Tragedy are a few of
the plays sampled.

These were presented originally as "... programs not intended for the expert or even the student but for the person who
likes plays. " But for expert as well as student, these nineteen records make clear the historical, sociological and religious implications of early drama.

John Barton's comments, especially at the beginning of the
third album, and his recapitulation on the final record help the listener to recognize each new development of playwriting as it appears.
With this directed anticipation, the listener spots the arrival of
humor in the characterization of Noah's Wife, the beginnings of
probing dialogue in that between Abraham and Isaac, and the pipings
of poetic beauty in English drama through such morsels as the Nativity lullaby and the Crucifixion lament. A merry England has its
chance in the playful rounds, the gay songs and other musical resources lavishly used throughout the programs. The set of records
is too expensive for most individuals but is so valuable for independent study that it should be made available by libraries. The
tediousness of long moralizings will be discovered by young playwrights and they will better appreciate what it takes to create dimensional characters in a play. They will also grow in understanding the thinking of those of different religious beliefs. The albums
would be well placed in seminary libraries.

A useful compact introduction to the history of drama will be
found on an early Caedmon recording, The Wellsprings of Drama,
Vol. 1. [2] The material comes from Quem Quaeritis, Banns, The
Deluge, Abraham and Isaac and Robin Hood.

A beneficiary of the wellsprings of drama was Christopher
Marlowe. The Tragical History of Dr. Faustus[3] shows a sensitivity
to the "fluid line in which the poetry and thought dissolved into one
another and moved according to their harmonious urgings." From
"How am I glutted with conceit" to "look not so fierce on me," one
is impressed by the music of speech, especially that of Faustus and
the Chorus. At times the words soar with singing vowels as in
"...now is his fame spread through every land..." and at other
times they conform to the limitations of the crisp consonants as
"Faustus' restless course draws nigh its end..."

John Webster's The Duchess of Malfi,[4] first produced in 1612,
has rarely been produced in modern times. Because it is so significant in the history of drama, the recording of this turbulent tale
of malignant horrors is a bonus from modern recording. The anguish, terror and evil are all present to saturation point. It is

courageously directed by Howard Sackler and played to the hilt by
Barbara Jefford as the Duchess of Malfi. She is supported by Robert Stephen, Alec McCowan, Jeremy Brett and Douglas Wilmer,
and by unusual direction in the use of the sound possibilities in recording.

Eighteenth Century Drama

Love for Love by William Congreve[5] is the production of the
National Theatre of Great Britain directed by Peter Wood with
Laurence Olivier as Tattle and Joyce Redman as Mrs. Foresight.
Except for slightly indistinct scenes, especially in gossip between
the women, the popular play, written by the Irish dramatist in 1695,
holds up as delightfully realistic for a period in theatre not given to
the deep probing of human nature.

In 1964, under the title, Theatre Recording Society (T. R. S.),
Caedmon, which had already done most of Shakespeare as well as
several other plays, began a comprehensive program of recordings
of the theatre. An early release in this program of theatre from
its beginnings to the present time is Oliver Goldsmith's eighteenth
century comedy, She Stoops to Conquer.[6] The Hardcastles--family,
friends and servants--make amusing company for all ages. The
leading roles are played with lively creation by Alistair Sim, Claire
Bloom, Brenda de Banzie and Tony Tanner. A distinction of the
recording is the clear profile of the play structure.

In the introductory note to Sheridan's The School for Scandal,[7]
Sir John Gielgud, who directed it, comments on the production at
the Comedie Francaise where unusual liberties were taken with the
text, "...thus ruining the balance both of writing and construction
and completely destroying the careful way in which the author had
distributed his effects." Quite the reverse is his own respectful
probing of reasons behind the scene arrangement and crafty planning
of speeches by the playwright whose work he faithfully follows. The
elegant and frivolous period mise-en-scène, denied to our eyes,
reaches our ears through a surface elegance in speech. Later, human qualities emerge in Sir Peter's will scene and Lady Teazle's
capitulation. The inelegant human, too, comes through in coarser

grain when the sulphurous scandlemongers are fiercely ordered out
by Sir Peter's triple, "Leave my house!"

Gielgud as Charles Surface dominates the scene with stubborn
sentiment until he is completely unmasked. The scandalmongers vie
in a riotous competition of tale-telling: each one in character tops
a lie with his own addition until the peak of this ridiculous business,
reached by Sneerwell and Backbite, is halted by the entrance of Sir
Peter.

The play is fast-moving. A production brought to the studio
after much work by the company in live performances, it is minute-
ly timed in its business and quietly maestroed for an effective
whole.

Nineteenth Century Drama

Henrik Ibsen: Hedda Gabler,[8] in an abridged edition, is a
Theatre Masterworks production with Eva LeGallienne reliving Hedda's internal struggle. There is a good supporting cast with a narrator to give continuity to the play. Besides the objective dimension of heard dialogue which it provides for students often unable to
see the play, the reading keeps alive a performance by Miss LeGallienne, the plucky pioneer in repertory theater in America during
the worst years of the depression. For those wanting a more recent Hedda, there is the Caedmon recording with Joan Plowright.[9]

The Master Builder[10] (T. R. S.) by Henrik Ibsen is an adaptation by Emlyn Williams as presented by the National Theatre of
Great Britain. Voices convey the aspiration of Hilde Wangel (Maggie Smith), the sick conscience of Halvard Solness (Michael Redgrave) and the sick mind of his wife (Celia Johnson). Through the
use of stereo, the crowd gathered for the last scene can be easily
imagined watching from their several places.

Chekhov's Uncle Vanya[11] (T. R. S.) is also a recording of the
production by the National Theatre of Great Britain in which Laurence Olivier plays the doctor; Michael Redgrave, the younger brother; and Joan Plowright, the sister, who look together for the elusive happiness of this life. Chekhov's Three Sisters[12] also seek
that elusive happiness on another T. R. S. album.

The opportunity to hear the Minneapolis Theatre production of The Cherry Orchard, [13] at least on records, is welcomed by theatregoers unable to travel to see the production. The company plays well together in long established roles. Music and crowd scene sounds for arrivals and celebrations support the atmosphere. There are also times daringly empty for silence.

The original Broadway cast album of Ivanov,[14] adapted and directed by John Gielgud, has Sir John Gielgud as Ivanov, Vivien Leigh as Anna, and several first-rate players including Ethel Griffes as a marriage broker. The mood movements are planned to fit the heights and shallows of the play. The album is a good way to become familiar with this infrequently played lesser work of Chekhov.

Oscar Wilde's The Importance of Being Earnest,[15] first played in 1895, was subtitled "A Trivial Comedy for Serious People." It calls for gravely elegant style to carry off its fantastic nonsense. The mixture is achieved in this production by the excellent ensemble: Dame Edith Evans, Sir John Gielgud, Pamela Brown, Celia Johnson. An Angel recording it is on four records.

The Caedmon recording of The Importance of Being Earnest[16] is on two records. The very elaborate portfolio accompanying the spoken record album was designed by Frederich Hubicki, Oraston Brooks and E. William Kuch. A review by Max Beerbohm, written in 1912 when the play was revived after the premiere seven years before, is reprinted. The star-studded cast, with Gladys Cooper, Joan Greenwood, Richard Johnson, Alec McCowan and Lynn Redgrave, keeps to the Beerbohm dictum, "To preserve its style fully, the dialogue must be spoken with grave unction," like Cecily's, "If you are not too long I will wait here for you all of my life."

Robert Culp in Lady Windemere's Fan by Oscar Wilde[17] is directed and adapted by Elayne Carroll and Robert M. Culp. The adaptation and direction make this a tight, swiftly moving experience on one record. It is also well cast. For students of playwriting it is useful for experiencing Wilde's gifts for plotting and writing lines.

Edmond Rostand's Cyrano de Bergerac[18] (T. R. S.), the vehicle for a great performance by Constant Coquelin in 1897, had a

fragment recorded on Black Zonophone (11848) in Paris in 1901.
It is now recorded in English with Sir Ralph Richardson who was
widely hailed for his performance of the role in London in 1946.
This recording must also be hailed as a superb directorial achievement of Howard Sackler. The mobs and music in varied concoc-
tions tell the mood and reactions of playgoers, poets and Cadets of
Gascoyne. Each contrivance of the plot shuttles into place. It is
a well designed performance missing no quick jab of wit or poignant
revelation. The high level holds for minor speeches, such as the
speech to the Meddler, as well as for the famous nose speech. In
the latter, one readily follows the movements in the duel, recorded
with quick changing positions for the microphone; the relationship of
the microphone to the speaker is adjusted much as that of a camera
to an actor in cinematography, giving the listener a most dynamic
oral image.

Because it is so near, Cyrano's monosyllabic hope and despair in the early meeting with Roxanne is fully experienced. Ecstasy like Romeo's spills forth in the balcony scene, and a brilliant
crescendo of mad talk delays DeGuiche. The ebb and flow of Cyrano's persistent hope and despair are captured.

On this recording the many characters of the play mesh ex-
actly. Whether support comes from Anna Massey as Roxanne,
Peter Wyngard as DeGuiche, John Fraser as Christian, Ronald
Fraser as an ecstatic Ragueneau, Michael Gwynn as LeBret, or
Peter Bayliss, Eileen Atkins and Sarah Long in briefer roles, it is
always just right. Rostand's play has always been for everyone.
Now, on discs, it can move to faraway places.

Twentieth Century Drama
J. M. Synge: The Playboy of the Western World,[19] starring
Cyril Cusack and Siobahn McKenna, is Synge's controversial play of
1907. The combination of the music of Irish speech and romantic
daring create delightful lyric love-making. J. M. Synge: Riders
to the Sea and In the Shadow of the Glen[20] are two short plays
crafted and constructed in delicately beautiful language and tragic
humor. They are well executed by The Radio Eirann Players of

Dublin under the direction of Micheál Ó H-Aodha.   Another of the
classics of Irish theatre, Sean O'Casey: Juno and the Paycock, [21]
also has the able cast of Siobhan McKenna, Cyril Cusack, Seamus
Kavannagh and Marie Kean.

Of his Caesar and Cleopatra Shaw said, "Caesar is greater
off the battlefield than on it." On the Caedmon (T. R. S.) recording
of Caesar and Cleopatra[22] Caesar adopts Shaw's own outrageous
sense of humor.   In one case this means an ingenious mispronuncia-
tion of the already difficult Ftatateeta (Judith Anderson) by Caesar
(Max Adrian), used by Shaw in the crucial last scene to serve the
plot.   The director times the characters in brisk play with sharp
lines until Cleopatra's education is completed by Caesar's departure.
Especially successful is the stimulation of the listener's imagination to a sense of what must have happened when Cleopatra (Claire
Bloom) cries out, "Ftatateeta, Ftatateeta, it is dark; and I am a-
lone.   Come to me.   Ftatateeta.   Ftatateeta."

Hearing the Caedmon (T. R. S.) release of his Saint Joan, [23]
George Bernard Shaw, music critic and rhetorician, would have
been delighted with the casting of voices for the structure, parallel-
isms and rhetorical design of the many speeches.

The well chosen cast directed by Howard Sackler features
Siobhan McKenna, the rude-voiced Maid; Donald Pleasance, the
gentle speaking Inquisitor; Robert Stephens, the aesthetic Dauphin;
Felix Aylmer, the icy-voiced Bishop of Beauvais; Alec McCowan the
volatile Chaplain de Stogumber, in command of unusual vocal change
especially in the epilogue; and Arthur Hewlett, so rightly cast as
the aristocratic Archbishop who becomes irritable and harsh as he
grows in denunciation of Joan's "pride."

Her replies to him and to her accusers at the trial are stirring declarations.   Her words have many shadings and intensity.
Miss McKenna's Joan has grown more true with time.

Other characters in the play also provide moving moments.
A good example is the Dauphin's pitiful cry to the court: "You see
all of you; she knew the blood royal.   Who dare say now, that I
am not my father's son?"

Noel Coward and Margaret Leighton in Bernard Shaw's The

Apple Cart; Interlude and Poems by Noel Coward[24] gives a taste
of Shaw as well as of Coward. This acting team plays the quarrel
between the king and his mistress brilliantly. The candid poems of
Noel Coward are of unusual interest because they mirror a professional life so different yet basically the same as it is for other
men: the boy actor's struggle for a job, the cold beginning of the
honeymoon, the frank questioning of "do I believe?" and the philosophic acceptance of the changing of an era "when Queen Victoria
died." In the reading of the poems Margaret Leighton alternates
with Noel Coward for the poems of rather general concern and those
which are essentially feminine.

Anta Album of Stars, Vol. I, Great Moments from Great
Plays[25] includes scenes from Broadway successes between the
1930's and 1950's: Helen Hayes in Victoria Regina by Laurence
Housman; Frederic March and Florence Eldridge in Years Ago by
Ruth Gordon; The Skin of Our Teeth by Thornton Wilder; Eva Le
Gallienne in Hedda Gabler by Henrik Ibsen; John Gielgud in King
Richard II by William Shakespeare.

One-act plays are infrequently recorded. Very welcome is
the three-record album of Yeats: Five One-Act Plays. [26] Siobhan
McKenna, Cyril Cusack, Marie Kean and Patrick Magee enact
"Words Upon a Window Pane," "Only Jealousy of Emer," "Cat and
the Moon," "Pot of Broth," and "Purgatory." Also welcome is the
Argo two-record album of Yeats: At the Hawk's Well, Dreaming
the Bones, Cat and the Moon, Actors and Musicians. [27]

T. S. Eliot's Murder in the Cathedral, [28] with Paul Scofield
as Archbishop Thomas Becket, is directed by Howard Sackler.
Like a symphony conductor he knows the ambience of the characters
with which he plays. He manages the blend of women's voices in
the chorus in excellent readings by Cathleen Nesbit, Glenda Jackson,
Wendy Hiller and June Iago. They top each other in a fusion of
changing emotions, speak in sonorous prophetic notes or again in a
quiet mood which rises to hysteria.

There has seemingly been no limit to the casting of "best"
players to meet the needs of the material. The harsh-voiced
knights are of a timbre quite different from the others on the record.

Like new instruments on the scene they call out their accusations
and blasphemies in answer to the Archbishop's gentle, "Now what is
the matter?" Paul Scofield as the Archbishop is pastor of the flock
in the Christmas sermon "...and because our dear children I do not
think I shall ever speak to you again..."

The Cocktail Party by T. S. Eliot[29] was first presented at
the Edinburgh Festival in the summer of 1949. The poet himself
helped to rehearse the lines. When presented in New York in January, 1950, for a year's run, the play had the same cast, with only
one important change. The Decca recording, featuring members of
this New York cast, was made with the approval of the author and
was supervised by the director of both the Edinburgh and New York
productions.

Theater critics, without exception, hailed the brilliant acting:
Alec Guinness was "superb" and Irene Worth "beyond expertness."
They praised the whole cast of "lucid and accomplished players who
know how to speak the English language."

T. S. Eliot: The Family Reunion[30] is dominated by an atmosphere of depressed tone. The return home of the family is
overseen by Dowager Lady Monchensey. Dame Sybil Thorndike plays
the role as in the 1956 production and Paul Scofield, her son Harry,
Lord Monchensey. He doggedly answers his mother's oppressive,
"Where are you going?" with, "Where does one go from a world of
insanity?" The thinking of the members of the family is moodily
expressed at the ends of scenes in the choral refrains. At other
times the voices of beckoning Furies and Eumenides drive the play
on.

Christopher Fry's The Lady's Not For Burning[31] is another
verse play that has been recorded. With the original Broadway cast
headed by John Gielgud, it gives those who saw the play an opportunity to hear the verse at close range. The plot structure comes
through more sharply on the recording than it did on the stage.

The Human Voice[32] by Jean Cocteau, translated into English
by Maximilian Ilyin, is recorded by Ingrid Bergman. Before we
realize it, both sides of this record are over. It is a recording
which will interest a variety of listeners. The telephone conversa-

tion ranges through an astounding vocabulary of one woman's farewell.

Jean Cocteau: The Infernal Machine[33] is a translation by Carl Wildman, starring Margaret Leighton, Jeremy Brett, Diane Cilento, Alan Webb, Miriam Karlin and Patrick Magee. The recording communicates the sense of a real ghost on the ramparts, and of his comings and goings until the Cock's Crow at first light.

Margaret Leighton, as the overwrought, bad-tempered queen, dominates Jean Cocteau's drama of incest and patricide. There are very interesting dialects in speech, e. g. , for the common soldiers and the believable gossipy Matron of Miriam Karlin. At the end of the play, delicate, poignant Antigone guides her father away to exile.

Brief Encounter is presented in a tight adaptation for two voices by Noel Coward and Margaret Leighton in Noel Coward Duologues in Brief Encounter and Scenes from Blithe Spirit, Act II, Scene 1; Present Laughter, Act II, Scene 1.[34] For Brief Encounter the effect is that of starker tragedy than one gets from the play. With Act II, Scene 1 of Blithe Spirit and with Present Laughter, we have an impressive illustration of the range of Margaret Leighton's art. The author notes on the sleeve that her women "had more life and truth than he had ever seen in them before. "

Jean Paul Sartre: No Exit,[35] with Donald Pleasance, Anne Massey and Glenda Johnson, is an adaptation from the French by Paul Bowles. It is a successful directorial stint with daring pauses and silences. High dramatic intensity marks the speeches. The powerful build-up of passionate outcry and hideous insane laughter from Inez, as she is played by Glenda Johnson, resembles raw basics which are rarely heard. The other roles, each one a foil to the other two, carry the author's incisive thesis that hell is within ourselves and others.

Bertolt Brecht's A Man's A Man[36] is the cast album of the highly acclaimed 1962 production by the New Repertory Theatre. It is adapted by Eric Bentley, leading translator and interpreter of Bertolt Brecht, who also serves as narrator for what in this version becomes the travesty of the Organization Man.

In Endgame by Samuel Becket,[37] Alan Schneider has directed

his characters with special attention to distinctness. The rapid-
fire exchanges so essential to the piece can be understood. Ingenious and delicate sound effects tell about the silences. The two
actors in the ashcan roles, alone, are worthy of preservation.

Krapp's Last Tape, [38] by Samuel Beckett, with Donald Davis,
was directed by Alan Schneider. In the first minutes of the tape
one hears only coughs, crackling of papers and the drunken man's
feet dragging across the floor. Then the Canadian actor, Donald
Davis, moves from excerpts on tapes made annually over a period
of thirty years to interspersed comment by the dying man: "Past
midnight. Never knew such silence. Here I end this reel, box 3,
spool 5 ... Perhaps my best years have gone. When there was a
chance..." And then the dying man is heard, "No, not with the fire
in me. Now I wouldn't want them back." The recording has power.

Students of modern drama will welcome the three-record album of Eugene O'Neill's More Stately Mansions, [39] directed by Jose
Quintero and starring Ingrid Bergman, Arthur Hill and Colleen Dew-
hurst. There is also the album of the production by the Circle in
the Square of O'Neill's A Moon for the Misbegotten. [40] Introductory
notes by Howard Sackler, the director of Jean Genet, [41] describe
the evolution of this recording. They tell how the author, in several meetings in London during 1962 and 1963, selected the passages
and scenes from his work to be recorded. It recounts conversations with Genet giving his directions for the kind of voices to be
used and the manner in which his plays should be produced.

The material recorded comes from The Blacks, Our Lady of
the Flowers, The Miracle of the Rose, The Maids, The Balcony
and The Screens. The participants are Max Adrian, Alan Webb,
Brenda Bruce, Nigel Davenport and Sheila Burrell.

The unhindered animal cry of human violence is close. So
also are the thief and murderer. There is death experience and
the cries of women in terror and anger. Other sounds are of
horses' hooves, baying dogs and the funeral dirge reaching far
spaces. This listening experience is different from that on other
records. It is a transport into the core of the world of the un-
wanted and the violent.

Peter Weiss: Marat-Sade[42] is the original cast recording, directed by Peter Brook. A paperback text accompanies the album. The persecution and assassination of Marat as performed by the inmates of the Asylum of Charenton under the direction of the Marquis de Sade is a rhetorical piece of theatrical impressionism. A riot in an insane asylum is the soapbox for "We invented the revolution but we didn't know how to run it." The players make use of every theatrical device to create terror: music in rhythm for guillotined heads, horrible screams, mob singing together and apart, lunatic laughter, the jerky stressed speech of a broken mind and the terrible imaginative telling of a four hour execution "that was a festival." There are interruptions and explanations by the Marquis de Sade and always very understandable lines defending the action. For anyone who can take the combination of terrible sounds and imaginings, this is an extraordinary theatrical experience. It is an opportunity for those who could not attend the performance.

Benito Cereno,[43] the third play of Robert Lowell's trilogy, The Old Glory, with Roscoe Lee Browne, Clayton Corbin, Frank Langella and Lester Rawlins was produced at The American Place Theatre. It is a play in the van of the movement towards an American verse drama.

Jonathan Miller, of "Beyond the Fringe" fame, casts the roles with a good sense of vocal texture and rhythm. The play's confrontations with the roots of suffering and hate claw for recognition and involvement by the listener.

Although one wishes that there had been more of "...the necessary practice which makes verse come as naturally from the lips of the player as prose...," Lowell's appraisal goes as follows: "I think your record is the finest performance the play has ever had." Such concert readings of poetry as this, where every word is important, provide experience in depth for the listener. They are part of the fast expanding frontier of our oral culture. They may even change the quality of poetic writing, acting and listening.

The Quare Fella[44] by Brendan Behan was adapted for recording by Philip Rooney. It is a Radio Eireann Players' production directed by Micheál Ó H-Aodha. In adaptation and direction, especially in vocal casting and use of song, musical instruments, whistles, bells and walks, the production exhibits a knowing ear for the many means available for creating atmosphere.

Warden Henry Laws' writings described prison life and death; through drama, Behan's The Quare Fella moves one to deeper realization about that world. An unexpected break from the sighing of the prisoners is the humor of the scene where the bluffer who doesn't know Gaelic is caught. Brendan Behan's singing is the author's autograph.

With the exception of Julie Harris as Teresa, the cast for The Hostage[45] by Brendan Behan is almost entirely from the 1960 Broadway premiere and the award-winning off-Broadway version. That director, Perry Bruskin, also presided over the Bucks County Playhouse production from which this album was made. The delicate scene between Teresa and Leslie briefly slows the onrush of Behan's iconoclastic and chaotic spirit, but not for long. The recording is overwhelmed by a confusion of too many things, and so the play fails to maintain interest as a recording.

Tennessee Williams' The Glass Menagerie[46] (T. R. S.) brings back memories of the stage production with Laurette Taylor and Eddie Dowling who created the original roles. With the help of the author, the director, Howard Sackler, and a choice cast of Montgomery Clift, Julie Harris, Jessica Tandy and David Wayne, the recording notably makes up for their absence. Delicate direction and playing so engage the listener's sympathies that one almost believes the play was conceived with the intimacy of recording in mind.

The Rose Tattoo[47] (T. R. S.) by Tennessee Williams was the vehicle which raised Maureen Stapleton to stardom in 1950. The recording is of a recent revival with Miss Stapleton in the role she created. Others in the cast are Harry Guardino, Maria Tucci and Christopher Walker. Under the direction of Milton Katselas, the title role has all the wild Sicilian penchant for tragedy.

Arthur Miller's Death of a Salesman[48] (T. R. S.) records the work of the two stars who created the original roles during a long Broadway run. This production also has an introduction by the author.

The Subject Was Roses, [49] Pulitzer Prize winner for 1965, is a recording of the original group which worked together for the play's continuation and ultimate success on Broadway. Tense lines such as, "if it isn't too hot, it's too cold; if it isn't too strong, it's too weak," are handled as if on a tight rope. Realistic in language but not as animalistic as Albee's Who's Afraid of Virginia Woolf?, [50] it compels the same kind of nervous attention generated by Albee's hard working original cast under the direction of Alan Schneider. This is also recorded with Uta Hagen, Arthur Hill, George Grizzard and Melinda Dillon in their Broadway roles. Both of these records, along with the already mentioned Benito Cereno, are part of the Columbia program for recording current successes.

Some plays not possible to review on the ever growing list of T. R. S. play albums are Arthur Miller's Incident at Vichy and his After the Fall, the Stratford National Theatre of Canada production of Tartuffe, and the Repertory Theatre of Lincoln Center production of In the Matter of J. Robert Oppenheimer. There is also The Great White Hope, [51] recently released by a new name in spoken recording, Tetragrammaton of Beverly Hills, California.

One of the great events in over ten years of New York theater history was a financial loss; the one-man Christmas 1968 show of Aubrey's Brief Lives [52] with Roy Dortrice. Still a sell-out in London (1969) parts can now be heard on a Major Minor Record.

Available through Decca is the John Gielgud vehicle, 40 Years On, [53] written by Alan Bates. There is also an A and M recording of the complete version of The Boys in the Band [54] by the New York cast.

Some Beginnings on Play Frontiers

Folk drama of the American South is to be found on Paul Green Discussing and Reading from In Abraham's Bosom and Roll Sweet Chariot. [55] This has already been discussed under Authors' Readings but a reference here is apropos.

Modern activity on the Scottish front is recorded on The Real Macrae: A Man of the Theatre. [56] "The Three Estates" was first performed in 1540 and revived in 1948 as the first official

Scottish contribution to the Edinburgh International Festival. The
old morality was adapted for the modern arena stage of the Assembly Hall by Robert Kempe.   Sir Tyrone Guthrie brought the
whole to life.   In the excerpts for the record Duncan Macrae plays
his original role of Pardoner.   Also on the record are excerpts
taken from "Let Wives Tak Tent," a translation into Scots of Moliere's L'Ecole des Femmes, and excerpts from a modern Scóts play,
"The Warld's Wonder" by Alexander Reid.   All these plays were recorded before an invited audience in the Scottish Film Council Theatre in Glasgow in March, 1964.

Sive,[57] by John Keane, a young Irish playwright, was produced by Michéal Ó H-Aodha.   It is in County Kerry speech.   It
won the All-Ireland Drama Festival Award in 1958.   Very strong
characterizations make the tragedy.   Mona Glavin (Nora Relihan),
in fierce lines, argues for the marriage of young Sive to Sean Dota
who is "as old as the hills" but is after a young wife.   The author,
John Keane, plays the tinker, using warning music and comment,
as might a Greek chorus.   The play is for the connoisseur who en-
joys discovering talent.   It is an early effort by Mr. Keane who
continues to write.

The Poacher[58] appeared at the turn of the century and is one
of the first Welsh comedies in the English language.   A one-act
comedy of country life in Wales, it was produced by Dafydd Greef-
fydd with actors schooled in the Welsh accent.

Greek and Other Foreign Dramas

There have been very few recordings of Greek plays in English.   The best known are the two releases in free adaptations with
Judith Anderson in Medea.[59]   Both have the merit of her savage
creation of that ancient role.   The Oedipus Rex by the Stratford
(Ontario) Players sound fatiguingly aware of being recorded.

Attempts by university groups remain amateur, because they
are without the vocal and interpretive resources experienced artists
might bring to the plays.   The performance of Oedipus King[60] in
the translation by David Greene, done by members of Cambridge
University, is one of the best.   But even here, with the exception

of Creon in the prophecy scene and the two shepherds in their confrontation, the actors are recorded without a sense of addressing listeners. The recording is worthy of notice, however, because of its majestic and lyric line-readings and the fine music by Derek Bourgeois.

The handsome brochure accompanying Antigone, [61] one of the plays in The Theatre Recording Society Project, sets the play in history with photographs of the great amphitheater where it was first presented. The several confrontations between Antigone and Ismene, Creon and Haimon, and Antigone and Creon come across well. Very effective, too, is the quiet sobbing of Ismene and the quick heartbreak cry from Eurydice.

The fourth side, which should carry the terrible burden of the tragedy, is somewhat flatted. Coming off with the Puritannical efficiency of the translation, it is a sermon rather than the original play's tragic happening.

Greek Tragedy [62] is itself on records through some scenes from Hecuba, Oedipus, The Persians, and Electra, performed by Katina Paxinou and Alexis Minotis in modern Greek. Communicated with tremendous epic power, these readings, nurtured in Greek soil, can be followed with the accompanying translation much as one does opera. Fuller recordings of the plays are desirable. Of utmost value would be a recording of a Greek chorus with descriptive material about its function in Greek drama and the way the chorus is prepared for this role in the Greek theater.

Through the records, for those to whom the language of the National Greek Theatre is "Greek," the movement, interplaying echoes and cadence of the swinging lines becomes a universal language for understanding epic joys and woes. Wild power rarely experienced in English theater is hurled at the listener. It starts one thinking of what could happen to Shakespeare's language under Greek theater tutelage.

This Caedmon recording of passages from Greek Tragedy done by the leaders of the National Greek Theatre, as well as Noh: Two Major Dramas, [63] sung and performed in Japanese by players of the Komparu and Kange Schools of Noh in Tokyo, have placed

within the hearing of ages to come some of the great theater experiences of our time.

The Noh plays of Japan have a blending of musical instruments and opening of human tone in sympathy with "beauty and sorrow." More than with the Greek plays, these require listening
tastes only gradually acquired by the occidental ear. A recording
makes it possible to listen often and long for discoveries in sound
which can be achieved only through such practice. The language
sounds can be noted only in passing in a theater where a radio
transistor simultaneously conveys the translation, valuable and necessary as this is for most people. One wishes that there was some
provision for following the accompanying text for those lost with the
Japanese.

The Golden Treasury of French Drama[64] attests to the alert-
ness of Spoken Arts in recognizing the value of such a recording.
Scenes from Molière, Beaumarchais, Marivaux and Musset are introduced by Barrault and enacted by him and Madeleine Renaud.
One detail of this intricate craftsmanship is the last line of the
passage from Moliere's Amphitryon: "Bon jour la nuit," "Adieu-
Mercure."

Theatre Souvenirs

The group of records of special interest to people of the theater is being added to from time to time. Some of these have been
processed in limited editions, like Edward Gordon Craig: Radio
Talks,[65] (O. P.); some are out of print and an unknown number a-
wait processing.

The Theatre Today[66] is a discussion among several stage
personalities expressing keenly felt opinions. Noel Coward, Albert
Finney, Peter Hall, Sean Kenny, Siobhan McKenna, Harold Pinter,
Sybil Thorndike, Kenneth Tynan and Peter Ustinov participate.

Babes in the Wood,[67] written in 1934, was originally presented in a woodland glade at Fair Oak, Reigate. An authentic English pantomime with rhyming couplets, ludicrous and ingenious puns,
it is "a family entertainment." George Speaight, in the Bulletin of
the Society for Theatre Research, says: "It would be a great mis-

take, however, to regard this as merely a clever parody of English pantomime. It is nothing of the kind. It is English pantomime. Pantomime always has been a parody of itself. No one could do the job better or more ludicrously than the ingenious rhymsters and punsters who evolved this peculiar art from extravaganza out of fairy tale. Mr. Clinton-Baddeley is the heir to a great tradition. "

Directed by the author, an authority on the English pantomime who also plays the wicked role with an ear-picked company, Babes in the Wood is for the student the only available experience on record of a true English pantomime. The style is right, from the over-elegant Babes' first steps into the woods of creaky twittering birds, past the wicked guardian's "Tis safe enough. Who'd guess the children's guide / Had been indulging in infanticide?", to the final safe return to Euclid and other serious joys. An amusing quarter of an hour to us, one can imagine the witty extravagances of a live production with music, costumes, lights and dance and understand why Englishmen of all ages flock to the Christmas pantomime. The gay cover makes the seven inch record a festive gift.

In spite of background noises, the recording of Sir Herbert Beerbohm Tree[68] by the Gramphone in 1907 manages to pass on a sampling of his art. Antony's lament over the body of Caesar comes from depths ringing with rarely heard vibrato and passion. The fade-out in last lines and the sometimes missed vicious bite for the "butchers" are imperfections of an otherwise seldom matched performance.

In other passages, the characters of Richard II, Falstaff, and Svengali come remarkably true to the modern ear. One is impressed by Tree's wide range of roles and vocal versatility. The list of passages gives some notion of his undertaking on the record: Antony's Lament Over the Body of Julius Caesar, Soliloquy on the Death of Kings (Richard II), Falstaff's Speech on Honour (Henry IV, Part I), Hamlet's Soliloquy on Death, Svengali Mesmerizes Trilby (Trilby, DuMaurier).

The Great Actors of the Past, Shakespeare, Vol. I[69] (O. P.) contains dubbings of speeches by Dame Ellen Terry, Edwin Booth, Lewis Waller, Sir Herbert Beerbohm Tree, Arthur Bourchier, Ty-

rone Power, Sr. and Alexander Moissi from the collection of Mr.
Leonard Petts.

Most of these recordings, made in 1911 or earlier, are surprisingly clear. Anyone who has heard the early Tennyson recording may not expect much from the 1890 Edwin Booth recording of
Othello's "round unvarnished tale" to the senate. But "...if one
listens with text in hand there is no difficulty in hearing even subtle
inflections." Mr. Leonard Petts, who owned the original copy,
calls it "the rarest item on this record."

From the extensive sleeve notes one also learns that the five
Dame Ellen Terry speeches "...were all made in a single day in
1911 in New York by the Victor Company when she was sixty-three
years old." Her vivacious Beatrice is a treasure. The four passages by Sir Beerbohm Tree recorded in 1906 support his reputation as a versatile character actor. Antony's Lament Over the Body
of Julius Caesar uses the words of Shakespeare, the actor, with a
fellow guildsman's understanding of their place in tragedy and in la-
mentation in the theatre. The soliloquy on the death of kings is
absolutely right for Richard II on a histrionic spree of self-pity.
It has all the watching in a mirror of the "star." One gets Lewis
Waller's need for support as he leads his soldiers "once more unto
the breach."

Range, schooled daring and nuance, not to mention careful
stress and phrasing, mark the work of these past masters of the
theater. Transmitted on one record is the audial experience of an
acting style from the past, known heretofore only through wordy descriptions.

Listeners conditioned by the quiet acting of a less barnlike
theater than that represented on The Great Actors of the Past may
at first criticize these performances as pretentious and even ludicrous. Once the prejudices pass, and one hears their basic sincerity, depth and range, he can appreciate the greatness.

Shakespeare

If one could only have recorded Shakespeare! For since recording arrived it has been possible to hear Edwin Booth, Dame

Ellen Terry, Sir Beerbohm Tree, John Barrymore and a host of
others. Besides, though out of print, there are such treasures as
the two Columbia 78 RPM records by Sir Johnston Forbes Robertson on How to Speak Shakespeare: Richard II, Macbeth, Hamlet,
Henry VIII.

All of Shakespeare has been put on records by Argo (Marlowe
Society) and Caedmon (The Shakespeare Recording Society). There
have been many brief editions of the plays and collections of scenes
and speeches. There are at least five albums of Macbeth, Romeo
and Juliet, Hamlet and Othello. For those interested, A Selective
Discography of Shakespeare Plays prepared by Arthur J. Weiss in
1966 will be found at the end of the chapter. Reviewed here will be
those albums which together suggest the achievement in Shakespeare
recordings.

By the Quartercentenary of Shakespeare's birthday, April 23,
1964, the Marlowe Society of Cambridge under the direction of
George Rylands had completed recordings of all of Shakespeare's
works using the John Dover Wilson texts. A token of love, the
early releases were marred by amateurism. This was before a
policy of more extensive use of professionals was adopted.

The Marlowe Society's Shakespeare's Sonnets is an example
of the amateur metronomic reading which deadens listening. Some
of the plays fare better, for example Othello and Timon of Athens.
One persistent weakness in the recordings is the use of a small
group of standbys for all minor roles, a practice common on the
stage for producing large cast plays. Without costume changes or
other disguises, however, having the same person portray several
different roles is confusing. It is also disconcerting to the listener
to find himself trying to remember: "Where was that voice heard
before?"

On the plus side for the Marlowe recordings are the casts of
professional actors and the musical direction by Thurston Dart. One
is sure that the use of trumpets, drums, zither, and lute is consistent with the theatrical practice throughout Europe during Shakespeare's time.

Much pioneering effort in opening new sound frontiers through

stereo went into the Shakespeare Recording Society albums which use
G. B. Harrison's texts.   One good example of successful sound exploration is heard in the reverberating calls in Romeo and Juliet,[70]
as Romeo's gay blade friends shout to each other in the cobbled
square.   The listener, brought so close, hopes against the wrath of
awakened neighbors.   On these recordings, too, as in arena the-
aters, the listener becomes a part of the "surrounding" sound: of
the "caterwauling" party, for example, or the suppressed laughter
of Malvolio's braying torturers.   Through stereo we are made intimate witnesses of the Troylus and Cressida[71] perfidy and of Othello's
tortured soul.   But in the latter case, where the problem has not
been completely solved, the listener may feel uncomfortably close to
the murder.

The closeness of recording brings added meaning to lines,
often enlivening the pace of the plays.   Many intimately realized insights are made possible because one is so close.

Characteristic of the Marlowe Society recordings is the clear
emerging structure of the plays.   In A Midsummer Night's Dream,[72]
for example, the three separate groups--court, craftsmen and
fairies--are sharply defined.   In the first group, a Theseus with a
dashing military voice opens the courtly nuptuals and is well supported by the courtly lovers.   A second group, the Athenian craftsmen, delight with speech of humble origin.   But the third group,
consisting of the Fairy King, Queen and Puck, though also easily
discernible as a group, succeeds in transporting the magic of the
dream only occasionally beyond suburbia.

Movement of lines, strong point sense, line endings and the
ring of echoing sounds reach the ear with no loss in meaning.   At
times the Spartan dedication to making clear an argument seems to
hold in check some lines which should leap with lyricism.

The dialogue moves with crisp timing and crescendo.   There
are exciting quarrels between young voices rich in vocal resource-
fulness.   Believable are Hermia's frightened awakening, Bottom's
variations in bray, and the hunting horns which wake the lovers.

On the Caedmon recording of A Midsummer Night's Dream[73]
there is an Oberon (Paul Scofield) who, after a weak "I know a

bank," rises to fine lyricism in the reconciliation with Titania:
"Sound music; come my queen, take hands with me / And rock the
ground whereon these sleepers be. "

The musical movement for scenes in Fairyland has magic
and works well for the transitions and entrances it marks.   There
is also gloriously conceived sound support for the duke, and much
spoken music in such lines as: "And mark the musical confusion /
Of hounds and echo in conjunction. "

The scenes with the players are full of fun and are refresh-
ingly conceived, free from the exaggeration with which amateurs so
often endow them.   The natural relief-filled welcome to Bottom, just
in time to "go on," is a case in point.

A most valuable contribution for future producers of the play
is the marvelously designed response of the courtly audience as it
listens to the play (side six).   Commedia del' Arte in conception,
this is by itself a delightful improvisation of bursts of laughter, sur-
prised chuckles, smothered titters and "sh's. "   With its lines, timing, touch, and grouping of voices, it is a meaningful story.   What
the audience sees as it listens to the play is related to the listener
through sounds; and there is a bonus too because of the closeness:
a character for the audience--by turns compassionate and snobbish.
Perhaps those near the small stage in Shakespeare's time had a
similar treat.   Indeed, this new world of sound, with the speech detail it permits, is making contributions to our understanding of
Shakespeare in the 1960's much as the newly popular science of psy-
choanalysis did in the 1930's.

The character of Iago on the Marlowe Society Othello[74] is
conceived as "a consummate villain entrapping a noble nature... a-
gainst which no discernement was available. "   To all appearances a
normal human being, this Iago (Donald Beeves) bears down relent-
lessly to crush the dignity and joy of Othello's marriage and the
peace of his soul.   Satanic cold which freezes the tragedy is the
pervading quality of an album hard to take but most sophisticated in
the understanding of evil.

Equally right casting and character conception is found in the
clean-cut and physically strong General Othello (Tony Church).   There

exists a sense of generalissimo importance in his characterization and of his being most attentively listened to as he tells of how "she loved me." Effortlessly, he moves from the suffering intensities of a whipped soul to the peak of the last scene. The women are felicitous supports: the new bride, Desdemona (Wendy Gifford), a hard voiced Emilia (Irene Worth) and an over-ripe Bianca (Mary Fenton).

We are involved in the drama at many points: in the suspenseful wait at Cyprus for "a sail," in the outright lie of "Cassio's dream," "Strangle her in bed" and the delicate plaint of "Sing Willow."

The music of the lines is there in the "sport and profit" of Iago as the "public coffin" is prepared for Othello. Always conveying the sense, the vocal yielding of these speakers to the poetic elements never intrudes: "I never knew a Florentine more kind"; "Thus credulous fools are caught"; "Thou hast set me on the rack."

The last scene, in the interplay between the men's parts, is adroit in the minute handling of plot movement and exquisite in its bitter accomplishment of the catharsis. So fine to a hair's breadth is the direction that after hearing the recording one wants to pay a deserved tribute to the director, the late George Rylands.

Laurence Olivier in Othello,[75] the presentation of the National Theatre of Great Britain, was completely sold out for the years of its run in the Old Vic. Eventually it was made into a movie. But here on records is the performance recorded with the actors re-enacting all the stage movements as they speak. What the fortunate theatergoers witnessed, we hear in the remarkable isolation of sound; the Othello voice with characteristic tonalities, Desdemona's girlish but firm dignity, the quiet mouthed Iago (Frank Finley), and the final shrill heroic declaration of Emilia (Joyce Redman).

One must agree with the wildly enthusiastic viewers of this Othello. It is probably the greatest so far. The recording is always in character but it includes the record listener too. Whether in the addresses to the council or in gentle loving to each other, Laurence Olivier as Othello and Maggie Smith as Desdemona reach our ears and hearts. Backgrounds for scenes move in and out. A

most striking example is the revelry before Roderigo's death.
Close, but mercifully not too close, is the final scene.
Everything appears to have been planned in the execution of
the album to bring the perfection of a "greatest" performance of
Othello to ears ready to listen. The accompanying text and illus-
trated brochure complement a very great experience in listening.

The Old Vic Company Macbeth[76] makes use of many sounds,
especially those of night: the tolling bells announcing the murder,
the knocking at the gate, the sounds of festivity escaping through
open doors and then closing off. The voices, too, change with the
dark plot development and the ear finally hears, "What a sigh is
here." There are many whispered scenes made all the better for
close listening: between Macbeth and his wife, the parting of the
two brothers after the murder, Macbeth's instructions to the mur-
derers of Banquo, and the smothered grief of MacDuff: "My wife
killed too?" Few records can boast of as many responsive and well
trained voices as are to be found on this one, e. g., "Stands Scotland where it did?"

One can hear Macbeth vocally hardening in his chosen path
in the lines from Alec Guinness. Pamela Brown decreases amaz-
ingly in vitality and inner strength, and in Robin Bailey as MacDuff
there is all the range from terrible sorrow to lunatic rage when he
finally confronts the murderer. This is a true Macbeth, the mon-
strous tragic figure, communicated solely through sound.

Notable on the Marlowe Society album of Timon of Athens,[77]
the play which is partly Shakespearean, is the third scene of the
Fourth Act where there is undoubted Shakespearean writing. The
scene is brilliantly played by all the characters and very excitingly
built in the confrontation in the forest between Timon and Alcibiades.
Also beautifully done is the final meeting between Timon and the
faithful Flavius.

The directing by George Rylands holds in check the many
flare-ups of Timon until the powerful volcanic eruptions which make
the play so worth hearing. Because it has been so rarely done, it
is especially good to be able to hear a recording of the play.

In A Study of Shakespearean Versification, M. A. Bayfield

wrote:

> In Antony and Cleopatra he embodies in its utmost perfection that ideal of dramatic verse at which he had long been aiming; more than from any other play one receives the impression of an art completely mastered. The sureness and touch and the ease, one might almost say, the nonchalance with which the thing is done are so marvellous... the result is such as none would have believed possible unless it had been achieved. Here indeed he was 'on the heights.'

The Marlowe Society _Antony and Cleopatra_[78] has a vigorous down-to-earth General Mark Antony and excellent movement of troops and people between scenes with the support of the music prepared by Thurston Dart. But the Caedmon Antony and Cleopatra[79] essays the lyric lode of the play with operatic fervor and maintains it in high gear throughout. Committed to belief in this as high romance, valid in the opulent Egyptian world as Romeo and Juliet is in its world, it but skims the mud beneath. Anthony Quayle and Pamela Brown soar with the glory of verse about a Mark Antony whose "legs bestride the ocean" and a Cleopatra of "infinite variety."

Anthony Quayle's hero is regally dashing and worth hearing in these poetic lines and Pamela Brown's Cleopatra does have variety and depth, especially in the last scene. Her concept of the role is too circumscribed by the minx, however, and misses the mysterious allure and rare beauty of Egypt's queen which must have penetrated even to words. The gifted Irene Worth on the Marlowe record also misses here. One wonders if a director of spoken records will someday hear the right Cleopatra, perhaps Miriam Makeba.

A large and varied cast, carefully chosen, and absorbed into the play, supports the principals in generally realized characterizations. This is especially true on the Caedmon record for the women about the dying Cleopatra. Tiny details of sound also stimulate imagination of the unseen action on this album and only the stark ping-pong-pung of three gongs separates the acts. This abbreviating device also conveys an apt finality. Together with the swift movement of the whole, it also manages to get the meteoric play onto six sides.

The extraordinary worth of The Old Vic Company in Hamlet[80] lies in having a permanent recording of John Gielgud, one of the greatest Hamlets of our time. Almost alone, the soliloquies sustain the interest of this Hamlet until the middle of the play. Then excitement mounts with the action and interplay among Hamlet, his mother, Polonius, Ophelia, and Claudius, as well as with others who would "play upon" him. The ears prick up for the discovery of murdered Polonius, the plotting of the King, Ophelia in madness, and the Queen's lyric dirge for her.

Word scenes like those around "alas poor Yorick" and the detail of the foil and poison deaths are new experiences because of recording closeness. Briefly narrated continuity, sound of revelry, of alarum and cannon, together with generally well done supporting roles, especially Paul Rogers as an older-voiced Claudius, make for great theater magic here.

The beginning of the Caedmon The Winter's Tale[81] gives the distracting impression of an assembly line of actors fronting microphones in tenth row theatrical stance. The company does not seem to be working together fluidly or to be seriously engaged in the business of "the play's the thing." But the power of a recording to establish and sustain illusion is definitely present in the last act. The ear then begins to relish and discover the ever new wonders of the lines within the action. "There was speech in the dumbness" as the King and Camilio heard the shepherd tell how the child was found. Paulina (Dame Peggy Ashcroft) "lifted the Princess from the earth," and "so locks her in embracing, as if she would pin her to her heart, that she might no more be in danger of losing." And Leontes with "my daughter" is "almost transported" before the statue. Gielgud in the Leontes role is at his intensive best.

The title is accurate for what Zeffirelli, the Italian director and designer, has done with or for Shakespeare's Much Ado About Nothing.[82] While not a "Much Ado" to end all such, for fun and invention it will long hold the record. It is the injection needed for much anemic Shakespeare.

From the first, there is no doubt that brave soldiers have returned from the war and that there is a war still going on between Beatrice and Benedick. Much surrounding merriment and noisy mu-

sic at times blurs the spice of early lines. We also miss the fabu-
lous and outrageous shennanigans with costumes, scenery, and action, which are described in the handsome brochure containing the
text. But once one has settled for what sound can convey, a rollicking opera bouffe takes the stage. And there is always sympathetic help from Nino Rota, the musical director. Shakespeare himself might have tried to best this leap of Zeffirelli if he too had
lived after Rossini.

The wine is intoxicating. Maggie Smith shrieks "Kill
Claudio!" It is superb, as are her lyric love passages. Robert
Stephens is a truly doting bachelor and Albert Finney struts the gallant Italian Don Pedro. One suspects that his exaggerated accent
was not as artificial in the trappings of a Zeffirelli performance as
it is in the isolation of a sound recording.

The scene between the two noblewomen on the morning of
Hero's wedding is harshly, and most realistically, interrupted by
the excited screams of Margaret announcing the arrival of company
to take Hero to church.

The concentration of essential flavors of the fantastical banquet will be found on side four by directors, actors and Shakespeare
buffs. The performance of Frank Finlay as Dogberry closely
matches the director's dream. He must always have two or three
extra cymbals and musical fanfares to accompany whatever he does
and then he regularly breaks the solemnities with a tin whistle!
Dogberry extends lines at will into arias from La Traviata. "For
the ewe that will not hear her lamb" is one of these which, aided
by choral effects from his watchmen, must have stopped the show!

Shorter Recordings of Shakespeare

For some, John Barrymore was the greatest of Hamlets.
The Audio Rarities release, John Barrymore Reads Shakespeare
with Commentary, [83] one of the older Shakespeare recordings, contains some of the speeches from Hamlet. It is therefore a special
delight to many who remember the 1922 production and a unique opportunity for others to hear the genius they were not born to see.
What one quickly admires is Barrymore's command of range, swift-

ness in lyricism, and truly Shakespearean rhetorical intensity. Beyond the human sound barrier goes the hurled power of Richard III, in his ambition for the Crown: "I'll pluck it down..." and again in his "You lie!" to Richmond's "Nay Richard, death hath found thee." There is his terrible sardonic laugh at the end of the wooing of Lady Anne and his later sob, and crying out in sleep. At the other pole of this disciplined art are the almost inaudible depths of Hamlet to the Ghost, "I'll follow thee." Subtle significance through phrasing and delicate handling of words is heard in Macbeth's "Tomorrow, and tomorrow..."

Seldom has it been the lot of an artist of the theater to be able to present, and on an extended tour, a program made up of the great roles he has played. This Sir John Gielgud did at the peak of his career in 1958-59 in a grand tour which included the United States when Ages of Man,[84] made up of passages from Shakespeare's plays and sonnets, was recorded. Ordinarily, this would have been described for posterity in annals to be imaginatively reconstructed by later readers. But in this our time the live presentation, with all its range, variety and intensity, has been made permanent through recording. The recording also had the benefit of the warmth which came to the performance through long trial before audiences.

The lyric, tragic and deep human in Shakespeare are discovered with new meaning in word, phrase and sentence: "brag," "ever till now," and "in the base court come down." The tricky underhandedness of a word: "Cousin, seize, the crown," the phrased timing of: "As Brittle as the glory/ is the face" and the plea in "Cordelia, stay a little" contain much for study by younger artists. For everyone's experience are the vowel cries from outraged animal to finite human in the final anguish of King Lear. Masterpieces of art in the theater can at last be passed on, and this record qualifies as one of them.

In passing, Gielgud has also recorded the best album of the complete Sonnets of William Shakespeare.[85] There is also a record of nine scenes with Sir John Gielgud and Miss Irene Worth in Men and Women of Shakespeare.[86] Each is a fresh confrontation

between two of Shakespeare's characters.   It covers the remarkable
sweep from Titania and Oberon to Lear and Cordelia, and brilliantly displays the forever fresh resources of two most gifted artists.

Another phase in the development of Shakespeare recording
is the presentation of many of the plays in shortened form, especially useful for young people.   The Living Shakespeare King
Lear, [87] directed by the late Sir Donald Wolfit, is one such modern
condensed performance and stars Sir Donald Wolfit as King Lear,
Rosalind Iden as Cordelia, Barbara Jefford as Regan, and Coral
Browne as Goneril.

There is behind Sir Donald Wolfit's direction of this King
Lear an understanding of the play and of Lear which rings true.
Most Lears have foundered in vocal shallows.   The complete King
Lear, [88] on Caedmon, is excellent but Scofield is too young voiced.
Wolfit's Lear meets the extraordinary vocal demands of the role
with something to spare.   Two wishes arise in the listener to the
performance on records: first, the desire to hear the whole play
done by this group, then the wish that the number of sound effects
and the amount of music had been limited so as to permit greater
concentration on the play.

In the vocal casting, Wolfit has juxtaposed with his own Lear
a warm-voiced Kent and Cordelia, a romantic-sounding France, a
delicate fool and two vulture daughters.   These last, fire and ice,
register without overtaxing their voices, a fault which is all too frequent in other portrayals of the roles.   Wolfit's own vocal quality is
not unlike that of Dylan Thomas on the Caedmon recording Dylan
Thomas Reading Shakespeare: King Lear, and Webster: The Duchess of Malfi. [89]

There are many singularly beautiful passages on the record:
Lear's "... Poor naked wretches," "True my good boy, come bring
us to this hovel," "Where have I been where am I' and "Thou wilt
come no more."   To the point for any Lear are the famous scenes
on the heath and also in the ranging "Oh, reason not the need."

Dames Sybil Thorndike and Sir Lewis Casson are featured in
the Folio Theatre Player's production of Henry VIII, [90] put out by
Spoken Arts and cast with Russell Thorndike, Christopher Casson and

William Styles under the direction of Christopher Casson and William Styles.

"I oppose you as my judge and appeal... I will not tarry," sets the tone for a recording of key speeches from a production of Henry VIII which today is a memory of the privileged few who heard the original. That the members of this great theater family could take as many as four different speeches within the brief time of two sides of listening without once betraying themselves is a phenomenal proof of great acting. The recording of Dame Sybil Thorndike's Anne Bullen and an Old Lady as well as her Queen Katherine, together with Sir Lewis' Buckingham and Griffith, place us in debt to their son Christopher who conceived the record.

Also worthy of notice, and this is in the Spoken Arts program of Shakespeare recordings, is the production of Julius Caesar.[91] The plotting of this fifty-minute streamlined version of the play is surprisingly convincing. With exact cuing, the important role of the mob in the play comes clear. At home with the music of the lines, the characters clearly relate to each other as Brutus to Cassius for "Portia is dead." There is cunning fire in Marc Anthony's speech. One hopes it is not mean to want, in something so well done, more lunatic incitement for: "Cry havoc! And let slip the dogs of war!"

Recordings Discussed

1. The First Stage. A Chronicle of the Development of English Drama from Its Beginnings to the 1580's by John Barton. Originally issued by Spoken Word, these albums are now issued by Dover in Four albums: Boxes L, M, N, O.

2. The Wellsprings of Drama, Vol. I: Quem Quaeritis, Banns, The Deluge, Abraham and Isaac, and Robin Hood. Caedmon (1-12") TC 1030.

3. The Tragical History of Dr. Faustus. Caedmon (1-12") TC 1033.

4. The Duchess of Malfi. Caedmon (3-12") TRS 334.

5. Love for Love by William Congreve. The National Theatre of Great Britain Production by Peter Wood. RCA Victor (3-12") VDS 112 Stereo.

6. She Stoops to Conquer. Caedmon (3-12") TRS 309.

7. Sheridan: The School for Scandal. Tennent Production Company. Directed by Sir John Gielgud. Command Records (3-12") RS 33 13002.

8. Henrik Ibsen: Hedda Gabler. Theatre Masterworks (3-12") GRC 861.

9. Hedda Gabler with Joan Plowright. Caedmon (3-12") TRS 322.

10. The Master Builder. Caedmon (2-12") TRS 307.

11. Chekhov's Uncle Vanya. Caedmon (2-12") TRS 303.

12. The Three Sisters. Caedmon (3-12") TRS 325.

13. The Cherry Orchard. Jessica Tandy and the Minnesota Theatre Company. Caedmon (3-12") TRS 314.

14. Ivanov. RCA Victor (2-12") VDS 199.

15. The Importance of Being Earnest. Angel (4-12") 3504 P.

16. The Importance of Being Earnest. Caedmon (2-12") TRS 329.

17. Robert Culp in Lady Windermere's Fan by Oscar Wilde. Library Editions (1-12") 4001.

18. Cyrano de Bergerac. Caedmon (3-12") TRS 306.

19. J. M. Synge: The Playboy of the Western World. Angel (2-12") 35358.

20. J. M. Synge: Riders to the Sea and In the Shadow of the Glen. Directed by Mícheál Ó H-Aodha. Spoken Arts (1-12") 743.

21. Sean O'Casey: Juno and the Paycock. Angel (2-12") 3540 B.

22. Caesar and Cleopatra. Caedmon (2-12") TRS 304.

23. Saint Joan. Caedmon (4-12") TRS 311.

24. Noel Coward and Margaret Leighton in Bernard Shaw's The Apple Cart; Interlude and Poems by Noel Coward. Caedmon (1-12") TC 1094.

25. Anta Album of Stars, Vol. I, Great Moments from Great Plays. Decca (1-12") D. 9002.

26. Yeats: Five One-Act Plays. Caedmon (3-12") TRS 315.

27. Yeats: At the Hawk's Well, Dreaming the Bones, Cat and the

Moon, Actors and Musicians.   Argo (2-12") 5468-9.

28. T. S. Eliot's Murder in the Cathedral.   Caedmon (2-1_) TRS 330.

29. The Cocktail Party by T. S. Eliot.   Decca (2-12") DL 9004 S.

30. T. S. Eliot: The Family Reunion.   Caedmon (3-12") TRS 308.

31. The Lady's Not for Burning.   Decca (2-12") DX 110.

32. The Human Voice.   Jean Cocteau.   Caedmon (1-12") TC 118.

33. Jean Cocteau: The Infernal Machine.   Caedmon (3-12") TRS 321.

34. Noel Coward Dialogues in Brief Encounter and Scenes from Blithe Spirit, Act II, Scene 1; Present Laughter, Act II, Scene 1.   Caedmon (1-12") TC 1069.

35. Jean Paul Sartre: No Exit.   Caedmon (2-12") TRS 327.

36. A Man's a Man.   Spoken Arts (1-12") 870.

37. Endgame by Samuel Beckett.   Evergreen (2-12") EV 400.

38. Krapp's Last Tape.   Spoken Arts (1-12") 788.

39. More Stately Mansions.   Caedmon (3-12") 331.

40. A Moon for the Misbegotten.   Caedmon (3-12") TRS 333.

41. Jean Genet.   Readings by the author and cast.   Caedmon (1-12") TC 1134, TC 1134S.

42. Peter Weiss: Marat-Sade.   Caedmon (3-12") TRS 312.

43. Benito Cereno.   Columbia (2-12") DOL 319/DOS 719.

44. The Quare Fella.   Spoken Word (2-12") A 24.

45. The Hostage.   Columbia (3-12") DOL 329/DOP 729.

46. The Glass Menagerie.   Caedmon (2-12") TRS 301.

47. The Rose Tattoo.   Caedmon (2-12") TRS 324.

48. Death of a Salesman.   Caedmon (3-12") TRS 310.

49. The Subject Was Roses.   Columbia (4-12") DOL 308/DOS 687.

50. Who's Afraid of Virginia Woolf?   Columbia (4-12") DOL 287/ DOS 687.

51. The Great White Hope. Tetragrammaton (4-12") TDL 5200.

52. Brief Lives. By Aubrey. With Roy Dortrice. Major Minor
    (1-12"). MMLP 48.

53. 40 Years On. Decca (3-12")

54. The Boys in the Band. A and M (3-12")

55. Paul Green Discussing and Reading from In Abraham's Bosom
    and Roll Sweet Chariot. Spoken Arts (1-12") 719.

56. The Real Macrae: A Man of the Theatre. Scottish Records
    (1-12") SR 123.

57. Sive. Nealon (1-12") 002.

58. The Poacher. Qualiton (1-12") BMP 2026.

59. Medea. Judith Anderson in free adaptation by Robinson Jeffers.
    Decca (1-12") DLP 9000.

    Medea. Adapted from the English translation by Rex Warner.
    Caedmon (2-12") TRS 302.

60. Oedipus King. From the translation by David Greene. Per-
    formed by members of Cambridge University. Millers of
    Cambridge (2-12").

61. Antigone. Caedmon (2-12") TRS 320.

62. Greek Tragedy. Performed by Katina Paxinou and Alexis
    Minotis in Modern Greek. Caedmon (1-12") TC 1127.

63. Noh: Two Major Dramas. Sung and performed in Japanese
    by players of the Komparu and Kanze Schools of Noh in
    Tokyo. Caedmon (2-12") TC 2019.

64. The Golden Treasury of French Drama by Jean Louis Barrault
    and Madeleine Renaud. Spoken Arts (1-12") 715.

65. Edward Gordon Craig: Radio Talks. (O. P.) Extracts from a
    Diary, Woodcuts. Discurio (3-12") Edition Limited to 99.

66. The Theatre Today. Argo (1-12") RC 279.

67. Babes in the Wood. Jupiter (1-7') jep oc 35.

68. Sir Herbert Beerbohm Tree. Selections Records (1-7') 45
    RPM jec 505.

69. Great Actors of the Past. Shakespeare, Vol. I. (O. P.)
    Delta (1-12") Del 120 20.

70. <u>Romeo and Juliet.</u> Caedmon (3-12") SRS 228S.

71. <u>Troylus and Cressida.</u> Caedmon (3-12") SRS 234.

72. <u>A Midsummer Night's Dream.</u> Marlowe Society. Argo (3-12")
    ZRG 5250-2.

73. <u>A Midsummer Night's Dream.</u> Caedmon (3-12") SRS 208.

74. <u>Othello.</u> Marlowe Society. Argo (4-12") RG 121-4.

75. <u>Laurence Olivier in Othello.</u> R. C. A. Victor (4-12")

76. <u>Macbeth.</u> R. C. A. Victor (2-12") LM 610.

77. <u>Timon of Athens.</u> Marlowe Society. Argo (3-12") ZRG 5253-5.

78. <u>Antony and Cleopatra.</u> The Marlowe Society. Argo (4-12")
    ZRG 5307-10.

79. <u>Antony and Cleopatra.</u> Caedmon (3-12") SRS 235.

80. <u>The Old Vic Company in Hamlet.</u> RCA Victor (4-12") LM 6404.

81. <u>The Winter's Tale.</u> Caedmon (3-12") SRS 214.

82. <u>Much Ado About Nothing.</u> RCA Victor (3-12") VDS 104.

83. <u>John Barrymore Reads Shakespeare with Commentary.</u> Audio
    Rarities (2-12") 2280, 3380.

84. <u>John Gielgud: Ages of Man.</u> Columbia (1-12") OL 5390.

85. <u>Sonnets of William Shakespeare.</u> Caedmon (2-12") SRS 241.

86. <u>Sir John Gielgud and Miss Irene Worth in Men and Women of</u>
    <u>Shakespeare.</u> RCA Victor (1-12") VDS 115.

87. <u>King Lear.</u> The Living Shakespeare (1-12") SKL 354.

88. <u>King Lear.</u> Caedmon (4-12") SRS 233.

89. <u>Dylan Thomas Reading Shakespeare: King Lear; and Webster:</u>
    <u>The Duchess of Malfi.</u> Caedmon (1-12") TC 1158.

90. <u>Henry VIII.</u> Spoken Arts (1-12") 881.

91. <u>Julius Caesar.</u> Spoken Arts (1-12") 809.

A Selected Discography of Shakespeare's Plays

by Arthur J. Weiss, M. A.

Despite the brief history of spoken records, the accumulation of Shakespeare is already such that it bids fair to take its place sometime in the near future alongside the vast Shakespearean printed literature--a body of work too large for complete comprehension except by professional scholars. This is as it should be, of course, for somewhere in the miles of microgroove is recorded for posterity the Betterton or Garrick of the twentieth century, our legacy to as yet unborn ears. The average listener of today, however, will perhaps best be served by a selected overall view of what is currently readily available, and that is what the following charts attempt. The discography is limited to the plays: Chart 1 deals with them as entities, Chart 2 with some representative collections of scenes, and Chart 3 with a few rare or difficultly obtained recordings.

All recordings are 12-inch 33 1/3 rpm unless otherwise indicated. Those marked Marlowe Society are uncut and directed by George Rylands; those marked Caedmon are also uncut with perhaps two exceptions. Where the director has been given credit by the producers in cases other than the Marlowe Society, he is listed with the cast. This credit is not consistent, however. Where prominent professional players perform leading roles they are listed.

Key

Record Companies		Performing Companies	
Audio Rarities	AR	Dublin Gate Theatre	DG
Caedmon	C	Marlowe Society	MS
Columbia	CU	Old Vic Company	OV
Decca	D	Shakespeare Recording	
Educational Audio Visual, Inc.	EAV	Society	SRS
Living Shakespeare	L. S.	Swan Theatre Players of	
London (McGraw Hill now)	L	London	ST
Spoken Arts	SA		
Spoken Word	SW	Miscellaneous	
Victor	V		
		Stereophonic availability	(s)
		Complete	CP
		Excerpts	EX

Chart 1

Company	Record No.	Scope	No. of Sides	Cast
All's Well That Ends Well				
1. C	212, 212S	SP	3 (s)	SRS: Claire Bloom, Flora Robson, John Stride, Eric Portman.
2. L	M4370, S1370	CP	3 (s)	MS: Michael Hordern, Max Adrian, Prunella Scales.
Antony and Cleopatra				
1. C	235, 235S	CP	3 (s)	SRS: Pamela Brown, Anthony Quayle; Howard Sackler, dir.
2. C	TC 1183	EX	1	SRS: same as complete.
3. L	M4427, S1427	CP	4 (s)	MS: Irene Worth, Richard Johnson.
4. L. S.	SAC - 9	EX	1 (s)	Peter Finch, Vivien Leigh.
As You Like It				
1. C	210, 210S	CP	3 (s)	SRS: Vanessa Redgrave, Keith Michell, Stanley Holloway, Max Adrian; Peter Wood, dir.
2. L	L4336	CP	3	MS.
3. SW	SW-A4, 123-4-5	CP	3	DG: Micheál Ó Mac-Liammóir; Hilton Edwards, dir.
4. SA	880	EX	1	Dunne, Watkinson.
5. Angel	35220	EX	1/2	Edith Evans, Michael Redgrave, Ursula Jeans. (reverse=20 sonnets).
The Comedy of Errors				
1. L	A4524, OSA 1252	CP	2 (s)	MS.

Chart 1 - Continued

Company	Record No.	Scope	No. of Sides	Cast
2. SA	888	EX	1	Folio Theatre.

Coriolanus

1. C	226, 226S	CP	3 (s)	SRS: Richard Burton, Jessica Tandy, Kenneth Haigh; Howard Sackler, dir.
2. L	4415	CP	4	MS: Irene Worth.
3. SW	SW-A17, 154-155-6-7.	CP	4	DG: W. Bridges-Adams, dir.

Cymbeline

1. C	236, 236S	CP	3 (s)	SRS: Claire Bloom, Pamela Brown, John Fraser, Boris Karloff; Howard Sackler, dir.
2. L	4425, 1416S	CP	4 (s)	MS.
3. SA	889	EX	1	Folio Theatre.

Hamlet

1. C	232, 232S	CP	4 (s)	Paul Scofield, Diana Wynyard; Howard Sackler, dir.
2. L	4507	CP	5	MS.
3. CU	OL-8020, OS-2620	EX	1 (s)	Richard Burton.
4. V	LM-6404	CP	4	OV: with John Gielgud; dir. by John Richmond and John Gielgud.
5. V	LM 1924	EX	1	Laurence Olivier: scenes from film sound track (with HENRY V).
6. AR	AR -2201	EX	1	John Barrymore.

Chart 1 - Continued

Company	Record No.	Scope	No. of Sides	Cast
7. L. S.	N804-8833	EX	1 (s)	Barbara Jefford, Michael Redgrave, Margaret Rawlings.
8. SA	SA -781	EX	1	DG: Micheál Ó Mac-Liammóir; Hilton Edwards, dir.
9. V	LM -6007	EX	2	Gielgud.
10. SW	6002-3	Adaptation	3	Baylor Theatre.
11. D	9504	EX	1/2	Gielgud (soliloquie) + Romeo & Juliet excerpts with Pamela Brown.

Henry the Fourth, Part One

1. C	217, 217S	CP	3 (s)	SRS: Harry Andrews, Pamela Brown, Edith Evans, Richard Johnson, Anthony Quayle, Michael Redgrave, Paul Rogers.
2. L	M4421, S1409	CP	4 (s)	MS: Paul Scofield, Gary Watson, William Squire.
3. SA	815	EX	1	ST.

Henry the Fourth, Part Two

1. C	218, 218S	CP	4 (s)	SRS: Max Adrian, Harry Andrews, Felix Aylmer, Pamela Brown, Edith Evans, Richard Johnson, Anthony Quayle, Joyce Redman.
2. L	4422, 1410S	CP	4 (s)	MS: Gary Watson, William Squire.
3. SA	816	EX	1	ST.

Henry the Fifth

1. L	M4424, 1415S	CP	4 (s)	MS: Gary Watson, William Squire.

Chart 1 - Continued

Company	Record No.	Scope	No. of Sides	Cast
2. SA	817	EX	1	ST.
3. V	LM-1924	EX	1	Laurence Olivier, film sound track (with HAM-LET).

Henry the Sixth, Part One

1. L	4374, 1374S	CP	3 (s)	MS.

Henry the Sixth, Part Two

1. L	4428, 1428S	CP	4 (s)	MS.

Henry the Sixth, Part Three

1. L	4429, 1429S	CP	4 (s)	MS.

Henry the Eighth

1. L	M4226, S1426	CP	4 (s)	MS: Robert Speaight.
2. SA	881	EX	1	Thorndike, Casson.

Julius Caesar

1. C	230, 230S	CP	3 (s)	SRS: Ralph Richardson, Anthony Quayle, John Mills, Alan Bates.
2. L	4334	CP	3	MS.
3. SW	SW-A15, SW	CP	3	DG: MacLiammóir, Edwards, Casson. Anew McMaster, dir.
4. SA	809	EX	1	DG: same as no. 3.
5. MGM	E3033	EX	1	Film track, scenes with Gielgud, Brando, Mason, Calhern, Kerr, Garson.
6. EAV or	LE 7570, 7575	CP (edited)	2	Orson Welles and Mercury Theatre Co.
CU Entre	RL -13089	CP (edited)	2	

Chart 1 - Continued

Company	Record No.	Scope	No. of Sides	Cast

King John

1. C	215, 215S	CP	3 (s)	SRS: Donald Wolfit, Kenneth Haigh, Rosemary Harris.
2. L	M4418, S1413	CP	4 (s)	MS: Michael Hordern.
3. SW	A9	CP	4	DG.
4. SA	784	EX	1	DG.

King Lear

1. C	233, 233S	CP	4 (s)	SRS: Paul Scofield, Cyril Cusack, John Stride, Pamela Brown, Rachel Roberts.
2. C	TC 1158	EX	1	Dylan Thomas reading selections.
3. L	4423, 1414S	CP	4 (s)	MS.
4. SW	SW-A9, SW 134 135-136-136X.	CP	4	DG: Anew McMaster, dir.
4. L. S.	SKL-3, 4	EX	1 (s)	Donald Wolfit, Coral Browne, Barbara Jefford.

Love's Labour's Lost

1. L	M4363, S1363	CP	3 (s)	MS: Gary Watson, Max Adrian.

Macbeth

1. C	231, 231S	CP	2 (minor cuts)(s)	SRS: Anthony Quayle, Gwen Francon-Davies, Stanley Holloway; Howard Sackler, dir.
2. C	TC 1167	EX	1	Same as no. 1.

Chart 1 - Continued

Company	Record No.	Scope	No. of Sides	Cast
3. L	4343, 1316S	CP	3	MS: Tony Church, Irene Worth.
4. V	LM 6010	condensed	2	OV: Alec Guinness, Pamela Brown.
5. SA	782	EX	1	DG: Dir., Hilton Edwards.
6. AR	LPA 2202	EX	1	John Barrymore.

Measure for Measure

1. C	204, 204S	CP	3 (s)	SRS: John Gielgud, Ralph Richardson, Margaret Leighton; Peter Wood, dir.
2. L	4417, 1411S	CP	4 (s)	MS.
3. SW	SW-A19; 176-77-78	CP	3	(in preparation).

The Merchant of Venice

1. C	209, 209S	CP	3 (s)	SRS: Hugh Griffith, Dorothy Tutin, Harry Andrews, Jeremy Brett; dir. by Peter Wood.
2. C	TC 2013	minor cuts	2	Michael Redgrave.
3. L	4416, 1412S	CP	4	MS.
4. SA	810	EX	1	DG.
5. Lexing-ton	7540	EX	1	Paul Sparer, Nancy Marchand.

The Merry Wives of Windsor

1. C	203, 203S	CP	3 (s)	SRS: Anthony Quayle, Micheál MacLiammóir, Joyce Redman.

Chart 1 - Continued

Company	Record No.	Scope	No. of Sides	Cast
2. L	4372 1372S	CP	3 (s)	MS.

A Midsummer-Night's Dream

1. C	208, 208S	CP	3 (s)	SRS: Paul Scofield, Joy Parker.
2. L	M4349, S1321	CP	3 (s)	MS.
3. SW	SW-A5, 131-32-33	CP	3	DG, with Micheál Mac-Liammóir. Dir. by Hilton Edwards.
4. SA	882	EX	1	Dunne, Watkinson.
5. V	LVT 3002 or LM 6115 O. P.	CP	3	OV, with Shearer, Helpmann, Holloway. Full Mendelssohn score.

Much Ado About Nothing

1. C	206, 206S	CP	3 (s)	SRS: Rex Harrison, Rachel Roberts. Dir. by Howard Sackler.
2. L	M4362, S1362	CP	3 (s)	MS: Peggy Ashcroft, John Gielgud, Gary Watson, Williqm Squire, Michael Hordern, Peter Pears.
3. V	VDM-104 VDS-104	CP	3 (s)	Great Britain's National Theatre, Directed by Franco Zeffirelli. With Albert Finney, Maggie Smith, Frank Finlay.
4. SW	SW-A6, 141-42-43	CP	3	DG: with Micheál Mac-Liammóir. Dir. by Hilton Edwards.
5. SA	883	EX	1	Dunne, Watkinson.

Chart 1 - Continued

Company	Record No.	Scope	No. of Sides	Cast

Othello

1. C   225, 225S   CP   3 (s)   SRS: Frank Silvera, Cyril Cusack, Anna Massey. Dir. by Howard Sackler.

2. L   4419   CP   4   MS.

3. CU   5SL-153   CP   3   Paul Robeson, Uta Hagen, Jose Ferrer.

4. V   VDM-100 VDS-100   CP   4 (s)   Great Britain's National Theatre, with Laurence Olivier, Frank Finlay, Maggie Smith, Joyce Redman. Dir. by John Dexter.

5. V   VDM-108   EX   1 (s)   same as no. 4.

6. SA   783   EX   1   DG: Micheál MacLiammóir.

Pericles

1. L   4377 1377S   CP   3 (s)   MS: William Squire, Prunella Scales.

Richard the Second

1. C   216, 216S   CP   3 (s)   SRS: John Gielgud, Keith Michell, Leo McKern; Peter Wood, dir.

2. L   4335   CP   3   MS.

3. SA   891   EX   1   Folio Theatre.

Richard the Third

1. L   4430M 1430S   CP   3 (s)   MS.

Chart 1 - Continued

Company	Record No.	Scope	No. of Sides	Cast
2. V	LM 6126	CP	3	Sound track of film, with Laurence Olivier.
3. V	LM 1940	EX	1	same as no. 2.
4. AR	2203	EX	1	John Barrymore.
5. L. S.	SR 111; 35/36	EX	1 (s)	Peter Finch, dir. by Dennis Vance.

Romeo and Juliet

1. C	228, 228S	CP	3 (s)	SRS: Claire Bloom, Albert Finney, Edith Evans. Dir. by Howard Sackler.
2. L	4419M; 1407S	CP	4 (s)	MS.
3. SW	SW-A16, 147-48-49-50	CP	4	DG: dir. by and starring Anew McMaster.
4. V	LVT 3001 or LM 6116	CP	3	OV: Claire Bloom, Alan Badel, Peter Finch. Dir. by Hugh Hunt.
5. Epic	LC 3126	EX	1	Film track: Laurence Harvey, Susan Shentall, Flora Robson.
6.	Atlantic Set No. 401; (102/5)	condensed	2	Eva LeGalliene, Richard Waring, Dennis King. Dir. by Margaret Webster.
7. SA	812	EX	1	ST: dir. by John Blatchley.
8. D	9504	EX	1/2	Gielgud, Brown (soliloquies from HAMLET on reverse).

The Taming of the Shrew

1. C	211, 211S	CUT	2 (s)	SRS: Trevor Howard, Margaret Leighton. Howard Sackler, dir.

Chart 1 - Continued

Company	Record No.	Scope	No. of Sides	Cast
2. L	4367, 1367S	CP	3 (s)	MS: Derek Godfrey, Peggy Ashcroft.
3. SW	SW-A7; 151-2-3	CP	3	DG: Micheál MacLiammóir, dir. by Hilton Edwards.
4. SA	884	EX	1	Casson, Watkinson.

The Tempest

1. C	201, 201S	CP	3 (s)	SRS: Michael Redgrave, Vanessa Redgrave, Hugh Griffith, Anna Massey.
2. L	4346M, 1318S	CP	3 (s)	MS: Michael Hordern.
3. SW	SW-A10; 137-8-9	CP	3	DG: with Hilton Edwards, dir. by Micheál Mac-Liammóir.
4. SA	886	EX	1	Carrol, Casson.

Timon of Athens

1. L	M4350; S1322	CP	3 (s)	MS: William Squire.

Titus Andronicus

1. C	SRS2271	CP	3 (s)	SRS: Howard Sackler, dir.
2. L	4371M 1371S	CP	3 (s)	MS: Jill Balcon.

Troilus and Cressida

1. C	234, 234S	CP	3 (s)	SRS: Jeremy Brett, Diane Cilento, Cyril Cusack, Max Adrian. Dir. by Howard Sackler.

Chart 1 - Continued

Company	Record No.	Scope	No. of Sides	Cast
2. L	4413	CP	4	MS: Tony White, Irene Worth.
3. SA	892	EX	1	Folio Theatre.

Twelfth Night

Company	Record No.	Scope	No. of Sides	Cast
1. C	213, 213S	CP	3 (s)	SRS: Paul Scofield, John Neville, Vanessa Redgrave, Siobhan McKenna. Dir. by Howard Sackler.
2. L	M4354; S1326	CP	3 (s)	MS: Peter Pears, Dorothy Tutin, Jill Balcon.
3. SW	SW-A3; 116-7-8	CP	3	DG: with Micheál MacLiammóir, dir. by Hilton Edwards.
4. SA	887	EX	1	Folio Theatre.
5. AR	22-4	EX	1	John Barrymore.

The Two Gentelemen of Verona

Company	Record No.	Scope	No. of Sides	Cast
1. C	202, 202S	CP	3 (s)	SRS: Wyngarde, De Souza.
2. L	M4344, S1315	CP	3 (s)	MS.
3. SA	893	EX	1	Folio Theatre.
4. SW	SW-A23; 173-4-5	CP	3	DG.

The Winter's Tale

Company	Record No.	Scope	No. of Sides	Cast
1. C	214, 214S	CP	3 (s)	SRS: John Gielgud, Peggy Ashcroft.
2. L	M4420 S1408	CP	4 (s)	MS: William Squire.
3. SA	894	EX	1	Folio Theatre.

Chart 2

Included in this listing are a few of the most interesting collections and one anthology. The Argo, EMI and Philips recordings are only available in Great Britain. For tracing other works of English origin, including many anthologies containing Shakespeare excerpts, the best source is The Gramophone, a monthly catalogue published at 177-9 Kenton Road, Kenton, Harrow, Middlesex, England.

Company	Record No.	Title, Reader(s), No. of Sides, Plays Included
Argo	DA-1	Highlights from the Tragedies, Volume I; Marlowe Society; 1 LP; "Julius Caesar," "Romeo and Juliet," "Othello," "Macbeth."
Argo	DA-2	Highlights from the Comedies; Marlowe Society; 1 LP; "Merchant of Venice," "Mid summer Night's Dream," "Twelfth Night," "The Tempest."
Argo	DA-3	Highlights from the Histories; Marlowe Society; 1 LP; "King John," "Richard II," "Henry IV, 1 & 2," "Henry V."
Argo	DA-4	Highlights from the Tragedies, Volume 2; Marlowe Society; 1 LP; "Hamlet," "King Lear."
Argo	ZNF-4	Homage to Shakespeare; a quartercentenary anthology including his own works and the homage paid him by other poets (Johnson, Milton, etc.); 1 LP (s); Laurence Olivier, Michael Redgrave, Paul Scofield, John Stride, Alan Bates, Peter McEnery, Ralph Richardson, Richard Johnson, John Gielgud, Donald Wolfit, John Masefield, Dorothy Tutin, Sybil Thorndike, Peggy Ashcroft, Irene Worth, Edith Evans, Vanessa Redgrave and others; "Measure for Measure," "Othello," "Macbeth," "King Lear," "Antony and Cleopatra," "Cymbeline," "The Winter's Tale," "King Henry VIII," "The Tempest."
Caedmon	TC 1170	Shakespeare: Soul of an Age; narrated by Ralph Richardson, read by Michael Redgrave; 1 LP; "Richard II," "Richard III," "Twelfth Night," "Merry Wives," "Henry IV," "Henry V," "Henry VI," "Henry VIII," "King John," "Macbeth," "As You Like It," "Hamlet," "The Tempest."

Chart 2 - Continued

Company	Record No.	Title, Reader(s), No. of Sides, Plays Included
Columbia Master- works	OL 5390	The Ages of Man; Sir John Gielgud; 1 LP; "As You Like It," "The Merchant of Venice," "The Tempest," "Romeo and Juliet," "Measure for Measure," "Henry IV, 1," "Richard II," "Sonnets," "Henry IV, 2," "Julius Caesar," "Hamlet," "King Lear," "The Tempest."
Decca	DL 9041	Immortal Scenes and Sonnets from Shake- speare; Sir John Gielgud, Pamela Brown, Arnold Moss, R. E. Johnson; 1 LP.
EMI Records, Ltd; Laureate Series.	CLP 1738	Scenes and Speeches from Shakespeare; Paul Rogers, Coral Browne, Anna Massey, Corin Redgrave; 1 LP; Vol. I; "Richard II," "Richard III," "Henry V," "Macbeth," "Merchant of Venice."
EMI Records, Ltd; Laureate Series.	CLP 1739	Scenes and Speeches from Shakespeare; Corin Redgrave, Anna Massey, Robert Hardy, Roger Livesey; 1 LP; Vol. 2; "Ham- let," "Julius Caesar," "Midsummer- Night's Dream," "Twelfth Night," "As You Like It," "Much Ado About Nothing."
London Library of Recorded English	Album No. 2	Book IV: Shakespearean Dramatic Poetry; eminent critics, poets, authors; 1 LP; "Henry V," "Midsummer-Night's Dream," "Richard II," "Merchant of Venice," "The Tempest," "Hamlet," "Henry VIII," "Macbeth," "Othello."
Philips	ABL 3331	One Man In His Time; Sir John Gielgud; 1 LP; "The Passionate Pilgrim No. 20"; "A Midsummer-Night's Dream," "Sonnets," "Love's Labour's Lost," "Taming of the Shrew," "Troilus and Cressida," "King Henry V," "Richard II," "Julius Caesar," "Macbeth," "Cymbeline," "Much Ado A- bout Nothing."
Spoken Arts	723	Scenes from Shakespeare; Paul Rogers; 1 LP; Falstaff, John of Gaunt, Mercutio, Bottom, Macbeth.

Chart 2 - Continued

Company	Record No.	Title, Reader(s), No. of Sides, Plays Included
Spoken Arts	766-7	Scenes from Shakespeare; Anew McMaster; 2 LP's; "Taming of the Shrew," "Othello," "Merchant of Venice," "Romeo and Juliet," "Hamlet," "Macbeth," "As You Like It," "Julius Caesar."
Spoken Arts	836-V. 1	Shakespeare Scenes and Soliloquies for Actors; Micheál MacLiammóir and Hilton Edwards; 1 LP each; Vol. 1: "Hamlet," "Macbeth," "Othello," Vol. 2: "Julius Caesar," "Merchant of Venice," "King Lear."

Chart 3

Finally, a group of interesting and rather special recordings, all of which require some ingenuity to obtain, some of which are rare indeed. They are included as spicy tidbits to whet the appetites of both the connoisseur and the dilettante-antiquary.

Company	Record No.	Speed, Size No. of Records	Reader, Selection
Selection	JEC 505 A	1-7' 45RPM	Sir Herbert Beerbohm Tree reads Antony's lament over Caesar, Falstaff's speech on honor, Hamlet's soliloquy on death, Richard II's soliloquy on the death of Kings; also, Svengali mesmerizing Trilby. Recorded in 1907.
National Council of Teachers of English	RS 80-3	1-10" 78 RPM	Harry M. Ayres reads "To be or not to be" and Portia's speech on mercy, in "Elizabethan" accent. Also a few lines of "Speak the speech. . ." and a passage from Love's Labour's Lost.
SW	202	1-10" 78RPM	Walter Hampden in excerpts from Henry V.
SW	067	1-10" 78RPM	Antony's funeral oration from Julius Caesar read by DeWolf Hopper (side 1) and Baliol Holloway (side 2).

Chart 3 - Continued

Company	Record No.	Speed, Size No. of Records	Reader, Selection
Columbia Masterworks	C-33	9-12" 78RPM	Macbeth (condensed) read by Orson Welles, Fay Bainter and members of the Mercury Theatre.
Columbia Masterworks	MC-6	12-12" 78RPM	The Merchant of Venice (condensed), with Orson Welles and members of the Mercury Theatre.
CU	Set 303	5-12" 78 RPM	Scenes from Richard II read by Maurice Evans and company.
Harvard Vocarium	HFS 1906-7	1-12" 78RPM	Flora Robson in excerpts from Macbeth.

* * * * * * * * *

New issues and withdrawals are as constant in the field of Shakespeare recordings as elsewhere. This selected discography, therefore, is necessarily a picture frozen in time; to be specific, spring of 1966. Many other lists are extant (this one, however, was compiled from original sources). For example, the Canadian periodical, Record News, available in the rare book section of the Music Division of the New York Public Library at Lincoln Center, contained listings of Shakespeare recordings before it went out of print. Its section on Hamlet went on for five pages, including such special items as the preserved work of London school children (Vol. 2, No. 1). Between them and the likes of John Gielgud rises the growing mountain of Shakespeare for the phonograph.

Appendix A

In the study of spoken records much data of historic and human interest became available. The following pages contain some of these materials. They are here presented with the permission of the writers, for which the author is deeply grateful.

Contents

I. The Origin of a Sound Collection

Milo Ryan, University of Washington, Phonoarchive

The collecting of monuments of sound is the twentieth century's unique extension of archaeology, even though it has not yet been dignified by appropriate recognition within that world of fossils, pots and baskets, temples and instruments of war. It is so new as to still be groping for a suitable scholarly noun with which to identify itself. For reasons that require no explanation, the term "recorded sound" falls flat.

But what is one to do? Wait for a word?

Fortunately, the inadequacy of the language has not dampened the zeal of the art historian; and perhaps it is out of respect for what language we have that collectors of sound recordings have refrained from such corruptions of the spirit as invented the term "musicology." The world goes bravely on its way in spite of the want of suitable words for many things, and so it is with sound collectors, who remain content to live with such drab terminologies as the "Association for Recorded Sound Collections" and that desperately uneuphonious name, the "British Institute of Recorded Sound."

The name chosen for the collection at the University of Washington School of Communications--"Phonoarchive"--represents little inventive restraint, which may be why it has never seemed to catch on. It was chosen quite deliberately, to prevent the collection from becoming known as a library, which it is not, since it has nothing to do with books nor is its mission the circulation of recorded information. It is not a "collection" in the sense that it was not deliberately brought about by a zealous searcher. It is an archive, the repository of radio programs of a particular period in the art and technology of broadcasting, programs that constitute monuments of a time when the principles of broadcast journalism were being set down. It is a monument in the sense that a Roman arch is a monument, or the Eiffel Tower, the U. S. S. Olympia or Volpone. It is there for those who want to know in detail what a broadcasting organization, the Columbia Broadcasting System, was ingenious enough to develop in the way of forms and practices in order to reveal the nature of one of man's disasters, the Second World War.

Some sound collections, such as the Spoken Record Collection at Brooklyn College and that of the National Voice Library at Michigan State University, the brainchild of G. Robert Vincent, have been deliberately gathered. In fact, most of the great collections have come about by devotion and determination. Not so the Phonoarchive at the University of Washington. It came about by a chain of accidents, and its curator, the present writer, is merely a by-product of the accidents. The story of its discovery has been told before, in the Journal of Broadcasting, in the author's book, History in Sound, which catalogs the collection, and in numerous newspaper and magazine articles. The setting for the story is Puget Sound and Vashon Island, a pleasantly rural body of land approximately equidistant from Seattle and Tacoma, Washington. Geographically it would be more proper to say Maury Island, though few make the distinction. Maury is a small island acreage adjacent to Vashon, very much like a baby kangaroo in Vashon's sac-like eastern shore. There, because of long-ago real-estate values and because of the proclivity of salt water for giving an additional boost to radio waves, four of Seattle's most powerful radio stations maintain transmitter operations, one of them KIRO, an affiliate of CBS and now owned by a subsidiary of the Church of Latter Day Saints. At the time of the "accidents" KIRO was still owned by its originator, the Queen City Broadcasting Corporation, of which Mr. Saul Haas was president.

A successful broadcaster, Mr. Haas is also a man of wide-ranging social interests, including a sense of history not always found in the rush-rush of commercial radio. As the clouds of war began to glower, Mr. Haas and members of his staff felt themselves frustrated by one of the facts of time-geography peculiar to the West Coast--the three-hour differential between their area and New York City, where much of radio was dominated, as television is today.

The story of the war, as it was being told by that magnificent news organization being built by C. B. S. under the impetus of Mr. William Paley through the talents of the late Paul White, was not reaching concerned listeners in KIRO's coverage area at a time when they could tune it in. A supper-hour news roundup built for New York was a mid-afternoon broadcast in Seattle; a newscast at 7 a. m. EST was a newscast at 4 a. m. PST, or 3 a. m. when New York was on Daylight Time.

What seems today to be the obvious solution to the problem was equally obvious then, but almost impossible to bring about. For one reason, the technology of instantaneous recording was comparatively primitive--even the wire recorder was to become industrially available only after the war--and for a second reason, there was a network regulation to the effect that everything sent out had to be carried live and instantaneously. To get a sense of what this regulation involved, one should read William L. Shirer's Berlin Diary and note how time after time he had to go to the studio in Berlin at such improbable hours as 1 or 2 a. m. in order to take part in an early evening program being anchored in New York. (They were giants in those days, not yet softened up by the facilities of the era of tape.)

In spite of the network regulation, KIRO began to connect incoming network lines to a disc-recording apparatus its engineers had improved upon as to sound quality. The discs were then broadcast at a suitable time, and the problem was solved.

When the broadcast was over, what then? Now comes another aspect of the series of accidentals that resulted in the Phonoarchive. Recording discs for instantaneous cutting had initially been made of aluminum, and after use could be returned to the supplier for a credit entry. The supplier could then resurface the discs and return them to the market. But aluminum went early into the war, and disc suppliers began to use glass, among other materials, as a substitute. What do you do with such discs when you're through with them? As apparently many broadcasters did, you could destroy them; after all, you're not in the archive business and space is always at a premium in a broadcasting station. KIRO shelved them as long as it could, and when the war was over, sent them into storage in the

basement of its transmitter building on Vashon (Maury) Island.
And there they remained, almost forgotten.

In 1956, this writer and a colleague were engaged in a series of educational television programs dealing with the art of
propaganda and needed some examples of the wartime oratory of
Prime Minister Winston Churchill and President Franklin D. Roosevelt. It was a frustrating search until this writer recalled that
while employed at KIRO in the later 1940's, he had seen boxes of
recordings being carried out of the station's filing area. Where
were they now and would there be any Churchill and Roosevelt a-
mong them?

Those now in charge at KIRO didn't know, and those who
might remember were either out of town or no longer employed at
the station. This writer himself was now on the faculty of the University of Washington. There were many cases at the transmitter
but no one there knew of their contents. Perhaps, it was suggested,
we would be interested in going to the island to have a look. We
agreed and set Washington's Birthday for the trip. The day before
that there came a second phone call from KIRO, suggesting that if
there were any recordings there that might be useful in our classes
we would be welcome to them. We took a University-owned truck
and brought back 51 packing cases full. The Phonoarchive resulted.

The C. B. S. news, actualities, special reports, talks, interviews, documentaries and discussions have been dubbed to tape--the
largest part of the collection--thanks to a grant for the purpose
from the C. B. S. Foundation Inc. Taping has enabled us to bypass
the fragility of the glass-base discs and yet make the content useful
to scholars and to teachers, and to undertake the very wearisome
and expensive task of cataloging.

The Phonoarchive is housed in the School of Communications.
Everything possible to preserve both the discs and tapes from loss,
breakage or deterioration has been undertaken, though as of summer
1969 some necessary steps still remain to be put into effect. Guide
for housing and storage has been the Taylor-Lemcoe study, with
supplementary advice from the National Archives.

By practicing judicious exchange with other collections we

have been able to add to the tape files such as entertainment and
cultural broadcasts as to make the Phonoarchive even more representative of the age when radio was attempting to be all things to
all men.   There has also been a gift of a substantial number of
discs, many of them of N. B. C. origin, given to the Phonoarchive by
another Seattle radio station, KOMO.   The heart and soul of the
collection, however, will always by the day-by-day record of World
War II as told through the enterprise of the Columbia Broadcasting
System by Edward R. Murrow, Eric Sevareid, Howard K. Smith,
Charles Collingwood, Winston Burdette, John Charles Daly and their
brilliant contemporaries.

        The detailed description of the content of the Phonoarchive
is to be found in Milo Ryan's History in Sound--q. v.

II. The Story of the National Voice Library,
     And the Man Who Made It

G. Robert Vincent, Director, National Voice Library

Until the birth of sound reproduction, chronicles about the past consisted mainly of words--carved in stone, painted on papyri, written on parchment, or printed on paper. They were precious heirlooms of learning but they lacked a dimension. Sound provided that dimension, reaching beyond the intellect to the emotions.

We can understand a man's ideas through our intellect but to know him really, to know him as a full, vivid, rounded personality, we must respond to him not only intellectually but also emotionally. This response can often be immediately evoked when we hear his voice. The timbre of the voice, the inflections, the accents, the very hesitations and imperfections of his utterance tell a story which cannot be conveyed by mere alphabetic symbols. Print stands for the word, but it never is, it never can be the word itself. Only the spoken voice can bring the word fully to life.

Today, more and more public and private schools and universities are supplementing their libraries of books with recorded voice libraries. Foremost amongst these is the National Voice Library at Michigan State University in East Lansing, Michigan. This organization is dedicated to the preservation of the spoken word in every field of human endeavor, and to making it available for students and research workers.

The desire to halt the fleeting moment, to give those who come after us a more intimate understanding of the men and women of our own time, was an instinctive feeling when I was a youngster and became a confirmed, reasoned conviction as the years went by. A few incidents which occurred during these years may help to explain the origin, scope, procedure, aims, and aspirations of the National Voice Library.

184

Way back in 1912, when Teddy Roosevelt turned down an invitation to address a boys' club of which I was a member, I did not quite give up hope that he would be heard at our meeting. He was a rather busy man in those days; he was running for President of the United States on a brand new party ticket whose emblem was the head of a bull moose.

Through our friendship with young Charles Edison (son of the inventor), we were able to borrow a cylinder recording machine to bring with us on a journey to Sagamore Hill, Oyster Bay, Long Island, where T. R. lived. Four boys made the pilgrimage in a Model-T Ford.

To get an audience with Colonel Roosevelt was no easy matter. It required the combined efforts of the newspaper correspondents stationed at the Oyster Bay Inn and of some of the Roosevelt kids. When he finally received us, Teddy at first demurred at speaking into the horn but, as he didn't wish to disappoint us, he consented to make a two-minute talk. It became the only ad-libbed recording T. R. ever made. It was clear, precise, full of vitality. I remember his every expression and hearing him go into a falsetto, as he concluded with: "... don't flinch, don't foul, and hit the line hard!"

Because of this accomplishment and my boyish enthusiasm for recording, the Edison Labs presented me with the cylinder machine. One of the first things I did was to ask a man by the name of Job E. Hedges, a well-known New York attorney, whose oratory greatly appealed to me, to let me set up a recording session with him. To my astonishment, he flatly refused, on the grounds that it was undignified. "It may be all right for a rough and ready individual like Teddy Roosevelt to speak into one of those things," he said, "but not for me." If Mr. Hedges had lived to witness the era of radio, he might have changed his viewpoint.

The three-cornered presidential campaign of 1912 was a dramatic one. The entire country took an intense interest in the candidates and the issues. Sometimes the public displayed an almost religious fervor and huge crowds sang "The Battle Hymn of the Republic" and "Onward Christian Soldiers." A crank shot Teddy

Roosevelt while he was on his way to a speaking engagement in Milwaukee, but a bullet in his chest did not deter Teddy from delivering his address. That talk was later recorded and so were speeches by Governor Woodrow Wilson and President William Howard Taft, T. R. 's opponents. They were added to my group of speech records. It would be years before the appearance of sound motion picture newsreels, radio, or television were using the medium of the phonograph to tell the candidates' story to those voters who were deprived of seeing them in person.

Talks by William Jennings Bryan, known throughout the land as the Silver-Tongued Orator, had been recorded even before 1912; also a fiery and impassioned campaign speech by Eugene V. Debs, the Socialist. But all of the spoken phonograph records in those days were not only about politics. They included the voices of stage personalities: Joseph Jefferson recorded scenes from Rip Van Winkle even before the turn of the century; Sarah Bernhardt did excerpts from well-known French dramas; famous Shakespearean actors and actresses made records; comedians like Weber and Fields, Nat Wills, Raymond Hitchcock, all engraved their talent onto wax.

There were evangelists and preachers, poets, explorers. James Whitcomb Riley, the Hoosier poet, recited his homespun verses: "Little Orphan Annie," "The Happy Little Cripple," "The Raggedy Man," "Out to Old Aunt Mary's," in a weak but kindly voice. Hearing his delightful interpretations gave you the feeling that you really knew this beloved, ailing old man.

What had excited me greatly, three years before the Teddy Roosevelt incident, was the race for the discovery of the North Pole, a goal many countries had tried to attain for years. It had just been accomplished by an American. But by whom? The whole country was divided on that question. Was it Commander Robert Edwin Peary, United States Navy, now on his eighth polar expedition; or his former ship's doctor, Frederick A. Cook, who found himself a millionaire sponsor and took off for the Arctic the year before--ostensibly on a hunting trip? Enthusiastic people everywhere wore celluloid buttons on their lapels, indicating either COOK or PEARY. It was like an election campaign. Dr. Cook

had returned home before Peary did. He was feted in Denmark--
from whence he made the announcement--and hailed in America by
President Taft and cheering crowds. The New York Herald strongly supported his claim.

When Commander Peary and his crew were homeward bound,
they received word of Dr. Cook's assertion. Peary cabled to the
New York Times--which had the serial rights to his story--"Do not
trouble about Cook. He has not been to the Pole on April 21, 1908
or at any other time. He simply handed the public a gold brick."

There were geographic societies which demanded something
tangible from Cook, for he said that he had lost his notes and,
moreover, his polar observations were vague. Finally, he was
completely discredited, cancelled his lecture tours, and dropped out
of sight--but not before he had made a recording about his alleged
adventures on the expedition.

The Peary Arctic Club of New York induced Commander
Peary also to speak into a recording machine. His crisp, matter-
of-fact, authoritative description is in sharp contrast to the suave
words spoken by Dr. Cook. Visit the National Voice Library and
hear them for yourself.

It was my privilege, decades later, to play Admiral Peary's
recording for a former member of his expedition, Captain Bob Bartlett, the Master of the steam yacht "Roosevelt" on which the historic voyage was made. He was deeply moved at hearing the voice
of his old commander through the veil of years and agreed to say
a few words of his own about the story of the discovery of the
North Pole on April 6, 1909. I recorded it on the spot.

There were still unexplored frontiers on earth for man to
conquer in those early days of the 20th Century. Of his south polar
experiences, Sir Ernest Shackleton told a thrilling story on a recording which found its way into my steadily growing collection.

As war broke out in Europe, I started a new category:
British, French, and German war songs and speeches. Without
quite realizing it, I was becoming documentary minded. In 1917,
shortly after the United States declared war against Germany, I interrupted my schooling to join the 27th Division of the New York

National Guard and was sent overseas. Following the armistice, I remained in France as an attaché at the American Embassy, doing decoding work.

It was fascinating to attend a grand reception given by Ambassador Sharp for the visiting United States President Woodrow Wilson. There I had the opportunity personally to see President Poincaré, Georges Clemenceau, Marshal Foch, General Joffre, Lord Derby, General Pershing, and many other dignitaries. Later, not only their recorded voices but also those of King George V, Kitchener, Haig, Jellicoe, the two Kaisers, Hindenburg, and Ludendorff were added to my sound-relics of World War I.

The troopship "Leviathan" returned me stateside to complete my classroom education in engineering but I studied the world scene with keen interest, as the Roaring Twenties approached. Normalcy. Harding's Disarmament Conference. The Klu Klux Klan. Prohibition. The newfangled radio. The stock market craze. Modernism. The League of Nations debates. The Teapot Dome scandals. Hey-day of the silent screen. Channel swimmers. Sacco and Vanzetti. Sound reproduction becoming electrified. The monkey trial at Dayton, Tennessee. Lindy's flight to Paris. Movies beginning to talk. The Big Bust on Wall Street.

And then came the Thirties. Life now more complex. Apple sellers at the corner. Hoover out and F. D. R. in. The First Hundred Days. Quintuplets. The King of England abdicates. A new Pope. The rise of Hitler and Mussolini. Huey Long. Gandhi's fasts. The Radio Priest. The Martian invasion. Fred Allen. Munich. Another war begins. ...It is possible to relive those memorable days by listening to the actual voices and events that were recorded on the spot and are now filed in the archives of the National Voice Library.

I had been associated with the Thomas A. Edison Recording Division during the latter Twenties and, when they ceased operation, I set up my own sound and recording studio--a penthouse studio in Radio City, New York. There, I worked on devices to electrically rerecord the old experimental wax cylinder records that I had inherited from Mr. Edison's own collection.

When the phonograph was in its infancy, in the late 1880's and early '90's, Edison invited many distinguished people to try out the new talking machine. That was before the development of duplicating matrices so that those old waxes were the only ones in existence of the guest speakers. Among them were Henry Morton Stanley, Nelson A. Miles, Porfirio Diaz, Garrett A. Hobart, Hudson Maxim.

To promote the phonograph in England, Colonel George E. Gouraud, Mr. Edison's representative, set up recording sessions with celebrities in that country. Gouraud quite often received instructions from the Boss, via "phonogram" (a thin wax cylinder of one-inch diameter, sent out in a cardboard container that was being used as a substitute for letter writing). One of these spoke to him in poetic words. It said:

> Gouraud, agent of my choice,
> Bid my balance sheets rejoice--
> Send me Mr. Gladstone's voice.

Colonel Gouraud not only succeeded in having Prime Minister Gladstone send a greeting to America by phonograph; he was also instrumental in recording Florence Nightingale, Sir Henry Irving, Queen Victoria, and P. T. Barnum. And he sent an aide to Rome to deliver a spoken message to the Pope from Cardinal Gibbons. Pope Leo XIII, in turn, blessed the people of the United States on wax.

It was Gouraud who thought of inviting the only surviving trumpeter of the Charge of the Light Brigade to resound that famous "Charge," to have the notes of the very bugle reproduced through this new medium of communication.

The famous bugle--which had also been used in the Battle of Waterloo in 1815--was loaned by the British Museum for the occasion. Trumpeter Landfrey came to Edison House on Northumberland Street, London, to make the recording; the date: August 2, 1890. Actually, it was some 45 years later, in 1935, when I first came upon this priceless relic in the cellar of Walter H. Miller (formerly director of the Edison Recording Division) at his home in South Orange, N. J.

That same night, some of my friends and I worked for hours
at the studio in New York to grind the proper sapphire stylus and
make a filtered, electrical duplication on disc of this historic cylinder record. It seemed rather spooky, at about 3 a.m., to listen
to the loud-speaker play back an unbelievably clear reproduction.
We felt like sound-archaeologists and celebrated the feat by going to
an all-night drugstore for chocolate sodas.

Sometimes people will say that these rare old waxes are
really only novelties and have little historic significance. This I
vehemently deny. Much can be learned about these speakers of the
past. Take the voice of P. T. Barnum, for instance. Here was
the only specimen of the timbre and voice inflections of a legendary
figure who was born in 1810--only a year after Abraham Lincoln.
His voice and his words are a distinct reflection of his personality.
He expressed the hope that: ..."my voice, like my great show, will
be heard by future generations, long after I have joined the great
and, as I believe, happy majority."

The income-producing activities of the sound studio, which
was named The National Vocarium, included studio and location recording on disc and film, public address work, radio program production, commercial work for advertising agencies. I spent most
evenings and weekends on the historic record collection. It was becoming somewhat unwieldy for the available space.

People would come in, asking to hear certain voices--actors
from the March of Time and the Radio Networks, the BBC, schools,
colleges. Messages would be received from institutions throughout
the country and also from Europe, asking for information or copies
of records. Sometimes VIP's would arrive and had to be received
cordially even during working hours.

I remember one particular incident which amused me. An
energetic little old lady stormed into the studio and said she was
told that I had a recording of her husband's voice. "Quite possibly," I remarked, "May I ask your husband's name?" She replied
impatiently: "President Benjamin Harrison," as though I should
have known. We spent two pleasant hours together and I recorded
her points of view on the old and the new American scene.

Then, one day, --through the French doors leading from the roof garden--a most attractive woman appeared. She was in her thirties, spoke softly, and inquired if she might hear her father's voice which, she had read, was included in the collection. She turned out to be Hope Davis, the daughter of Richard Harding Davis.

Some of the longer sessions took place in the evening (generally accompanied by refreshments). It was fun to watch such dignified personages as Frederick Lewis Allen, the editor of Harper's Magazine, and his wife, Agnes Rogers, acting like two happy kids when they listened to voice after voice of people they knew and wrote about in their books.

At times I was requested to furnish voice specimens for movie stars, Spencer Tracy, Fredric March or others, when they were impersonating individuals from the past. Their portrayals were good but somehow they never sounded quite genuine to me--at least, not from the standpoint of character analysis.

Now the collection was growing so large and the expense for recording discs, sapphire styli, and miscellaneous equipment was becoming a decided financial burden. I thought that stronger hands should take up the quest, constantly supplementing the nucleus that I would contribute and which would fill a time gap that it would be hardly possible to duplicate.

So I set out for the nation's capital to get the cooperation of the United States Government. I met old Dr. Putnam at the Library of Congress and he briefly informed me that he had no authority to take on new projects and that the President was about to appoint his successor. National Archives said that they were interested only in Americana--no European subjects at all--but that they could not accept even parts of the collection because the Government would be put in the position of endorsing someone in the commercial recording business. Smithsonian Institution had no room or facilities to play records. "We have a replica of the early phonograph and a few cylinder records and that will suffice" was the gist of their response.

I visited Statuary Hall in the U.S. Capitol Building, saw the beautiful structures of the city, looked at monuments and oil paint-

ings of famed individuals, some of whose living voices could and
should be made available for earnest research workers, students,
and historians.   I regretted that our government did not visualize
this cultural asset as some European governments have done in their
own countries.

Before leaving Washington, I arranged for personal recording sessions with most cabinet members of the F. D. R. administration, with Senators and members of Congress.   Among them were
the first woman U. S. Senator, Hattie W. Caraway of Arkansas, and
the gentleman from Ohio, Senator Robert A. Taft, who graciously
came over to the Hay-Adams House where my equipment was set
up.   He gave his impressions of the current scene and his ideas on
the rights of labor.

Not long after this Washington trip, the New Yorker Magazine decided to write a "Profile" about me and my activities.   After
it appeared, a telegram arrived from the librarian of the Sterling
Memorial Library at Yale University.   It stated that Yale would be
happy to provide a home for the voice library and that he--Mr.
Bernard Knollenberg--would like to meet with me in New York to
discuss what requirements were necessary for this arrangement.

We agreed on some temporary provisions but not many
months thereafter, Mr. Knollenberg was appointed Assistant Lend-
Lease Administrator, resigned as librarian, and went to Washington.   The National Voice Library never moved to New Haven.   And
soon America was at war again.

It was a quiet Sunday morning and I reached the studio early
in order to catch up on a lot of unfinished recording work.   Everything seemed so peaceful at Rockefeller Center, the only sounds
came from the skaters on the ice rink in the Plaza.   When I turned
on the studio equipment, a news flash came through from an NBC
commentator that a small group of Japanese paratroopers was reported to have landed on Waikiki Beach and that the Japanese Consul
in San Francisco, who had been reached on the phone, gave assur-
ances that it must be an error.   Probably, this far eastern expert
concluded, it was a trick by the Germans, dressed up as Japs, to
cause tension.   They would be apprehended shortly and the true

story would then come out.

I recorded this strange news analysis and warmed up all the
other equipment, preparing for a long session. Sure enough, within minutes the air was alive with news. It was horrifying but exciting. I remained at my post for the next 48 hours, recording
everything that transpired. Bill Shirer of CBS, later that Sunday
afternoon gave a resumé of the tragic events, starting with: "Sanka
Coffee--the coffee that always lets you sleep--will dispense with its
usual commercial because of the present emergency..." There is
thus a fairly complete sound documentation of our entrance into
World War II at the National Voice Library.

During the early months of the war, I was able to assist the
Office of War Information with program material and in April 1942
was offered a commission in the Army Signal Corps. My assignment as one of the original group which formed the Radio Section--
later Armed Forces Radio Service--was exciting. A year later I
created a phonograph record project for the armed forces which released musical records that were sent to our troops all over the
world. The records were called "V-Discs." By war's end, over
30 million of these unbreakable discs were distributed. The project
made phonograph record history and, since many name artists, including Arturo Toscanini and Glenn Miller, made spoken introductions on these records, their voices have been included in the voice
library.

In 1945 I was "requisitioned" by the State Department to take
charge of all sound activities for the United Nations Conference on
International Organization in San Francisco. It resulted, among
other things, in a great deal of fascinating documentary sound recordings for the historical archives. At my suggestion, representatives from each country were asked to say a few words in their native language upon affixing their signatures to the UN Charter.

After VJ Day, I was sent to Germany, assisted by a small
group of enlisted men, to install and technically operate the multi-
lingual interpreting system at the Nuremberg War Crimes Trials.
We also "fed" the broadcasters and motion picture crews with live
sound and with recordings. Highlights from these proceedings are

now an interesting part of the voice library.

A two-year appointment as Chief Sound and Recording Officer
for the United Nations at Lake Success, N. Y. , started upon my
separation from the army. As more nations were admitted to the
UN, my staff numbered in excess of 50 engineers. This interlude
added an abundance of formal and informal voice material to the collection, of especial value to students wishing to study some of the
dramatic episodes which took place during that period.

But it was nice to get back to the cozy penthouse studio. At
the half century mark, I produced a long-playing record album of
outstanding events which occurred during the first three decades of
the 20th Century, featuring the actual voices of the principal participants of these events, with narration by Fredric March. It was
originally distributed through Capitol Records and later reissued by
the National Voice Library at Michigan State. Library Journal, in
a review, commented: "...It may well be that there could never be
another audio-documentary as valuable as this one."

For the next few years, working on documentary motion pictures took up much of my time. Hopes of ever establishing a national institution to preserve and disseminate oral history were getting dimmer. But I never lost faith, reflecting that P. T. Barnum
did not start his Big Circus until he was 60. My time would yet
come!

The 60th birthday arrived and then another year passed by
before the phone in the den rang. "Would you consider," said the
voice on the other end, "a friendly haven for yourself and your famous collection of voices, on the beautiful campus of Michigan State
University?" It was Dr. Richard E. Chapin, the Director of Libraries, calling from East Lansing, Michigan. "Is it cold out
there?" I asked. To which I received a cautious reply: "Well,
rhododendrons, roses, and tulips are planted all around the Library."

The National Voice Library was launched in the spring of
1962. A suite of carrels on the fourth floor of the Main Library
building on the MSU campus were shaped into offices, control room,
and rerecording studio. There was much to be done.

First, there was the work of transferring the sound from

cylinders, discs, and electrical transcriptions onto heavy-duty recording tape.   The equipment at our disposal was modest--most of
it dating back to my recording studio days in Radio City.

Thirty hours per week of student help was assigned to the
National Voice Library.   My own work time ran closer to 80 hours
a week.   The voice library was active the entire day, every evening and weekends.   "At this rate," I calculated, "we ought to catch
up on dubbing the existing collection by the time I'm 96 years old."

But there was more to the job than rerecording and equaliz-
ing.   Even the voices of the Apostles would hardly be of value, if
they couldn't be found.   A comprehensive index file in the form of
a card catalog had to be started at once--and that meant not just
numbering and indicating the name of a speaker and marking the
approximate date.

The gist and subject matter of a speech is most important,
as there might be many talks by the same speaker.   A student or
teacher desiring to hear a certain person discussing a particular
subject covered in an address which includes various topics might
spend hours trying to locate it and even then not succeed, without
an index card showing a synopsis of the contents.

We copied, for example, 320 broadcasts and other speeches
by the late Fiorello H. La Guardia about the problems faced during
the 12 years of his administration as mayor of New York City.   It
was a significant period that included the Big Depression and the
War Years.   It would hardly be practical for a researcher to listen
to all the resulting half-hour tapes in order to locate a short reference to a specific situation.

This problem applied to other speakers and events as well.
Winston Churchill, Franklin Roosevelt, Wendell Willkie, the Army-
McCarthy hearings, the War Crimes Trials, United Nations sessions, Herbert Hoover, Harry Truman, and so many more recordings have to be auditioned by our small staff (which changes constantly, due to graduations), and they have to be summarized and
cataloged.   I wish that a wise computer could do this job--one that
can spell flawlessly.   Book libraries obtain their index cards already printed from the Library of Congress; we have no such help.

Correspondence, too, greatly curtails the day's production. Schools, broadcast networks, documentary motion picture companies, industrial organizations constantly phone or write to request our services. Generally we comply with these on a reciprocal basis. An article in the Education section of Time brought in over 500 letters from all parts of the world; a piece in the Sunday Magazine Section of the New York Times about half as many. All sorts of ideas, suggestions, or commendation are being received daily. All of them have to be answered.

Then there are requests for lectures on and off campus. They sometimes require considerable preparation, to show the scope of the National Voice Library. Invitations for appearances on nationwide television programs have also been received. The NBC "Today" show devoted half an hour to the National Voice Library and Michigan State's WMSB-TV is working with us in the production of a series of documentary programs, consisting of anecdotes with pictures and voices of the past.

Schools and libraries all over the United States are clamoring for the use of National Voice Library tapes, which we are unable to send them at this time because of lack of funds and facilities. On occasion, however, we have released long-playing phonograph record albums of interesting historical events and speakers, and these can be supplied at a nominal cost.

Trips to New York and Washington and Hollywood have resulted in the acquisition of an abundance of valuable documentary sound material of all descriptions. Our "reciprocity" arrangement with CBS, whom we have repeatedly helped with excerpts from early broadcasts or past presidential campaigns, has procured for us greatly desired historical tapes. And the Voice of America sends us dubs of overseas broadcasts covering all important current events that contain the voices of outstanding Americans. Now the United Nations is making a similar agreement.

Knowing that we are authorities on the subject of historic voices of the past, the National Voice Library was selected by the Westinghouse Electric Corporation to produce a documentary recording for the Westinghouse "time capsule" which was buried in the ground at the site of the New York World's Fair in the Fall of 1965, for the next 5000 years.

Progress has been made but a lot more help is needed in order to fully realize the possibilities for service to this generation and to posterity by the National Voice Library. Librarian Chapin's foresight in enabling the voice library to be started at MSU, to furnish a new dimension in learning resources, deserves much praise. He has been most friendly and cooperative and phones frequently to give me the benefit of his advice--generally with the salutation: "Hello, Voice? this is Book..."

* * * * * * * * *

About the Author: A native of Boston, Mass. , G. Robert (Bob) Vincent studied at schools in New York City, and at Yale University. In 1962 he donated the National Voice Library to MSU to be used as a national resource for the collection of priceless historic sound-documents. Mr. Vincent and his wife recently moved their permanent residence from Santa Monica, California to East Lansing.

The author has produced two 12-inch LP recordings of some of the voices from the National Voice Library collection: "Hark! The Years," an anthology of voices and sounds from 1890 to 1933; and "Patience and Fortitude," a selection of talks by the late Fiorello La Guardia, former mayor of New York City.

III. Recording James Joyce

by Sylvia Beach, from Shakespeare and Company.

In 1924, I went to the office of His Master's Voice in Paris to ask them if they would record a reading by James Joyce from Ulysses. I was sent to Piero Coppola, who was in charge of musical records, but His Master's Voice would agree to record the Joyce reading only if it were done at my expense. The record would not have their label on it, nor would it be listed in their catalogue.

Some recording of writers had been done in England and in France as far back as 1913. Guillaume Apollinaire had made some recordings which are preserved in the archives of the Musée de la Parole. But in 1924, as Coppola said, there was no demand for anything but music. I accepted the terms of His Master's Voice: thirty copies of the recording to be paid for on delivery. And that was the long and the short of it.

Joyce himself was anxious to have this record made, but the day I took him in a taxi to the factory in Billancourt, quite a distance from town, he was suffering with his eyes and was very nervous. Luckily, he and Coppola were soon quite at home with each other, bursting into Italian to discuss music. But the recording was an ordeal for Joyce, and the first attempt was a failure. We went back and began again, and I think the Ulysses record is a wonderful performance. I never hear it without being deeply moved.

Joyce had chosen the speech in the Aeolus episode, the only passage that could be lifted out of Ulysses, he said, and the only one that was "declamatory" and therefore suitable for recital. He had made up his mind, he told me, that this would be his only reading from Ulysses.

I have an idea that it was not for declamatory reasons alone

that he chose this passage from Aeolus. I believe that it expressed
something he wanted said and preserved in his own voice. As it
rings out--"he lifted his voice above it boldly"--it is more, one
feels, than mere oratory.

The Ulysses recording was "very bad," according to my
friend C. K. Ogden. The Meaning of Meaning by Mr. Ogden and
I. A. Richards was much in demand at my bookshop. I had Mr. Ogden's little Basic English books, too, and sometimes saw the inventor of this strait jacket for the English language. He was doing
some recording of Bernard Shaw and others at the studio of the
Orthological Society in Cambridge and was interested in experiment-
ing with writers, mainly, I suspect, for language reasons. (Shaw
was on Ogden's side, couldn't see what Joyce was after when there
were already more words in the English language than one knew
what to do with.) Mr. Ogden boasted that he had the two biggest
recording machines in the world at his Cambridge studio and told
me to send Joyce over to him for a real recording. And Joyce
went over to Cambridge for the recording of "Anna Livia Plurabelle. "

So I brought these two together, the man who was liberating
and expanding the English language and the one who was condensing
it to a vocabulary of five hundred words. Their experiments went
in opposite directions, but that didn't prevent them from finding
each other's ideas interesting. Joyce would have starved on five or
six hundred words, but he was quite amused by the Basic English
version of "Anna Livia Plurabelle" that Ogden published in the review Psyche. I thought Ogden's "translation" deprived the work of
all its beauty, but Mr. Ogden and Mr. Richards were the only persons I knew about whose interest in the English language equaled
that of Joyce, and when the Black Sun Press published the little volume Tales Told of Shem and Shaun, I suggested that C. K. Ogden
be asked to do the preface.

How beautiful the "Anna Livia" recording is, and how amusing Joyce's rendering of an Irish washerwoman's brogue! This is
a treasure we owe to C. K. Ogden and Basic English. Joyce, with
his famous memory, must have known "Anna Livia" by heart.

Nevertheless, he faltered at one place and, as in the Ulysses recording, they had to begin again.

Ogden gave me both the first and second versions. Joyce
gave me the immense sheets on which Ogden had had "Anna Livia"
printed in huge type so that the author--his sight was growing dim-
mer--could read it without effort. I wondered where Mr. Ogden
had got hold of such big type, until my friend Maurice Saillet, ex-
amining it, told me that the corresponding pages in the book had
been photographed and much enlarged. The "Anna Livia" recording
was on both sides of the disc; the passage from Ulysses was contained on one. And it was the only recording from Ulysses that
Joyce would consent to.

How I regret that, owing to my ignorance of everything per-
taining to recording, I didn't do something about preserving the
"master." This was the rule with such records, I was told, but for
some reason the precious "master" of the recording from Ulysses
was destroyed. Recording was done in a rather primitive manner
in those days, at least at the Paris branch of His Master's Voice,
and Ogden was right, the Ulysses record was not a success technically. All the same, it is the only recording of Joyce himself
reading from Ulysses, and it is my favorite of the two.

The Ulysses record was not at all a commercial venture. I
handed over most of the thirty copies to Joyce for distribution a-
mong his family and friends, and sold none until, years later, when
I was hard up, I did set and get a stiff price for one or two I had
left.

Discouraged by the experts at the office of the successors to
His Master's Voice in Paris, and those of the BBC in London, I
gave up the attempt to have the record "re-pressed"--which I believe is the term. I gave my permission to the BBC to make a
recording of my record, the last I possessed, for the purpose of
broadcasting it on W. R. Rodger's Joyce program, in which Andri-
enne Monnier and I took part.

Anyone who wishes to hear the Ulysses record can do so at
the Musée de la Parole in Paris, where, thanks to the suggestion of
my California friend Philias Lalanne, Joyce's reading is preserved

among those of some of the great French writers.

IV.   From An Adventure In Sound

by Roland Brockhurst, Linguaphone

Linguaphone was created at the turn of the century when im-
proving means of communication was making the knowledge of languages a necessity in all aspects of life: social, diplomatic and
commercial, as well as cultural.

Mr. Jacques Roston, the founder of the Linguaphone Institute, was himself a considerable linguist and a professional language
teacher.   Early in his career he had been confronted with the problems of bringing the sound of the language to his students, and of
training them to understand the language when it was spoken, and
to speak it correctly.   He realized, too, that, as an integral part
of language, the sound of the language was something which his students needed, and something which would help them to use the language more correctly and appreciate it more fully.

In the course of his thinking, it occurred to him that the
gramophone--then a new invention--could solve this problem for
him.

Once he had this idea, he embarked upon many years of
careful, scientific experiment, and in this work he enlisted the help
of specialists, including the help of Professor Paul Passy, the famous French phonetician.   A plaque in the Linguaphone headquarters
in Regent Street, London, commemorates the important part that
Paul Passy played together with Mr. Roston.

After many years of careful research, the first Linguaphone
Courses were produced.   They were an instant success--because
they were just what people needed.   Teachers sought them eagerly
for use in schools because they gave to these teachers the opportunity of bringing the living language itself to the classroom, and
private students everywhere recognized in these courses something
which would enable them to study a language at home.   The coming
202

of wireless, the ever growing facilities for travel, the ever increasing need for commercial and cultural intercourse made people
want to speak languages, and Mr. Roston's invention made this possible in a new and exciting way.

The fundamental principle behind Linguaphone is a simple
one: you learn a language exactly as you learned as a child--by
hearing it spoken. But, of course, with Linguaphone there are several advantages. In the first place the Courses are designed so
that you learn the most important aspects of the language first, and
secondly, you are able to repeat individual sentences or lessons as
many times as you wish. This constant repetition constitutes the
important ear-training which is so vital to successful language study.

An important aspect of the language courses is that they are
alive and about subjects of every-day interest. The conversations
are in ordinary, every-day idiom, so that the psychological approach to the language is correct as well as the linguistic approach.

Since the creation of Linguaphone, over two million people
studying in their own homes have learned a language by this method. Linguaphone Institutes have been established in thirty-two countries, and Linguaphone Courses have been published in thirty-eight
different languages. Altogether over 15,000 schools, colleges and
universities use the Linguaphone material as audio-visual material
both in the classroom and in the language laboratory.

In addition to the standard material, the Linguaphone Institute has from time to time produced special series of records to
meet special needs. Among these is the series "English Through
the Centuries" spoken by Professor H. C. Wyld, B. Litt. , M. A. ,
Professor of English Language and Literature, Oxford University;
Professor Daniel Jones, M. A. , Dr. Phil. , Professor Emeritus of
Phonetics, University College, London; and Miss Eileen M. Evans,
B. A. , Lecturer in Phonetics, University College, London. These
records provide an authoritative attempt to reproduce, as accurate-
ly as is now possible, the original pronunciation of Anglo-Saxon,
Middle English, Early 17th Century English and Early 18th Century
English. They include extracts from Aelfric's Life of King Ed-
mund, Chaucer's Prologue to "Canterbury Tales," extracts from

Shakespeare, and from Congreve's "Way of the World," and Pope's
"Epistle to Robert Harley."

Another interesting series is a series on English poetry en-
titled "English Landscape Through the Poet's Eyes" spoken by
Stephen Usherwood and David Lloyd James.

There is, of course, an American English Course which is
used throughout the world by individual students and by teachers.
The speakers of this Course are:

W. Cullen Bryant, Ph. D., Director of the American Lan-
    guage Center, Columbia University;
Dwight Cooke, M. A., Correspondent, Columbia Broadcasting
    System;
George W. Hibbitt, Ph. D., Associate Professor of Speech at
    Columbia College, Columbia University;
Paul Merrick Hollister, B. A., former Vice-President of the
    Columbia Broadcasting System;
Allan F. Hubbell, Ph. D., Associate Professor of English,
    New York University;
Roswell Magill, A. B., L1. D., J. D., Professor of Law,
    Columbia University;
James F. Mathias, Ph. D., Associate Secretary, John Simon
    Guggenheim Memorial Foundation;
Inez G. Nelbach, M. A., Instructor in English, Barnard
    College, Columbia University;
James F. Sirmons, B. A., Lecturer in Radio, Speech and
    Announcing, New York University;
Jane Dorsey Zimmerman, Ph. D., Professor of Speech,
    Teachers College, Columbia University.

In addition to its use as described above, Linguaphone has
been used for special purposes. During the war the American
Armed Forces used Linguaphone Courses to teach their own person-
nel European and Far-Eastern languages, and to teach Allied Forces
English. The Linguaphone Institute cooperated in the organization
of this scheme. After the war a vast number of refugees were left
in camps in Europe, and the United Nations, through the medium of
their special agency, The International Refugee Organization, embarked upon a scheme for teaching necessary languages to the refugees. For this purpose they used the Linguaphone Courses and sec-
onded specialists from the Linguaphone Institute to the IRO to ad-
vise on the organization of this scheme and to supervise its successful outcome.

And, of course, business men whose time is short find
Linguaphone especially useful, as they can take it about with them,
and study in times of their own choosing, and for periods which
suit their convenience.

A glance through the names of some of the 200 distinguished
people who have contributed to Linguaphone makes interesting reading. One sees names of distinguished professors and phoneticians,
like those of Professor Daniel Jones, and Dr. David Lloyd James,
and of eminent broadcasters and actors like John Snagge, M. Bas-
sompierce, and Sir John Gielgud. They are all people who speak
their own language well, and who are, therefore, perfect examples
for the student.

Many famous people have used Linguaphone too. Among them
are Prince Bernhard of the Netherlands, who bought a Linguaphone
Spanish Course in Holland in preparation for his business tour of
the West Indies and South America. His trip was, of course, made
in an aircraft carrier, and during the voyage he studied with Linguaphone. Mr. H. G. Wells, many years ago in his book The Salvag-
ing of Civilization, foretold the creation of Linguaphone when he out-
lined the ideal language-teaching method. Later, when he himself
tried Linguaphone, two years after the founding of the Linguaphone
Institute, he said of the Linguaphone records: "They are admirable
...you have made it possible for an attentive student with very mod-
erate expenditure of energy, to understand spoken French, and to
speak it intelligibly. Nothing of the kind has ever been possible before."

Maurice Maeterlinck, Sinclair Lewis, Sir Compton Macken-
zie, among others, have all used Linguaphone.

In the Boardroom at Linguaphone House, there are two things
of great historical interest. One is a photograph of George Bernard
Shaw, who was so impressed with the educational value of Linguaphone that he himself made two records--"Spoken English and Brok-
en English" for the benefit of Linguaphone students. The originals,
autographed by him, are now in the British Museum.

The object of interest is a bronze bust of the founder of the
Linguaphone Institute, Mr. Jacques Roston, by Epstein. When this

was presented to him, university professors, prominent linguists,
service men, business and professional men from all over the country gathered to honor him, and Professor Daniel Jones, the famous
phonetician, said: "Teachers of the spoken language realize the tremendous value of the idea which underlies the work which Mr. Roston has done. They realize the tremendous extent to which that
idea, in its practical application, has facilitated the study of the
spoken language... It may not be generally known that in order to
help us in our work, Mr. Roston has produced records of out of the
way languages, which were not a commercial proposition, but which
have been of considerable academic value... For all that Mr. Roston has done, both in promoting the study of specialized linguistic
subjects, and in the wider field of propagating the study of languages
throughout the world, I wish, on behalf of teachers, to express our
very sincere thanks."

Today, the Linguaphone Institute is watched over by Mr. Stanley Roston who is the nephew of the founder. Mr. Roston is a considerable linguist himself, has learned many languages by Linguaphone and has travelled throughout the world propagating the idea of
learning languages, and assessing needs. New Courses are always
being added to the Linguaphone repertoire, and, of course, earlier
Courses are under constant revision so that they are up-to-date.

Thus Linguaphone meets a new need, but not only does it
meet a new need, it brings a new and important dimension to language study--the sound of the language--because, after all, language
is a means of communication and all language is, in the first instance, speech.

* * * * * * * *

In processing his notes on the history and development of
Linguaphone, Roland Brockhurst observed: "... I have dealt largely
with the main language Courses which we do, because it is in the
field of language teaching that our major contribution has been made.
Indeed, I think it might fairly be said that when Mr. Roston invented the first Linguaphone Course he fathered the audio-visual approach to languages which is now accepted as the correct way of

teaching languages.   The subsequent use of electronic equipment in
the form of language laboratories is a development of the work
which he did, and the fact that existing Linguaphone Courses are
used for ear-training drill in language laboratories shows how right
their conception was. "

These observations are supported by a project, English by
Radio, which was instituted by BBC after World War II for those
studying without a teacher, and which became "English by Television" by 1962.   It has literally reached more than a million listeners.   From English by Radio has come a gramophone course which
uses twenty-one of the most suitable of the radio lessons.   The series is concluded with Readings from English Literature read by
eminent actors and actresses.   These readers are selected for the
clarity of their diction as well as for their dramatic ability, and
the readings are exceptionally well done.

V. Recordings Made for the National Council of Teachers of English

George W. Hibbitt, Columbia College

This project took form in the late '30's. Professor Packard had been making recordings at Harvard under his own initiative. Professor Cabell Greet had begun making recordings of poets between 1926 and 1929. It was in the latter year that George Hibbitt began to assist Professor Greet. There was no intercommunication between Harvard and Columbia on the work done at either place. Both Greet and Hibbitt believed the project at Columbia should be accelerated and should have a recognized sponsorship within the University. Professor Greet turned over the recording of poetry to Mr. Hibbitt because of the pressure of university work. Already Professor Greet, together with Professor Harry Morgan Ayres, had produced a set of recordings on American Dialects which had been published by the Victor Recording Company at Camden, N. J. Professor Greet thought that some organization or business enterprise should further the recordings of the poets reading their own verse. He got in touch with Mr. W. Wilbur Hatfield, the Secretary-Treasurer of the National Council of Teachers of English with headquarters in Chicago and made the arrangements through the National Council to forward the enterprise as part of the work of the Council. Dr. Hatfield then, through Professors Greet and Hibbitt, put the project into production with the group of recordings of Vachel Lindsay reading "The Congo."

Professor Greet had found Lindsay one day at Columbia University. Lindsay had just come from Camden, N. J. where he had tried to get the Victor Company interested in making some recordings of his readings. They had discouraged him from attempting such a project, saying there was no market for such records. Professor Greet persuaded him, through Professor Dorothy Scarborough,

to go to Milbank Hall of Barnard College where he recorded for
Professor Greet most of his readings of his poetry.   These recordings were made on eight-inch aluminum discs with all the imperfections that machines for such recordings possessed in 1928.   Professor Greet then found another poet wandering about the Columbia
campus.   He was none other than AE, the Irish poet.   AE recorded
for him and thus the initial body of speech recordings began at Columbia University.

The National Council of Teachers of English, with a special
committee appointed for the work of recording, took over and worked
through Professor Hibbitt and then Professor Henry Wells at Columbia University.   The first recordings after Lindsay were recordings of Robert Frost and then Gertrude Stein.   Archibald MacLeish
recorded for Professor Hibbitt in Washington, D. C.   W. H. Auden
recorded in New York City.   Professor Harry Morgan Ayres made
a recording of "How to Read Chaucer" and then read part of the
"Prologue" of the Canterbury Tales and part of another tale.   He
also read a passage from Beowulf with some notes on reading Anglo-
Saxon.

September 30, 1964

Author's Notes

Most of the recordings of the now defunct Harvard Vocarium
are out of print.   A few early recordings of the National Council of
Teachers of English continue to be available and the Council still
publishes some recordings.   In 1940, the Recording Laboratory of
the Library of Congress committed itself to the making of permanent
copies of poetry readings by visiting poets.   By 1943, supported by
grants, this had become a systematically planned program under
Archibald MacLeish, Librarian of Congress, and Allen Tate, con-
sultant on poetry in English.

Recordings which were begun in 1940 as 78's are now available on 33 1/3 RPM twelve-inch discs.   With time, considerable
overlapping with later commercial records and the recent Yale Series has taken place.   Although some of the older records have been
supplanted in the process, many of them remain important early
documents and are, of course, valuable for comparative study.

Twenty-eight of these records are available as well as an album of
nine Pulitzer Prize poets reading their own poems and edited by
Oscar Williams.   An album of three 12-inch 33 1/3 rmp records
has been issued by the Archive of Recorded Poetry and Literature,
Library of Congress.   American and British poets represented in
the album are:

Robert Frost	Gene Derwood
Wallace Stevens	George Barker
John Crowe Ransom	Vernon Watkins
Marianne Moore	Roy Fuller
T. S. Eliot	Edgar Lee Masters
Edwin Muir	Louise Bogan
William Carlos Williams	Stanley Kunitz
Robinson Jeffers	Leonie Adams
Edna St. Vincent Millay	Robert Lowell
Robert Graves	Theodore Roethke
Conrad Aiken	Delmore Schwartz
Archibald MacLeish	Jean Garrigue
Henry Reed	Richard Wilbur
Muriel Rukeyser	e. e. cummings
Allen Tate	W. R. Rodgers
Oscar Williams	Edwin Denby
W. H. Auden	Edwin Honig
Theodore Spencer	Howard Nemerov
Richard Eberhart	Ruth Herschberger
Stephen Spender	Joseph Bennett
Ogden Nash	Ted Hughes
Merrill Moore	John Thompson, Jr.
William Empson	W. S. Merwin

The more recent Yale Series of Recorded Poets was prepared
with an accompanying essay by a member of the Yale English Department on the poet's work together with a brief biography, a
printed text of the poems, and a striking portrait of the poet.

Allen Tate	CYP 300	R. P. Blackmur	CYP 311
Robert Lowell	CYP 301	Marianne Moore	CYP 312
Stanley Kunitz	CYP 302	Robert Penn Warren	CYP 313
Dudley Fitts	CYP 303	Richard Eberhart	CYP 314
George Starbuck	CYP 304	Theodore Weiss	CYP 315
Louis Simpson	CYP 305	John Hollander	CYP 316
John Crowe Ransom	CYP 306	Vernon Watkins	CYP 317
Conrad Aiken	CYP 307	Louis MacNeice	CYP 318
Louise Bogan	CYP 308	C. Day Lewis	CYP 319
Yvor Winters	CYP 309	Robert Frost	CYP 320
Lee Anderson	CYP 310	Winfield T. Scott	CYP 321

Today many record companies are undertaking the recording of modern poets.   Among these is the project by Jupiter Recordings of London to record contemporary English poets:

Edith Sitwell	C. Day Lewis
Robert Graves	Elizabeth Jennings
Laurie Lee	Christopher Logue
George Buchanan	John Wain
Ted Hughes	Kingsley Amis
Thomas Blackburn	Lawrence Durrell (Poems
	on Greece)

Authors and selections on The Columbia Literary Series of Recordings are: "The Three Fat Women of Antibes" and "Gigolo and Gigolette" by W. Somerset Maugham; Aldous Huxley reading the Introduction and Linda's Death (from Chapters 14 & 15) from "Brave New World"; John Collier reading "Mary," "De Mortuis," and "Back for Christmas"; "The Snake" and "Johnny Bear" by John Steinbeck; "Flowering Judas" by Katherine Anne Porter; Truman Capote's "Children on Their Birthdays"; and Edna Ferber's "The Gay Old Dog." Also represented is Christopher Isherwood with excerpts from "Prater Violet" and "The Condor and the Cows," plus "A Berlin Diary (Autumn 1930)" from Goodbye to Berlin, and William Saroyan "talking and trying to read from some of his plays, novels and stories" ("Common Prayer," "Rock Wagram," "Don't Go Away Mad," "Jim Dandy," etc.). All three of the Sitwells are found: Sir Osbert Sitwell reading from "Left Hand, Right Hand," Sacheverell Sitwell in Spain and Mauretania, among other places, and Edith Sitwell in excerpts both from "A Poet's Notebook" and "A Notebook on William Shakespeare" and selections from "The Canticle of the Rose" and other poems.

VI.   Folklore and Dialect Records

Helen Roach, Brooklyn College

Some Notes on Folklore Records

The collecting of folklife material by folklore commissions,
University research workers, and serious amateurs goes on in
many parts of the world.   The Folklore Institute at Indiana University is the most extensively developed work of this kind.   The primary need is to collect authentic pictures of life and traditions
which are fast fading out before these are lost with the older generation.

In the words of the holder of the first lectureship in Folklife
Studies in any British University, Stewart F. Sanderson at Leeds,
".. . subsequent generations may need to know and to draw fresh inspiration from the values of an older world than ours perhaps even
more than our own generation need to now. "

Much of the material being collected will take years to edit
and be made available to the public.   A few specimens especially
in the domain of folktales have been processed onto records; Jack
Tales Told by Mrs. Maud Long of Hot Springs, N. C. , edited by
Duncan Emrich and processed by the Library of Congress, is one
of these.

In her introduction, side 1, L47, Maud Long speaks of growing up on the Jack Tales as she did on the Great Smokey Mountain
air.   Of a long winter's evening as the girls pulled out burrs,
Spanish needles, bits of briars and dirt from a lap full of wool for
the next day's carding, their mother would tell the tales "to keep
their eyes open and their fingers busy. "

With vivid memory she recalls the original expressions in
the stories about how "The King put out an oration" to really "get
yourself killed, " and of the silver knife that the little old man with

the long grey beard had given Jack for "bedad it will come in handy. " The "regular Witch Gang workin" in the community had also to be discovered and routed with sparse, spontaneous mountain language.

The output of recordings by the Music Division of the Library of Congress (Washington, D. C. 20025), from which come the five aforementioned records of folktales, has over fifty other records of folk music from many different folk groups and parts of the U. S. A. One group of five records, The Ballad Hunter by John A. Lomax, Lectures in American Folk Music with Musical Illustrations, L49-53 covers Indian, Blues and Hollers, Cowboy songs, Woodcutter's songs and Prison Life songs, etc. L51 Part VI, Boll Weevil: songs about the little bug that challenged King Cotton, is packed with an economic peril of national importance.

The Folksongs of Britain, collected and edited by Peter Kennedy and Alan Lomax, has been processed by Caedmon, (5-12") TC 1142-46 under the following headings: Songs of Courtship, Songs of Seduction, Jack of all Trades and The Childe Ballads 1 and 2.

African Stories Told by Hugh Tracey, Music of Africa, Series No. 9. Decca, (1-10") LF 1174, has stories translated into English, keeping as closely as possible to the original Kamanga idiom. The five stories come from the Fort Victoria district of Southern Rhodesia: "The Bird of the Valley," "Mapandangara, the Great Baboon," "The Snake Who Bit a Girl," "The Lion on the Path," and "Tsimbarumbi, the Hardened Bachelor. "

A group of three records in 1960 came from the archives of the School of Scottish Studies of the University of Edinburgh. Produced in a limited edition, the records are now out of print but available for listening, in this case, at the Vaughan Williams Memorial Library in Cecil Sharpe House, London. Gaelic and Scots Folk Tales, A001/2, is the one spoken record of the group. On side one are told four Scottish Gaelic Tales. Side Two, understandable to non-scholars, contains Scots Folk Tales. Jeanine Robertson tells "Silly Jack and the Factor," Andrea Steward "Johnnie in the Cradle," and Bruce Henderson, "The Fairy Well of Shetland. " The second of these includes the approving grunts of the listeners.

There is an accompanying booklet with notes, text and translation.
The Irish Folklore Commission, established in 1924, has
long been engaged in collecting authentic existing folklife material,
with the Professor of Irish Folklore in University College, Dublin,
as Honorary Director. A group of six records in Irish was processed for the Educational and Poetry Series, available through Gael-
Linn, 54, Grafton Street, Dublin 2, Ireland. EEF007 in this series
is by a renowned story teller, telling the story of Cuchulain and the
loneliness of the son of the King of Greece. A textbook issued with
this record enables non-fluent speakers of Irish to follow the stories.

Now Is the Time for Fishing, songs and speech of Sam Lar-
ner of Winterton, England, compiled and edited by Peggy Seeger
and Evan MacColl, contains sea lore and rhymes about "The
Drowned Lover" and "The Dolphin," "Sea or Jail" and "Service or
Jail" with laughter and gay insistence: "now that's the truth... my
father used to tell me those old yarns." The Ritchie Family of
Kentucky (Folkways, 1-12", FA 2316), on which Jean Ritchie interviews her family, is another Folkways release. Here a Kentucky
mountain family talks and sings of its heritage, with Jean Ritchie
as the narrator.

The McPeake Family (Topic Records, 1-12", 12T87), recorded by Bill Leader in 1962, has an introduction and words about
Irish songs: "A Bucket of Mountain Dew," "Eileen Aroon," "My
Singing Bird," etc. Francis McPeake, Senior, sometimes puts in
a word: "The Lament of Anghorion" as he "played it for Roger
Casement," and "Ireland Boys, Hurrah" as he had it from his father.

A recording of William Kimber, player of the "Anglo" con-
certina made by Peter Kennedy, November 14, 1956, was published
in 1963 by the English Folk Dance and Song Society. It is mainly
concerned with the revival of Morris dances. Kimber takes on the
roles of musician, singer, and talker with a knack for putting ideas
into a nutshell. His account of the May Horn is of folklore interest as are also some of the local customs briefly discussed, e. g. ,
The Mummers Play. Of value to the distributors of the record

(Cecil Sharpe House, London) is William Kimber's reminiscence of his meeting with Mr. Cecil Sharp in 1899.

Dialect Records

Dialect surveys by teams of scholars have long used machines to record the local speech of people as they found it. All face the basic problem of getting on record a story or conversation in its own way of speech without unnaturalness caused by the disturbing presence of an outsider with a phonographic machine. The earliest and most extensive of these surveys was the Linguistic Atlas of the United States initiated by members of the Modern Language Association of America and the Linguistic Society of America and formally proposed at the MLA Meeting in December, 1928. In the preface to Volume I, No. 1 of the Atlas, Professor Hans Kurath, director of the Linguistic Atlas noted: "The field work for the Linguistic Atlas of New England was done between September 1, 1931 and October 1, 1933. Nine investigators went into the field the first year, four of them remained for a second year... the real editorial work was begun in the Fall of 1932 at Brown University while the field work was still in progress."

For many years recordings of the rat story used in this research as spoken in various parts of the United States have been available in the United States through Linguaphone. About half a dozen of these recordings are still in print.

After World War II, The Survey of English Atlas was begun in the British Isles under the supervision of Professor Harold Orton. At the present time, one copy of the numerous recordings from this research is preserved at the University of Leeds where it is based and another at the University of London. Copies are not commercially available.

In 1931 a resolution was proposed by Miss Elsie Fogerty and accepted by the Annual Conference of the British Drama League: "That it is desirable to undertake a regional survey of dialect throughout the British Isles."

Twelve records with twenty-four dialect variants were completed, issued early in 1936, and made available through Lingua-

phone.   An accompanying booklet in phonetic script transcribed by
Clifford Turner was published in 1937.   The series with American
additions was reissued in September 1964.   In most instances the
recordings are by actors with a knowledge of the dialect of the section represented.

One difficulty with this 1964 reissue is the very small thin
discs which can be used only on a machine with an extremely light-
weight arm.   They are available through the British Drama League,
9 Fitzroy Square, London, W. 1.

"It is no easy matter to describe a quality of sound by means
of written words" wrote Daniel Jones, the English phonetician, when
Jones, H. C. Wyld, and Eileen M. Evans entered into the early recording projects of Linguaphone records: English Pronunciation
through the Centuries.   The selected extracts come from Anglo-
Saxon, Middle English and later English of the early seventeenth and
eighteenth centuries.   "No man now living can possibly claim to
know beyond controversy how Chaucer and the Englishmen of his day
pronounced but we can form a conception perhaps not so far from
the truth of what the actual sounds were."

Readings from Anglo-Saxon Poetry by the Harvard scholar,
Francis P. Magoun, Jr. and Gretchen Paulus, issued in 1959 by
Harvard Vocarium, is read according to the early West-Saxon type
of pronunciation.   Of recordings by scholars, it is one of the most
attractive because it is so courageously narrated with a textural
quality fitting the rugged existence of the times.

VII. "Words, Words, Words."

H. P. Court, Rococo Records

About a couple of years ago, I happened to be in England
and caught a television show on the B. B. C. devoted to the life of
Bransby Williams. The high spot of the show, for me, was a
scene he did from that classic of the Victorian Theatre, "The
Bells." It was a fine performance; it recalled the high tragic
school of the great Actor-Managers--Beerbohm Tree, Arthur Bourchier and, of course, Irving--for "The Bells" was one of Irving's
great parts. It was a great performance in another way too, as
Williams was over 80 at the time. Not that age interfered with his
performance; that was only evident when he had finished--the nervous excitement generated by his acting completely obscured any
thought of age.

Bransby Williams was born in London on the 14th of August,
1870. He first recorded for H. M. V. in 1908 and his last record
was made in 1951 for Decca: forty-three years of record making,
from prewar acoustics to the high fidelity era of Long Plays. There
can be very few artists, even counting instrumentalists, who have
worn so well.

He started his career in the usual Stock and Touring companies of the period, in 1895, and graduated to London a year later.
He soon realized, however, that his métier was as a solor artist
and he went on to the variety stage, as a mimic of the actors of
the time. From this he developed his "act" into that field through
which he became famous--character studies from Dickens (his first
and last records are both in that category).

Later on in his career he became an actor-manager and
played in London and on tour all over the world such plays as "The
Lyons Mail," "David Copperfield," "Oliver Twist," and even

217

"Hamlet." As late as 1946 he starred in "The Shop at Sly Corner" in the London production.

All of Bransby Williams records bring a reminder of a past era of great acting, a style of acting which is completely different from our modern school. It cannot be dismissed as "ham" for his interpretations are so big and vital that they insure your attention by the vividness of the character and the emotion. Most important of his records is, perhaps, Columbia 408, "Henry Irving in the dream scene from 'The Bells.'" Williams was a wonderful mimic and, in the lack of a real Irving record, this must serve as well. This scene of the Innkeeper describing the murder of the Jew and his subsequent terror and remorse was one of Irving's great moments and, bad though the writing is, one can see why. This record, through all the melodramatic background, builds up a tremendous emotional impact and forces, for the moment, a willing suspension of disbelief. This is a high-spot of nineteenth century drama captured for us.

My favorite of the Dickens characters is the Wilkins Micawber advice to David Copperfield. All the plump earnestness of Micawber is here, and the famous lines, "Annual income ten pounds, annual expenditure nine pounds, nineteen shillings and sixpence. Result--happiness. Annual income, ten pounds. Annual expenditure ten pounts, ought, sixpence. Result--misery, etc.," are handled with wonderful comic spirit. More fine examples are the scenes from "The Christmas Carol," which are an object lesson in how this wonderful story should be handled. In fact, practically all of his Dickens is well worthwhile.

Another fine record is "The Showman," which must have been derived from a comedy routine he did on the "Hall," and is the "pitch" given by a showman to draw the crowd into the theater. Naturally it is very broad humor but very cleverly handled. More or less in the same tradition of the variety act is "The Stage Doorkeeper" who welcomes the actors into the theater. Perhaps this one is more interesting as it introduces very fine imitations of some of the stars of the Edwardian Theatre--George Alexander, Johnston Forbes Robertson, Chirgwin, etc.

For a wonderful piece of Victoriana I can recommend "The
Green Eye of the Yellow God" (Columbia 388). Even Williams cannot save this ballad from being funny; in fact, I have heard comedians trying to get laughs from this piece who have not been half as
successful as the original serious effort. Nevertheless, to anyone
interested in obtaining an authentic glimpse into the feel of another
age, I suggest that Bransby Williams' records will help.

The Records

H. M. V.

01011	Micawber and Uriah Heep - David Copperfield	C501
01012	Bob Cratchit telling of Scrooge - Christmas Carol	
01014	Sidney Carton's farewell - Tale of Two Cities	C500
01017	The old man's pipe	C501
01021	Devil-May-Care - Taylor	C501
01029	Scrooge - before the dream - Christmas Carol	C499
01030	Scrooge - the dream	C500
01031	Scrooge - the awakening	

Columbia - 12"

347	Scrooge - before the dream - Christmas Carol
	Scrooge - the dream
348	Scrooge - the awakening
	Micawber's advice to David Copperfield
350	The showman - Williams (two sides)
388	The green eye of the yellow god - Hayes
	The caretaker - Winter
400	Bill Sikes from Oliver Twist
	Tony Weller from Pickwick Papers
408	Henry Iving in the dream scene from "The Bells"
	The portrait - Lytton
594	The stage doorkeeper (two sides). Imitations of
	G. Alexander, G. P. Huntley, Forbes-Robertson,
	Chirgwin, etc.
9229	The Showman (two sides)
DX554	A Charles Dickens Christmas. With company
DX642	An old bachelor - Chevalier
	A fallen star - Chevalier

Columbia - 10"

2264	Death of Little Nell - Old Curiosity Shop
	Sidney Carton's farewell - Tale of Two Cities
2291	The murder in the forest - Williams
	The plumber - Wynne
2498	Spotty - Hennequin
	The coward - Hennequin
2560	Devil-may-care - Taylor
	Death of Uncle Tom - Uncle Tom's Cabin

Columbia - 10" (continued)
2636   The old country - The Village
          The old country - London
2645   The hero, the heroine and the villain - Newman
          The murder in the forest - Williams
2667   The Yukon - Hayes
          The Lounger - Winter
2680   Doctor Yank of Quackem
          Grandfather Smallweed - Bleak House
3062   The three bears
          Jack and the beanstalk
3063   The three little pigs
          Dick Whittington and his cat
3177   The sleeping princess
          Puss in boots
3774   The difference - Kelly
          Not old - Day
4013   The charge of the Light Brigade - Tennyson
          Henry V's speech before Harfleur
4836   Death of Little Nell - Old Curiosity Shop
          Sidney Carton's farewell - Tale of Two Cities

Decca
F9277   Wilkins Micawber - David Copperfield
          Dan'l Peggoty - David Copperfield
AK1963   A Christmas Carol, pt. 1
          Captain Cuttle - Dombey and Son
AK1964   A Christmas Carol, pt. 2
          A Christmas Carol, pt. 3
LF1033   Characters from Dickens. David Copperfield,
             Micawber, Dan'l Peggoty, Tony Weller, Scrooge

Pathé, Hill and Dale
5350   The Penny Showman. Both sides.
          There are probably more on this label. H. P. Court.

The following additions to the Bransby Williams list come
from Leonard Petts, English discographer.

2 min. wax cylinders - Edison Standard Gold Moulded Records
13508   Wilkins Micawber's advice to David Copperfield
13488   The Cynic - Recitation
13340   'is Pipe - Recitation
13348   Murder Scene - The Bells
13353   The awakening of Scrooge

Edison Amberol 4 min. wax cylinders
12452   Charge of the Light Brigade
12484   The green eye of the little yellow god.

British Blue Amberol wax cylinders
23031   Burial of Sir John Moore

Sterno Records (1934)
1394   The town crier (2 parts) - April 1934.

VIII.   On the Use of Shakespeare Recordings

A Letter From Elizabeth White, College Junior

About a year ago I found myself with sixteen Shakespeare
comedies and histories to read within a week.   I had had discourag-
ing difficulty trying to read through the plays for the first time, not
that the words were so hard, but mainly that the great dramatic
Shakespeare was actually boring.   I'm a fairly slow reader, especially since there were interesting footnotes to get bogged down in.
It took about 4 1/2 hours to read through an unfamiliar play for the
first time, a rate slower than speaking time and too slow to keep
interest and feeling of moving forward in a plot.   The less dramatic it seemed, the slower and more meticulously I'd read, getting
more and more bored and rushed.

Finally I realized that hearing the play would be faster than
reading.   (The Shakespeare plays take 6 or 8 record sides, 3 hours
or less.)   I took my text and a pencil for hasty underlinings and
sat down with an album and a phonograph.   The result was wonderful.   Even when the acting sounded phony, put on, the play seemed
more "dramatic. "   The actors knew the footnotes, read the line
with more or less natural intonations.   Temperamental scenes (like
Richard II, Act I, Scene 1, which clinks continually with gauntlets
hurled down) were quicker than slow poetic scenes (e. g. , Richard
alone, introspecting).   In visual reading they'd all proceed at the
same slow beat.   Men sounded different from women, Mercutio different from Romeo.   In visual absorption they tended to merge into
the same regularity of typed paragraphs with numbers after every
5 lines.   Elizabethan grammar and vocabulary became real speech.
The Marlowe Society (London Records) recording of As You Like It
reproduces the quickness of repartee between Rosalind and Orlando
in the lover's instruction scene.   (The Rosalind showed an aware-

ness of the shifts in tone between sprightly youth and lapses into
love-smitten maid, though she tended to sound artifically coy.)

Contrast between scenes was also much sharper aurally, as
in Measure for Measure where the low comedy of the stews and
Cockney-accented speeches alternates with the "lofty" affairs of the
Viennese state. Especially wonderful was the night scene at Bel-
mont (Merchant of Venice, Act V, "The moon shines bright; in such
a night as this...''), with the quiet of the poetic love dialogue briefly interrupted by the arrival of a messenger, and Launcelot Gobbo,
and then the call to the musicians, and then the actual music. (On
both the Marlowe Society and Caedmon records the music continues
lightly in the background, furring the verbal music of Jessica and
Lorenzo's dialogue. The Marlowe Society record came closest to
the quietness of the night, though the actors sounded a little too un-
real in speech. The voices rise too sharply at the end of a sentence, making the men slightly foppish and the women overly pert.)
The Caedmon recording, though not so delicate in volume, was
thankfully not so coy. Jessica especially kept the magic; Lorenzo
was a little too heavy. Music on many different recordings added
a great element to Shakespearean comedies. The Marlowe Society
As You Like It enhanced the pastoral scenes with very well done
songs ("Under the greenwood tree," "Blow, blow..."). The most
delightful record of all was A Midsummer Night's Dream (Old Vic,
1954, Moira Shearer, Robert Helpmann, Stanley Holloway, Philip
Guard), with the uncut Mendelssohn score providing interludes in the
uncut Shakespeare script. (My favorite place: where the scherzo
flits around as Oberon orders Puck off to get the love flower, Act
II, Scene 1.)

Another recording full of extra sound effects is the Polymu-
sic recording of the Tempest (Prospero--Raymond Massey; Ariel--
Lee Grant). It opens in full sound effects with "tempestuous noise
of thunder and lightning," plus wind and creaking yards which continue through the scene. After Prospero has made the thunder stop
aurally, Ariel enters to tinkly, not-too-obtrusive modern music.
This is one of the few recordings which is easy to appreciate without simultaneously reading the text of the play. (A narrator intro-

duces each scene, gives stage directions.) The other recordings, especially the Marlowe Society ones, where I got used to the cast's voices beyond their varying roles, were difficult to follow. For example, the end of <u>Coriolanus</u> is aurally very exciting, with its military drums and enraged "conspirators." ("Kill, kill, kill, kill, kill him!") However, without the book before me I got confused as to who was speaking--Aufidius, or Coriolanus or someone else.

When I got a chance to use the records for rereading, I could use the actors' character interpretations as a backboard against which to bounce my own (and the lecturer's) ideas. The next semester (mostly tragedies) I was less dependent on the records to read the plays for the first time. Still, it was interesting to hear <u>Othello</u> and compare the stern, modulated Robeson recording with the more hysterical Marlowe Society <u>Othello</u>, especially in the bedroom murder scene we'd written papers on. The records were helpful for renewing plays I'd read in high school, too.

Plays I'd listened to on records turned out to be easier to remember later. On exams or thinking by myself I'd recall people speaking as well as the blocks of type. The aural approach was especially helpful for the course I was taking, one in which Professor Brower's lectures and the written exercises emphasized language (sound as well as imagery).

* * * * * * * *

I am interested in finding some way to get students to read poetry aloud when they are alone for the sheer enjoyment of it... I wonder if there is some way to return to old-fashioned recitation methods without being elocutionary... with all the close analysis and intellectualizing, it's easy to lose the primary impact of language, sounds to listen to and to speak.

IX. Introduction to The Oral Study of Literature

Algernon Tassin, Columbia College

I. The Need of Teaching College Students to Read

In a more or less tolerable and tolerated way the study of
elocution has taken its place in the college curriculum, its Cinderella existence there being due to a vague popular demand, to a
somewhat lethargic academic recognition that without it the study of
the English language is not faring so well as the study of foreign
languages, and to an uneasy consciousness, unlocalized but vivid,
that something in the educational scheme is vitally wrong and possibly it may be that students have not sufficient command of English
to use it in their other studies. It has rather generally been supposed that the extended practice of writing would remedy the defect.
When it was found that it had not--that in spite of much theme work
students still remained unable to make use of the English language
as a tool to carve out other knowledge--Oral English was admitted
as a sister Cinderella. Students were given extended practice in
discussion and in public speaking. But in spite of the utility of
both written and oral composition, the trouble still persists.

What is wrong? Something is needed, it would seem, more
basic than either. Had the college faculties listened to the voice of
common sense, to the testimony of their occasional but invariable
experience, and to the testimony of the continuous special experience of the elocution teacher, they would have found out the trouble
long since. What is wrong is that students do not know how to
read. They do not get the meaning of the printed page. What is
needed is systematic laboratory work in the science of reading; in
short, supervised work in translating English.

For a college to teach students to write and not to read

would seem, on the face of it, an illogical discrimination. It is more rational to assume they can do both or neither. In actual practice, too, they do the latter a hundred times more than they do the former. Considerations of both common sense and utility, then, demand that education in English put more emphasis on the printed word and less upon the written.

These two aspects of the matter are so obvious, however, that if they possessed any power to convince they would have done so long ago. What is necessary, apparently, is to prove to colleges and to teachers that students read even worse than they write. Most teachers will agree that the average student arrives at college under-equipped in English. But though there is a widespread recognition that he is unable to make use of spoken and written English as an instrument for his own expression, it does not seem to have much urge about it in face of the many other things he should be learning at college. But this recognition, however uncompelling, is a grave understatement of the lesser part of the defect. The truth, as an elocution teacher sees it, is sensational. The average student cannot make use of English written or spoken as an instrument of anybody else's expression. He cannot read or even listen understandingly. If every college instructor could be made to see this, he would perceive the futility of prescribing reading to eyes that see not and of lecturing to ears that hear not. Every elocution teacher knows that students are unable to read, merely because he has an exact opportunity of finding it out. The teacher of anything else may discover it by asking his students to read aloud a page which develops thought they imagine they have mastered.

The Student Receives from the Page
Only Emotional Impressions

The ability of the average student to grasp anything beyond simple narrative of events cannot be counted on; it grows less in exact ratio as event and emotional association grow infrequent; it usually disappears entirely with the disappearance of these two. That is to say, he has received with definiteness only emotional impressions. Even if these should happen to convey the outlines of the thought, he has kept no relation and no proportion. In place of an articulated skeleton, he has only a heap of bones.

Oral reading every elocution teacher has found to be an exact test of previous apprehension. As the page presents emotional associations less familiar or more separated one from the other, the impressions made by it become more and more bodiless. As the inter-relationship of the thought becomes more intimate, the impressions produced become more misleading because necessarily more separated by their infrequency. If the text taxes the reader with the necessity of balancing and comparing ideas, keeping several in hand at once, he gets practically nothing at all. That is to say, just in proportion as connectives increase his apprehension diminishes. An expressed double antithesis, even when it presents emotional association, often floors an entire class. An antithesis which leaves one of its members to implication is likely to be undetectable by the average student on his first reading. Implication is, indeed, one of the last things to be grasped. The difficulty of making a class perceive that even the simplest speech implies as much as it asserts might well discourage any deliberate employment of subtleties on the part of the writer. The recognition that each sentence, as well as occupying its own position in space, has a backward and a forward glance, is a nicety undreamed of by the average student. Such are the disclosures of a class in elocution.

Emotional Skimming a Habit of Both Eye and Ear

This blithe art of emotional skimming--ladling off what appears to be the cream of the page--is certainly somewhat perfected by reading overyoung such writers as Shakespeare and Scott. Boys and girls on the lookout for emotional content only, especially when the intellectual content is outside of both their interest and their grasp, come naturally to feel from such writers that there is a vast deal on the printed page which is of no consequence to the main thought, and that it must be expected of the queer race of writers that they will pad out needlessly what they have to say. An exact counterpart of what a student receives from the printed page is furnished by his lecture note-book. Have you ever run through that

most depressing reading in the world? It is a box containing the
least important parts of a picture puzzle. Each part invariably
telescopes the illustration--the emotional association--with the idea
illustrated--the intellectual statement. Only the most highly colored
parts remain; and all the perspective, without which it is impossible
to reconstruct the picture, is gone. There is an emotional residue
of some striking nouns, adjectives, and verbs, but the background
has fallen out. In listening to a lecture, in writing notes into his
note-book, and in reading to himself the printed page, what the average student has failed to appreciate are the connectives. Like Alfred Jingle's his nature is too brisk, and like Gertrude Stein's it is
too soulful, to lose any time over such sluggish stuff. Not having
learned how ideas are built together into a structure, he has no
sense of the architecture of speech when he listens or reads. How
the chief words are welded into sentences by the little ones, and the
sentences are molded into a progressive development of thought by
means of connectives, is beyond him. By eye or ear, he gets isolated ideas substantive after substantive, as the early engravers
used to draw trees leaf by leaf; and like them he succeeds in getting
an entirely wrong impression both of the part and of the whole.

What he fails to perceive are the constructive relationships.
He generally appreciates the significance of "and" or "but"; he may
even see much virtue in "if"; beyond the coarsest of the conjunc-
tions, however, he seldom goes. The entire range of finer and less
formal affiliations might as well not be employed at all--or worse
still, they merely fumble the meaning of the major assertions already apprehended. When he listens, he cannot help hearing the
significance of even the subtlest of connectives in the lecturer's
voice; but unfortunately, since he understands their value instinctively, he does not feel the necessity of reproducing them--what is
so immediately apprehendable in the context seems to him to exist
in the assertions themselves. Consequently here, too, all relationship drops out. Thus the impression he receives when he crams
up on his notes for examination is as crudely inaccurate as that
which he gets from his other reading. In the one case he disre-
gards the connectives on the page; in the other there are none to

disregard.

The Voice the Best Medium for Teaching and Securing
the Relationship of Ideas

Now, all the connectives of written speech are expressed instinctively in the voice, and with subtleties and countless minor
variations and qualifications and dependencies which even the nicest
writer is incapable of indicating formally. These shades of relationship, however evasive to the reader, are immediately intelligible
to every hearer--merely because inflection is a natural language
which everybody possesses quite independently of his acquired vocabulary. So natural a language is it, indeed, that a hearer who
fails to comprehend any of your assertions perceives nevertheless
and at once the relationship which they bear to one another and your
intention in making them. If I am right, then, in thinking that the
failure of the student to apprehend his reading is caused by his failure to appreciate connectives, it should not be difficult to see that
the voice is the best medium by which to teach the significance of
the relationship of expressed ideas, precisely in the same way that
it is the best index of ideas ungrasped. It should not be difficult
to see that the best way to deal with the unapprehending student is
not to make him write but to make him read aloud, to give him
practice in consciously translating the connectives of written speech
into the inflections of spoken speech.

Reading aloud in an elocution class, then, discloses the habitual failure to have acquired the meaning on the first and silent
reading. It is an exact test of apprehension, and the only one that
does not involve the danger of ascribing to the understanding what
may after all arise only from the memory. It is the only exercise
which will correct the universal habit of assuming that because one
recognizes words one understands meanings.

Oral Reading an Exact Test of Apprehension

When you tell a student that the reason he cannot make you
understand what he reads is not your perversity but his ignorance,
he is indignant. He says that it is only because he cannot twist his

voice to it, and that this is what he is there to learn. You reply
that he is there to learn to be effective and that you cannot tell
whether he is or not until you understand what he is trying to say;
that you have no difficulty in understanding him when he is, as at
present, talking out of his own mind; if, then, you have such difficulty when he is using the words of another, it is merely because
the thoughts those words stand for have not as yet entered his own
mind. Still he insists, with a defiant determination not to look at
the worst in the face, that there are two ways of talking, his own
and the author's; and it is merely because he is unused to the language. Nor is he convinced until he is asked to put the author's
thought into his own words that hitherto he has really failed to grasp
it; nor even then will he own that the very moment he did so, he
was enabled to read this strange language aloud with perfect intelligibility. All this squirming is simply due to the fact that the student is unwilling to admit the drift of his present failure and its
enormity--that he is not in the habit of getting the thought of what
he reads, that his eye merely runs over lines of words and recognizes them separately, but that his mind fails to take them in as a
group. Well may he be unwilling to admit so radical a disability!--
less skipping and irresponsible spirits than his are apparently unwilling to admit it of him. He is only assuming what most colleges
at present assume, namely, that he knows how to read.

It must be owned that if I had not been there to nag him into it, he would have been entirely satisfied with his first reading.
Indeed, he does not at all doubt his ability now. The case was not
representative; the sentence was queer; the fault was in the unaccustomed language, not in himself. He still goes on believing that
he is reading books and has earned the right to judge them, when in
reality he has read only some of the more striking words and assertions, and these for the most part only in isolation.

But he is not the only one who claims that oral reading is an
inexact test of apprehension. Mouths more plausible, though perhaps actuated by a similar uneasiness, have said so. The trouble,
explain they, is merely a matter of translating an apprehended
thought into vocal expression of another person's words. But since

the thought came from these words in the first place, this does not seem reasonable. Or they say that the mind in reading a sentence by the eye alone suspends its decision as to the relationship of phrase with phrase until the sentence is completed, while the voice, having of necessity fixed what should remain fluid until the period, naturally makes some faulty inflections. But this specious contention is valid, of course, only with reading aloud at sight. Others say it is a matter of what might be called vocal self-consciousness through inexperience. For one reason or another they seek to explain how it is that goods which have just that instant been purchased by the mind are generally lost in delivery. The truth is simple and unescapable--whatever the mind understands it can, granted the words, make understandable.

There is one objection which appears for a moment more satisfactory. Some of the failure to express the thought may, it is true, proceed from the failure to bear in mind that speech is not subjective but objective in its intention. Since thought precedes speech, it, as it were, grows stale in the very instant of its acquisition; and, in the subsequent expression, the instinctive devices of the voice--inflection and emphasis--fail to manifest themselves correctly, merely because the ideas are not, at the precise instant of speaking, grouping themselves together for the first time. The mind of the reader, they say, having perceived the thought once and not being concerned as it should be with the objectivity of the oral act, is no longer exerting itself on the thought as new material and hence allows the voice to present it mechanically and thus, of course, wrongly. It is true that any language allowed to take care of itself generally acquires in utterance an inflection which betrays the fact by its greater or less unintelligibility. But while this distinction exists in public speakers and is real enough, it makes little difference in readers. Generally, false inflection and false emphasis indicate, not a mind which has temporarily absented itself, but one which was never present at all--uttering words which it recognizes but the significance of whose connection has not been grasped. A proof of this constantly occurs in an elocution class. If you tell a student there is only one part of his good reading which you fail

to comprehend, he will either admit or demonstrate by paraphrase
that this is the part he failed to comprehend himself.   There is
nothing capricious in the relation of the voice to the sane and presiding mind.   What the mind understands the voice, granted the
words, can communicate.   The voice may in a dozen ways deprive
the thing of interest and effect, but it cannot, except by deliberate
intention, deprive it of intelligibility, provided the thing is at the
moment of reading aloud being apprehended.

Neither Oral Nor Written Composition
Sufficient to Correct the Fault

Since, then, an inaccurate reading aloud means an inaccurate
silent one, it is apparent that Oral English, when it takes the form
of discussion on assigned reading, is not sufficient to correct the
fault.   It can do nothing more than demonstrate the fact.   Valuable
as returning the thought is, one must first have got it in order to
return it.   Even if the major thought has been acquired, returning
it is of course no equivalent for the exact rendering of the entire
passage aloud.   For, naturally, much must drop out on the smaller
scale.   And if I am right in saying that the failure to detect relationships is at the root of misapprehension, it is obvious that the
diminished return cannot disclose the bulk of the possible weakness
in what has of necessity been omitted.   As every student knows and
counts upon, an examination can hit only the high spots, and it takes
little astuteness to discover the low ones.

Nor is work in written composition sufficient.   An accurate
writer does not imply an accurate reader.   Naturally, any one will
take more trouble with his own work than with other people's.   But
aside from this human fact, many a student who can write well,
even to the exhibition of good structure as well as good diction, is
able to apprehend the printed page only esthetically.   He has merely that sublimated kind of emotional perception, the artistic.   That
this can be entirely divorced from the intellectual, both in perception and in expression, is crystallized in the familiar remark--
"beautiful, but what does it mean?"   Sometimes, it is true, students who write best may read best, but there is no necessary con-

nection between the two.

Even Good Writers Often Possess
Only Esthetic Perception

One of the best writers I ever had, whose writing was full
of the nicest discriminations, was unable to read a page so that it
could be understood. This was not because of a self-defeating vocal
monotony or of a lack of objectivity in reading, but because he
failed to apprehend the connection of the ideas as they came along,
and demonstrated it in his false inflections. The excellence of his
writing must be set down to a peculiar interest in expressing himself; but when it came to expressing another, he showed as skipping
and irresponsible a spirit as many who lacked his excellence in
writing. Diction, phrasing, rhythm were the things that contented
him in reading, since he perceived them emotionally; the exact intellectual content escaped him. Students who write well (unless, indeed, their excellence is obtained only by much use of knife and
file--two tools not to be found in the average kit) will, like this
man, always give a good account of themselves in oral composition
but not necessarily in reading. If we could teach all students to
write well, it appears that after a little exercise in the new medium they would show that they had been learning to speak well at the
same time; but we could not be sure that they were reading properly. Oral reading for the good writer as well as the poor one is
the needful test of apprehension.

The college, however, cannot teach all students to write
well. It can, for the most part, secure only a certain amount of
technical correctness. After this has been reached, further work
in writing for the most of them takes time that could be spent less
laboriously to both student and instructor and to better advantage.
Writing unfortunately will not enlarge a student's vocabulary or make
him think (except in the meager terms of writing not incorrectly),
unless he is the sort that would do both of these things anyway.
Accurate reading aloud will do both. At present and under the inevitable conditions of class work, only the best writers acquire that
necessary sense of proportion which written composition is capable

--though laboriously, it is true--of conveying. In oral reading, even the poorest student cannot escape it. Let us secure grammatical and intelligible writing by all means, but examine whether it is practical to try to go further.

Theme Work Unduly Specializes

The purpose of a college is to acquaint the student with the achievements of history, and to teach him how to observe and think. Obviously, theme work does nothing toward accomplishing the first purpose unless the student writes upon assigned reading. Even if he knows how to read correctly, his reactions upon his reading are either comparatively thin or are made so by the limitations of his ability or inclination to express himself. Obviously, too, when his themes are confined to discussions of what he reads, he does nothing toward accomplishing the second purpose of the college--teaching him how to observe and evaluate what goes on around him. But even when he has freer and more personal range, neither habits of observation nor habits of thinking are likely to be improved by theme work unless he has already the temperament demanding self-expression. And what he says is again so restricted by his concentration on the means of saying it and by the limits which time sets to his labor, that neither is exercised uncramped. The work devoted to theme writing, after the necessary amount of correctness has been attained, is, thus, work unduly specialized and diverted from the main purpose of the college.

Unless a person knows how to read he cannot become educated. It is the basic requirement of all education. It is the perception that to write properly, however desirable, is not the basic requirement of all education, which occasions the restlessness of the students and of the other departments of the college with the English department. Unless a person knows how to summarize properly he does not know how to think, which is the basic aim of education. It is the perception that all this theme work seems unable to teach students to read and think which makes the rest of the college feel that it is time spent unprofitably. There is a growing uneasiness as to its value and a growing discontent with the incom-

mensurate labor involved for both instructor and student.   But un-
desirable as it is, it seems necessary until we can find something
better.   The oral study of literature, which I propose in its place,
will secure both accurate reading and accurate thinking.

It consists of reading aloud, and a return in the student's
own words of what has been read.   Paraphrase should, if need be,
form a part of the reading exercise itself--so much reading, so
much paraphrasing, and at the end of each group of ideas, an abstract.   There is no better and more inexpensive training of the
mind than making paraphrases and abstracts of what has been read.
To get an idea in one set of words and give it in another set; to
get a progressive series of ideas on one scale and reproduce them
on a smaller--these two simple and universally available processes
require not only original accuracy of apprehension but a thorough
grasp of the primary principles of proportion and emphasis.   A student who can make an adequate and proportional abstract of a sonnet in one sentence has a grasp on the fundamental machinery of
thinking as well as on the sonnet itself.   If all college teachers
could hear how often a student will read a sonnet and be unable to
tell what it is about; how often on being questioned he will demonstrate ignorance of a large or even the principal portion of it (of
fourteen lines which he has prepared!), and reply that he did not
think it mattered, since he understood and liked the other part--they
would concede that the time given to such a class is given to all the
rest of the college.

In a "reading and returning" class a student receives the
highest mental training it is in the power of the college to give--
namely, the perception of what ideas are superior, what subordinate,
and what on a smaller scale negligible--and without this mental
training the knowledge and the culture with which we store the mind
are both unavailable and misleading.   Even the instructor of the college who refuses to admit that a man is known by the English he
keeps will readily admit that a study so basic to all studies may
justly occupy a place, especially since it takes up less time and energy than the English department does at present with written composition.   Even the English department should welcome the substitu-

tion. For at present, amusingly and illogically enough, for all the
time it takes, no student of English sets about reading an English
author with the same scientific spirit in which he demonstrates a
problem on the blackboard or performs an experiment in chemistry
under the eye of the teacher. Nor is any English work read and
checked up as carefully as one in a foreign language; and the intensive study given to Dante or Goethe, let us say, has its sole English counterpart in the labored recital of a student's meager reaction to campus topics or to some assigned essays.

The Special Values of the Oral Study
of Literature

I think, then, that this combination of elocution and composition which I have called the oral study of literature, will better
serve the purposes of the college and the English department than
theme work, in securing correct reading and thinking and in exer-
cising both upon more profitable material. But, in addition, it will
do what theme work cannot accomplish for even the best of theme-
sters. It will secure cooperation with the printed page--a perception of that fusion of emotional and intellectual content which goes
to make up what we call good literature. This is the aim of all
English teaching not exclusively compositional.

The Cooperation With Literature

To teach literature and not the appreciation of it is like presenting a picture gallery to the blind. It is well known that the
higher forms of literature cannot be appreciated by young people except when read aloud, and that reading aloud enriches the appreciation of even discerning minds. It is not necessary to remind the
lecturer on literature how much he must rely upon reading aloud
(even though, as too often, he communicates rational or emotional
values alone and not the two together). The subtler the art, the
more necessary is vocal embodiment to point it out. In a class in
the oral study of literature mere translation is important only as a
means to accuracy, since the habit of misapprehension is universal;
but its main business is the appreciation of literature. If to read

aloud accurately requires a closer thought analysis than the average
student ever gives to anything else, to read aloud illuminatively requires a sympathetic and imaginative cooperation which the average
student can cultivate nowhere else, and which is the aim of lecturing about literature when not merely biographical and historical.

The Appreciation of Poetry and Style

I have said that the subtler the literature, the more necessary is vocal embodiment to point it out.   Upon poetry the necessity rests with a two-fold obligation.   That this is an unpoetic age
may not be entirely because it is a scientific one.   It may well be
because the beauty of verse as verse lies in its rhythmic utterance,
and we no longer utter it.   In the general failure to appreciate oral-
ly its metrical values, it appears to be but a cramped and crabbed
sort of prose.   When the comic column of a newspaper prints verse
as prose, one reads it asking oneself why anybody should write in
so pointless, feeble, or peculiar a fashion, until some odd word or
arrangement reveals the presence of rhyme or meter and thus explains the puzzle.   The best sonnet written as prose is queer stuff
to the eye; and if read aloud in such a way as to sacrifice the fundamental quality of poetry, it is equally queer stuff to the ear.   On
the other hand, those oral readers of poetry who have any appreciation of it as such, fall for the most part into two divisions: the
one preserves nothing whatever but the metrical values and reads
with a scansion repellent to sense and humanity; the other reads in
a saccharine monotone equally devastating to humanity and sense.
Both shear away the intended sense from the sound, just as the
prosy readers shear away the intended sound from the sense.   If
the appreciation of poetry is as rare as the ability to establish oral-
ly its sound and sense values at the same time seems to indicate,
no wonder this is not a poetry-reading age.   But if the coming generation continues the process and cuts out poetry altogether, how
much of the treasure of the ages will it not forfeit!

Teaching the Principles of Literary Criticism
by Concrete Application

It is not only in helping on the appreciation of poetry and the subtler qualities of style, however, that a class in the oral study of literature is a valuable adjunct to the English department. It helps to teach the principles of literary criticism, which is also one of the concerns of lecturing about literature. Literary criticism deals with questions of material, structure, and workmanship. Is this the proper material for the effect intended, is it bound together into a whole, is it handled well? All principles of criticism cluster about these three things--choice of material, firmness of structure, appropriateness of handling. The principles cannot be elucidated so well by statement as by illustration. Rich and varied illustrations can nowhere be got at so inexpensively as in reading aloud passages of literature. This you may see from the practice of any lecturer or book which deals with criticism. If the student reads aloud the passages himself, his grasp on the principles is the surer. What we do ourselves we know better than when we are merely told it by others. The young silent reader is habitually inexacting. But even an actor, with special interest and eagerness to do his best with his material and with special equipment to enable him to do so, does not appreciate the good and bad point of his author's dialogue until he has learned it and tried to say it in action. It is not surprising, therefore, that the most uncooperating reader can perceive upon reading aloud how it happens that Shelley and Emerson are less clear than Byron and Macaulay. The good oral reader will find himself called upon again and again to compensate for slips in technique which he did not even suspect until he began to read aloud.

The good writer properly indicates his emphasis and inflection, makes his transitions, binds his sentences together. In all of these ways he will designate the movement of the voice in reading him aloud. Thus, doing so shows more clearly than any other way in which of these respects he fails to be good. To the silent reader, for instance, there seems no particular feebleness in Campbell's lines "And the battle did not slack Till a feeble cheer the Dane to our cheering sent us back." But when an oral reader is

compelled to find the precise meaning of the passage, he sees that
the entire point has been absurdly committed to an unimportant word
put in an unimportant place.   The battle went on vigorously until the
Danes stopped cheering in the usual manner and began to cheer
feebly.   It requires study in such an inept sentence to find the point
and the silent reader, unless conscientious, is content to gather that
the English felt in some fashion that they were winning.   Or take
another case.   Reading aloud discloses at once Wordsworth's invet-
erate habit, even in his best work, of not binding his thoughts together, a habit which some keen silent readers do not detect.   The
little verse called "Natural Piety" is flagrantly guilty in this respect.   The last line contains nothing new: he means that he wishes
his days to be bound together in the future as they have been in the
past.   The emphasis therefore, if any is needed, falls upon the un-
fortunate word "could" where it seems unnatural and awkward.   As
the whole thing has just been better said, this is an unhappy ending,
especially in so tiny a poem.   The same thing may be said of the
ending of the famous Ode.   Though majestic, it is not clear.   He
seems to be saying something new; he is in reality saying over a-
gain what he has said before; unless you give it the tone of implication, therefore, you falsify the meaning.   Yet even the critical silent reader fails to perceive the real meaning.   But more important than merely verbal slips are infirmities of structure which the
oral reader notes.   No silent reader is so conscious of redundant
matter and of digressions.   The student who reads aloud "The Scholar Gypsy" and "Lycidas" sees at once where these admit something
extraneous or at too great length for their purpose.   Indeed, one
may assert that no oral reader who has attempted to keep in the
main mood of "Lycidas" and found it impossible can have any sympathy with critical theorists who attempt to justify Milton's famous
digression, because he sees at once that it is destructive to the
main mood.   It is when you read Keats aloud that you perceive
most clearly that he did not excel in getting the right material to
prove his assertions.   Truth may be beauty, but an ode on how
much more beauty exists in imagination than in actuality is not the
place to say so; nor is it logical to compare himself to all the

nightingales that ever sang as if they went to make up one permanent bird, while he, on the other hand, did not constitute one permanent John Keats, as long as anyone was alive to hear his voice.
In short, then, just as it is the parodist who most tellingly shows
us the faults and mannerisms of the original, so it is the oral
reader who, in providing, as it were, another and livelier version,
points out the shortcomings of the writer. Far more than any silent reader, the oral one perceives pockets of vacancy in the meaning. Poets have been privileged and special offenders in this regard. I do not hesitate to say that he who reads poetry aloud to
others has a far higher standard of excellence in a poem. He perceives very emphatically that poetry is good not only on account of
its form but in spite of its form. Not many poems in the English
language will escape triumphant from the test of reading aloud--so
much feeble stuff has been admitted for the sake of meter and
rhyme.

Literary Interpretation Is Cultural and Creative

But the purposes of the college and the English department
are not all which such a class serves. Sympathetic reading aloud
is a fine art, and it is the only fine art within the gifts and the opportunities of every student. To many, it affords the only esthetic
and spiritual development they ever receive in college, or--in the
realm of art--in their lives for that matter. To this end, lectures
about literature are important, but they are not so important as
reading literature. They will of themselves only inform the mind;
they will not enrich the spirit. Nor will reading literature do so
unless it is read with cooperation.

Only to the rare youth does this sympathetic and imaginative
cooperation with literature come of itself. Or rather, it is only
the rare youth who retains it. It comes to all children apparently,
but early education--formal and social--seems to warp it out of
them. This need not be the case; but granting it is so, should it
not be the business of education to bring it back again? Upon
closer inspection it would appear that children have this cooperation

only when they fully apprehend. For the castles of giants and the revels of fairies are perfectly grasped--that is why they are appreciated. In childhood appreciation and apprehension go hand in hand. What is education if it fails to increase apprehension as it increases the number of things to be apprehended? But as children begin to read books they do not understand, their minds, though stimulated at first by mystery and vagueness, little by little grow dulled in response. Why not? The mystery and vagueness each day glitter less, because as they are approached they prove to be only obscurity; and as the outlines of the picture presented by their reading grow more blurred, the world of reality around them is each day unfolding more distinctly. By the time the child reaches youth, this sympathetic and imaginative cooperation with reading is gone. If the child's apprehension kept pace with the educative process, perhaps it would not be so. But since it is so, should not a special form of education bring back what education has taken away? Particularly when it is seen that unless a student possesses apprehension he is unable really to possess anything else that we offer him in college?

Lastly, illuminative oral reading should be taught because it is not only cultural but creative. It is the sole creative art which the average man has a chance at. Work of interpretation is work of creation for the worker. The difference is only one of degree and of the permanence of the concrete material result--the permanence of the spiritual result is the same. The interpreter, like the creator, gives shape and expression to something which was there before but had hitherto existed unperceived by him. The student who achieves a reading of Shakespeare unknown to him before, a meaning which may be implied but is not asserted by the author, is a creator. He has made something new out of old material, and Shakespeare could do no more than that. Such artistic creation-- the imaginative cooperation with what he reads--is the birthright of every child, and that he should lose it just as creation widens on his view is pitiable. We must bring back complete apprehension, a mental action, before we can bring back cooperation, a spiritual one.

II.   The Theory of Reading Aloud

This book is not an "elocution" book, and the lessons given
in the appendix are not "elocution" lessons.   They concern getting
the thought of the writer, and the oral reading contemplated is only
a test of whether one got the thought or not.   The lessons do not in
the least concern reading aloud artistically, except so far as any
comprehended and appreciated reading must be artistic.   They deal
with receiving and giving right information.   It cannot be too often
repeated that one can make anything understandable which one understands and anything appreciable which one appreciates, provided the
words are at command; and in reading aloud the words are supplied.
It is a psychological impossibility to convey wrong information, having just received right information; or for the voice to lie about the
state of the mind unless one wishes to make it do so.   If wrong information is given, then, it is because wrong information was received.   The hearer may puzzle out what the words ought to mean,
but if he does so he is more intelligent than the reader who handed
them on in the raw or half-baked mass in which they came to him.

The theory of reading aloud can be entirely summed up in
one statement.   The reader is taking the place of the writer and
simply talking what he has to say.   Literature is talk made permanent.   In the pithy contemporary phrase, it is "canned talk."   The
objects of the reader, then, are the same as the objects of the talker.   A person never talks without doing three things--saying something, revealing in his voice the attitude he takes toward what he
says, and showing the motive of each word as he is uttering it.   The
three things comprise all that is necessary for the reader to do in
order to communicate the thought of the writer accurately and effectively.

The instinctive, or automatic, devices of the human voice
when used to communicate are four in number--the tones of assertion and implication, emphasis, inflection, and color.   The tone of
assertion is the kind of tone we employ when we are answering a
question that calls for an answer, that is, it is the one we always

use when we are giving what we consider primary information. The
tone of implication we employ when we say something which has just
been said or involved in our preceding speech or in the situation itself. Inflection indicates the inter-relationship of the talker's
ideas. Emphasis indicates his notion of their relative importance.
Color indicates his attitude toward, or his motive in using, his
words. None of these devices are ever misused by a person who
speaks out of his own mind and selects his own words. If we mis-
use them in reading aloud, we cannot give, nor have we in silent
reading received, the author's meaning.

It is convenient to call these devices instinctive. But the
word is, of course, loosely used when it designates acts which have
long ceased to be consciously purposive, and now work of themselves. As people little by little, in the beginnings of a built-up
speech, found these devices necessary in order to understand each
other in the new art of words, they began to embody them in their
voices, until at last their voices acquired the habit. So, you may
hear a child acquiring the habit to-day as he learns to master
speech. None of the "instinctive" devices do you employ at once
with a foreign language. Little by little you learn to use them as
you increase your speaking acquaintance with it. And you find that
unless you do so, you cannot be understood except by one who is
perforce laboriously thinking like yourself word by word instead of
idea by idea, and using his mind to piece out what his ear fails to
hear and so to correct the false impression which it gave him. It
was, then, because people recognized that these vocal devices were
necessary to communication in words that they devised them. If
necessary in the speaking voice, equally necessary in the written
voice. The inaccurate reader is inaccurate because he has not
learned to recognize that these devices are all implicit in the written voice and he must embody them in his reading, silent as well
as oral. Without the recognition of when and where these devices
would be actually employed by the writer if he were talking the
words, there can be no accurate reading.

Assertion and Implication

Old matter--which is all matter previously said or involved
--is to be understood by the silent reader, and uttered by the oral
one, in the tone of implication. Only the new matter is to be read,
to oneself or aloud, in the tone of assertion; and in the new matter
always lies the emphatic word. The new material in each sentence
after the first one bears about the same proportion to the old as
the part of an iceberg above water bears to the part below water;
and as with the iceberg, it is not so much the part above as the
part below that is dangerous. For the reader, silent or oral, to
come in violent contact with it means shipwreck.

Emphasis

It is as necessary for the silent reader as for the oral reader to emphasize. Otherwise he cannot get the meaning and naturally will fail to deliver it. True, it may sometimes happen that he
will fail to deliver the meaning when he has got it. But that is
merely because the customary attitude of people in speaking printed
words is absurdly different from their attitude in speaking their own.
He fails to deliver the meaning he has seen because he really is not
talking, he is only pronouncing. A person never talks without saying something, but an oral reader never says anything when he is
just uttering words. He must utter ideas, and emphasize the important ones. It is not the words that contain the ideas; it is the
relationship of the words, their groupings. Shift the same words
and you get a new set of ideas; shift the emphasis even when you
retain the old grouping, and you get a new meaning. The trouble
with the inaccurate oral reader who has ever got the right meaning,
is that he thinks he is emphasizing when he is not; or when he has
emphasized the right word he immediately undoes what he has done
by emphasizing a wrong one, not realizing that any emphasis on a
wrong word deprives the right one of its emphasis. Not only is emphasis vital to the thought, it is vital to remembering. Without emphasis, words enter only the sight and not the mind. You can de-
pend upon the average inaccurate reader to forget at once a large

portion of the words he has read the moment he apprehends them.
This is because they came to him only as words. Words go, ideas
stay.

Emphasis in silent reading never of course interferes with
inflection, that is, it never disturbs the relationship of words.
With some very poor oral readers, there is a slight danger. Oral
emphasis cannot indicate the meaning if all the rest of the meaning
is dislocated. In oral reading as in silent, nothing should be emphasized but the point until the next point arrives. The unempha-
sized words should be heard, as they should have been seen, in
their proper relationship--and that is all. Any emphasis heard on
what is not the point does the same double damage that it did if it
were imagined to be there by the silent reader. It vitiates not only
the present meaning but the past emphasis also. Since the emphasis always falls in the new matter, it is apparent that when you
pass from one thing to another, the change must always be seen and,
in oral reading, heard. Readers who do not note the transition are
falsifying the meaning just as much as when they asserted on impli-
catory matter. In one case, they (and the listener) think the author is talking about something new when he is talking about something old; in the other, they (and the listener) think the author is
talking about something old when he is talking about something new.

Vocal Monotony and Lack of Personality

But having discovered the meaning in his silent reading and
emphasizing audibly only the chief assertions, still the oral reader
often fails to communicate. This is because of his vocal monotony.
No voice can communicate for more than a sentence or two without
movement. The ear of the listener becomes dulled. It is in reading aloud that the difference in the general attitude toward the
printed and the spoken word is most glaring. Few students would
be content to talk in the unanimated voices in which they read. If
they were, their hearers would not let them continue long. Every
normal talking voice has movement, its ups and downs. The rise
and fall in the voice is called modulation. It is dictated by the attitude of the speaker toward what he says, and is regulated by his in-

tention in the words he uses.   By reason of the artificial attitude
the oral reader takes toward the printed word--that is to say, no
attitude at all--he neglects to employ the movement that all voices
must take when naturally used and consequently what he says is
largely unintelligible.   Sometimes, however, he falls into the opposite fault.   He lacks intelligibility because he exhibits a false movement in his voice, through his instinctive or acquired appreciation
of the fact that no movement at all is unhuman and self-defeating.
The rises and falls in the voice should be dictated by the conscious
intention.   If they are not, the utterance gets into a pattern of ups
and downs, like song, and the sense is defeated.   Voice movement
should be impelled by rational and not by esthetic motives.   If rational, it is probably esthetic also; if primarily esthetic, it can
never be rational.

Yet reading may be accurate and intelligible, and still be uninteresting.   This, it is true, is generally because the reader has
failed to take an attitude toward the ideas that are coming out of his
mouth, and such a condition, were it possible, would make him
equally uninteresting in his own talk.   But sometimes a reader who
understands every idea he is saying and has the attitude toward
them one would have who said it out of his own mind, still fails to
be of interest.   That is because, though his attitude toward the
writer is correct, his attitude towards himself and his hearers is
wrong.   He has not sufficient interest in himself or his hearers to
talk as he would in conversation.   Consequently his ideas lack personality, or as the fine phrase of the day has it, there is no punch
behind them.   The best way for a reader to increase his vocal personality is to renew the realization of what happens in first-hand
speech.   In conversation no one ever speaks without revealing the
motive of each word he uses.   It was selected with a purpose and
it is expected to fulfill its function.   But in an impersonal reader's
delivery, there will be entire tracts of words which are, as one
might say, personality-less.   He fails in them to realize their purpose and they fail to fulfill their function.   Nevertheless, he is taking up as much space as if he were talking to the people before
him; and if he would hesitate to bore them then by talking absently,

why should he do so now?   He should read as if he considered the
three factors of the situation to be of equal importance, himself
and the audience as well as the author.   This will give him the attitude that something worth saying is being said by a person worth
listening to, and to people worth hearing it.

With accuracy and intelligibility and a proper sense of his
own importance, any reader can communicate the given information.
There remains only one obstacle in the path.   The rate of speed.
He may read either too fast or too slow.   This is so much a matter of the personality and vitality of the reader, however, that only
his own experience can direct him.   In general readers gallop.   One
should read much more slowly than he talks.   In the ratio that the
ideas are difficult to follow or out of the ordinary experience, he
should slow up still more.   If, indeed, the passage contains an unusual or peculiar word, or one liable to be mistaken for another,
the reader should call attention to the fact by a deliberate impulse
of the voice; and this for the same reason.   It requires an instant
of time for the listener to place the word, or if he has got the
wrong impression to replace it with the right one.

Effectiveness a Matter of Attitude

Accurate oral reading, then, means an exact conveyance of
the ideas.   Effective oral reading means conveyance of the emotion
also.   Accurate silent reading is thinking with the author; cooperative silent reading is feeling with the author.   Unless you perceive
his emotion as well as his thought, you cannot be said to cooperate
with him; and he is talking to you for that purpose.   If you would
talk to others in his words effectively, you must communicate his
emotion also.

In a sense there can be no accurate reading adequately pro-
jected to the listener, which is not at the same time effective.
Furthermore, there is a large body of rational content in most prose
and in all poetry which cannot be clearly conveyed without conveying the emotional content.   But as reading may be accurate without
being effective, it seems better to treat the two separately.

Here, also, the analogy with the talking voice is pertinent.

One can always tell in conversation whether the talker is approving or disapproving. If the talker indicated his emotional attitude in the neutral way the oral reader often does, we should think something was the matter with him. Yet students, invariably expressing in their voice far less emotion than in daily conversation, invariably fancy they are expressing far more and think they must tone down a bit lest they be accused of soulfulness. The tone in which they remonstrate with you is much more vivid and emotional than any they have been employing in their reading. If they used the tone they took to say a dance was a corker or a show was rotten, they would appear volcanic by contrast. Here is another glaring difference in the attitude toward the word written and the word spoken. It is of course not so glaring as that of reading in a voice altogether unanimated by evidence that the mind is present, for this is a voice which never occurs in life unless the nature is prostrate under some great shock or intense pain. But the animation prescribed by the presiding mind is no more essential and universal in the talking voice than is the color prescribed by the mood. Certainly the discrepancy presented between the colorless voice of the reader and the emotional idea it words is the more noticeable, because very few passages one can read aloud are merely expository; and even the scientific lecturer diagramming a process is passionate in comparison to the youthful reader who is afraid of expressing the emotion he habitually expresses in his talk.

The main thing in effective reading is to size up the mood of the passage and keep always in mind the purpose of the author. To depart from it is to be ineffective as well as confusing. When you pause to argue for a moment, read as if you were arguing merely to establish the matter and pass on to your main purpose. Few things exist in a passage for their own sake but for the sake of something else. Whatever this is, keep it in view. If any change of attitude is required by the immediate words you are reading, it must be a change completely assimilated with your main purpose. If the writer is expressing his sadness for the death of a friend, for instance, the friend is no less dead in the beginning when the writer is recalling him pleasantly than in the end where his death is explicitly mentioned. The attitude of the part is always prescribed by the attitude of the whole, except in a narrative of events; and here the attitude of the whole is prescribed by the fact that you are telling a story supposed to be interesting. Here each event that comes up must be narrated by the story teller from the mood of the person supposed to be affected by it, but all should nevertheless be kept in the key of the story teller who considers them all integral and himself wishes to interest. But in passages which express the emotion or belief of the writer, there is no such apparent (though not real) shift of the point of view. He is expressing the same emotion or belief all along; and if any part of what he says requires a change of attitude, it must be one subordinated to and colored by his main intention. If his motive in making this momentary departure be kept in mind, it will generally be found that he is not departing from it. If he really has done so (as in the case of 'Lycidas') the departure is likely to be an artistic mistake, however good the material is in itself. One must never be allowed to lose sight of the general intention because of the particular thing said at the moment. To do so is to get too close a view of something meant to be seen only in perspective; it is what we mean by not seeing the wood for the trees. A real digression exists when the author, like the talker, lays down his purpose and takes up another, when he stops going in one direction and breaks a new path. Effective reading is a matter of establishing one point after the other but always in a straight line.

The Writer's Valuation Not the Reader's

While we are on the subject of faithfulness to the mood of the writer, it may be pointed out that there is a kind of inaccuracy which, faithful enough to the ideas if they were really yours, is destructive to his. The average reader, student or adult, is unwilling to let a writer speak for himself. He puts his own valuation on the words according to his temperament, not remembering that the set of emotional associations intended by the writer may be different. This is of course aside from the case, of which there are a number in this book, where there exists a legitimate difference of interpre-

tation. I speak now of interpretation prescribed by the words used
and the ideas called up. If the author had the feeling of the reader,
he would not have employed those words, ideas, and images, but
others in their stead. The vast number of misreadings of Shakespeare on the stage caused by this elbowing the author out of the
way, is a good illustration. Let us take the "Seven Ages" speech,
for instance. It is apparent that Jaques is in every case calling up
ideas that belittle life; why then should he suddenly lapse into sentiment at the end? It is obvious that the temperament of the man
desires to belittle the last age at least as much as all the others--
that is why he selected those words to use about it. But because
the reader is sentimental about second childishness or because it is
thought to be more immediately effective as an ending, he forces
Jaques to take his own estimate. The reader should say to himself "Would the person who selects those words feel the same way
that I feel?" The wholesome old lady in "John Anderson, My Jo,
John," is not at all tremulous at the thought of death approaching
her and her old man. What she is saying is that they will be together in death just the same as they have been in life. But readers quaver or hush their voices here as if the old lady were not
contemplating it as rather pleasant under the circumstances. A
sentimental reading is not one which exhibits sentiment, but which
exhibits the wrong sentiment or the right one out of porportion to
the author's intention.

　　There is another kind of incomplete accuracy which destroys
effectiveness. The listener gets the separate affirmations but is at
a loss to discern their general aim. What is he to get out of this
bundle of interesting ideas you give him? What is the central idea,
the backbone to which all the others must be fitted? The reader
must size up not only the general mood of the writer but his general aim. There is not only a point to the sentence and to the paragraph and stanza, there is, even more importantly, a point to the
entire passage. This is where the value, to be discussed later, of
the one-sentence statement of the meaning comes in. Here lies the
central idea--all the rest is subsidiary. Find it and try in your
reading to make it stand out. Unless it does so, the listener will

Appendix A   251

again be seeing details too closely; in short, failing to see the wood
for the trees.

Lastly, effective reading demands that you indicate with an
air of completeness when you have reached your destination. Generally, the listener should know when the reader is approaching the
end, and he should certainly know when he has arrived. An abrupt
ending is untrue to the writer, and unless there has existed some
reason for concealing the fact, --as in a hoax, for instance--it is
unfair treatment. For the reader and the listener, too, it is un-
satisfactory. Either the reader feels dissatisfied with himself or
the listener with the reader. Everyone will recall the awkwardness,
physical and artistic, when a piano solo merely trails away. If the
author has not (as in the case of the "Intimations") provided a sufficient end, the reader can easily atone for the shortcoming by a
manipulation of his voice. In this connection, it may be said that
very few extracts or whole poems or articles can end on a question.
Even when there is a final interrogation mark, it will be found that
the mood demands an affirmation on some word that has occurred
earlier in the last sentence. Shelley's 'West Wind' by no means
ends on a question but on an assertion that winter being upon us,
spring must be near at hand. An authentic question is one which
asks for an answer; if you have already answered it, it is only a
vivid means of reaffirmation.

<u>Some Methods to Secure Good Reading</u>

A good way for the instructor to vivify the reader's voice is
to interrupt and ask "why," "what," or "how" whenever the passage affords him opportunity, and make the reader answer the question in the writer's own words. A good method to secure the right
attitude of the reader is to stop him and ask the class what they
think, judging from the tone of his voice, the reader is about to say
on the matter he is treating. Occasional reading at sight is highly
desirable, especially in satire. Sight reading is an instructive object lesson in the habitual failure of words to fill their function,
that is, to creat an impression the moment they are used. The instructor should require the impression of the student, new word by

new word, new sentence by new sentence.   This best of laboratory
exercises, soon demonstrates that no impression or the wrong one
vitiates all that follows.

At first all should follow the reading with the eye, in order
to profit by the corrections; but as soon as these become fewer,
one of the best readers may be appointed listener.   The account he
gives of the information received sometimes convinces the reader
how poor he is.   Sometimes, too, the good student may interrupt
with corrections himself, these being entirely restricted to wrong
emphasis since in other matters too much of the personal element
enters.   The more methods of keeping the class alert and the greater variety of usage the better.   The success of a course in any
kind of expression, written or oral composition or elocution, de-
pends on the tricks it employs.

III.   The Oral Analysis

An accurate and effective reading is only part of the work
in the Oral Study of Literature.   The student is required to precede
his reading with a one-sentence statement of its meaning, and afterwards to analyze and criticize the material presented.

A reader may master a sentence but not its connection with
the next sentence, and so on throughout; be, in short, unable to size
up the passage as a whole.   Hence the importance of formulating a
summary, after the first silent reading and in preparation for the
oral one, to determine the main point.   Take "The Blessed Damo-
zel" for instance.   Is it about a girl in heaven?   About this girl
looking forward to meeting her lover?   About a man picturing his
dead sweetheart in heaven?   Picturing her as looking forward to
their meeting?   As longing for a reunion which he fears is doubtful?
As longing like himself for a reunion which they both fear will never
take place?   Here are six summaries, and only the last one states
the main idea of the poem and hence dictates rightly how its details
should be proportioned.   Let us take another selection.   "Break,
Break, Break" does not merely give you some gloomy thoughts of
a man looking at the sea.   Tennyson says that the sea and all on it

can express themselves but he cannot. Or he says that everything
around him seems absorbed in the present while he lives only in
the past. Either of these statements covers adequately the ideas
called up. The oral rendering of the one will slightly differ from
the other in the stress and color of certain words; and it will be
instructive to ask the student to read the poem a second time with
the alternate thought in mind. But unless he has, after his silent
reading, tried to set the poem in order by one of them, he will get
out of it only an impression of its emotional drift and none at all
of its rational meaning.

An instructor cannot insist too often upon the fact that, in
general, a one-sentence statement is either right or wrong. Yet he
will, for an exasperating while, insist to somewhat mulish ears. A
student is, to be sure, forced to admit his mistake when his summary puts into the author's mouth precisely the opposite meaning,
--an occurrence of startling frequency--but short of so hopeless a
giveaway, it is difficult to convince him that "something along that
line" is not quite good enough. Here is where the need for brevity
comes in. It is impossible to locate a culprit behind a smoke
screen emitted on the time-honored academic principle that if one
says a mouthful some of it is sure to be right. The sentence must
be whittled down to a crisp wording of the writer's chief claim together with his chief reason for making it. These two are generally developed separately, and the student must find and combine them
for himself. If the instructor can ask why the writer is making
such a claim, the statement is not complete.

The analysis should generally come after the reading. Sometimes, a reader may be asked to designate the nature of the material beforehand, however, so that the class can be watching for it.
Occasionally, the analysis may profitably take the form of explaining
the exact function of each sentence in the passage, that is, what it
does with reference to the preceding one. This may be done after
the reading, or during it between the sentences according to the
method illustrated in Lesson VIII. An analysis of the material designates how the author supports his assertion or explains his mood.
What material has Ruskin assembled in "The Perfectness of the

Lower Nature" to make good his claim that we should not prefer it
to the imperfection of the higher? He levies upon not only the human world, of which he is speaking, but upon the animal and the
vegetable worlds, of which he is not speaking. It is his comparison and his analogy which make his case so strong.

Critical Comment of the Reader

Here it is even more necessary than in the summary to hold
the student to saying something precisely. But that something must
be critical. It is only too easy to secure a definite, though entirely unexplained, expression of his temperament. His tendency, of
course, is to confuse criticism of another's work with an assertion
of his own personality. This is a stage, indeed, beyond which the
untrained mind rarely goes. It is necessary to convince him that
this is merely a personal reaction and not an esthetic one at all;
that the critic deals not primarily with what is done but how it is
done; that the kind of thing one personally dislikes may be done well
just as the kind one likes may be done poorly; and that culture,
though it may indeed have preferences, seeks to appreciate all forms
of expression. A more sophisticated sort of student has annexed a
critical vocabulary without knowing how to harness it. It runs wild
over every passage read, when there is nothing in his mind that
corresponds to it. He must be choked off at once by challenging
him to explain concretely, in their immediate application, the empty
and specious phrases which he pronounces so trippingly on the
tongue.

With each kind of student, it is best to establish and make
articulate the critical faculty by inspecting words. In what words
has the writer indicated a desire to be interesting rather than merely to unfold his thought clearly and firmly? What words in their
mutual relationship bear out or frustrate an expectancy which has
been created? What word or idea appears well or badly chosen for
the purpose in hand? If the student can clearly explain the reason
for his selection, he is on the road to a substantial critical attitude.

The authentic critical attitude once established by such con-

crete methods, the now fairly-fledged critic may go farther. Has
the writer employed his words economically, smoothly, easily, flex-
ibly, rhythmically? Is his thought involved? Would you re-arrange
it? Has it any feeble matter? Does it mark time with too many
illustrations? And these, perhaps, too narrow in range? Has the
passage unity of thought and of mood? If a complete poem has it
begun and ended in the right place? Do the ideas seem to stand for
something natural and real, or are they only a literary pose or the
filling in of a prescribed pattern?

　　　Finally, a recitation should include when profitable the reader's personal opinion of the writer's ideas--that agreement or dis-
agreement, approval or disapproval which he had at first confused
with literary criticism. Whenever the material makes it worthwhile,
this should always be demanded. Do you agree with this claim or
approve this attitude? Would you modify it? Has the writer been
willing to exaggerate or overstate in order to justify? Is his material capable of establishing it? To make the talk of writers alive
to readers--this is the object of the instructor. What, for instance,
is Mr. Mencken doing in "The Declaration of Independence in the
American Vulgate"? Is he merely translating our historic document? Or also making fun of a popular conception of it? Or is he
making fun of the American ideal itself, that is to say, of us?

Training His Literary and Personal Judgment

　　　I have sought in all ways to select passages which, while of-
fering the two qualities of emotional and intellectual content, were
capable of training the literary and personal judgment of the reader.
For the latter reason, I have culled from as wide a field of opinion
as I could find at hand. For the former reason, I have included,
though space is precious, many selections which, while coming up
to a certain standard of merit, are not in their various kinds particularly admirable. For the same reason I have included many selections which would be better if edited. They are too long for
their content, they admit extraneous matter, they develop side issues unduly. It is my custom to ask the reader to condense such
selections before bringing them into class. With debatable editing,

I assign the passages to two readers; and they and the class compare their editions. Then, in this particular, there are other selections which, though possessing unity, can tell all they have to
say in less time. With these I ask the reader to omit all that he
thinks unnecessary before he comes to class, and then challenge his
excisions. The value of these two exercises in training the judgment is, I think, apparent; and is sufficient to justify the space
which makes them possible. I have included also several lengthy
poems of regular stanzas, because, being composed of uniform units,
they afford convenient material for a lively and illuminating exercise which I may call a reading bee. The entire section takes the
floor and I "spell them out" when they have falsified the meaning of
the author. I have seldom had a class in which at the finish of
Gray's Elegy or Omar, for instance, there was one surviving member.

In arrangement of the selections, I have generally proceeded
from the shorter to the longer, the first naturally presenting units
more adapted to the formation of the habit of careful reading and
the intensive analysis which secures it. For the rest, the arrangement contemplates only furnishing variety to a class period.

As I finish the long but pleasant task of selection, I am
struck anew with the substance, richness, and variety of the thought,
imagination, and emotion here contained. It is in setting before the
student such a collection as this, that the leading aim of college is
secured--to acquaint young men and women with the achievements
of mankind. As I look back upon my days of theme-writing in college and compare their poverty with these riches, I marvel at the
mistake of educating a student in English by writing rather than by
reading. When I read over the ponderous collection of my themes,
gathering dust now these many years on an out of the way shelf,
the impression is much reinforced. Why all this labor to produce
nothing? "As though Pharaoh should set the children of Israel to
make a pin instead of a pyramid," or, like Merdith's ocean, ramp-
ing with so thunderous a noise to make one thin line upon the
shore! Although I was a student who thought himself of unusual

literary appreciation and possessed certainly unusual desire for self-
expression, I am well-nigh appalled at their laborious vapidity, and,
what is worse, at their insincerity--although I had even more than
youth's usual share of the confidence of something to say.   Not until, somewhat late in life, I came to teach--that is, not until I
came to communicate precisely--did I realize how slipshod a reader
I had been.   This is how the students in a class in the Oral Study
of Literature may test, for themselves and under supervision, the
faultiness of their own habits of reading while their working lives
are still before them.   When I reflect how many years it was after
I left college before I came to recognize the fact that I did not know
how to read, I am tempted to indict an educational system which,
in assuming that I already knew how, although it knew very well to
the contrary, taught me Hamlet with Hamlet left out.

X. Sound Recordings and the Historians:
Needs and Opportunities

Richard W. Lenk, Bergen Community College

The question is often asked, why should the historian use
sound recordings to supplement written sources? As one leading
historian expressed his views in a letter to me:

> The tape recorder is invaluable for certain things such
> as recording the speeches of Winston Churchill and Gen-
> eral Marshall here. In the field of folklore, of course,
> it is an essential tool. It has never, however, been
> found of any particular use for historical research. The
> resulting records would be far too bulky, and the use of
> them compared with the use of printed works or files of
> manuscript would be impossibly slow.

Certainly these are serious problems which impede the use of sound
materials. Yet sound recordings provide a link to the past which
the written word cannot do; the sounds of the past bring a sense of
reality which enables the listener to recreate the past, an added
dimension which helps to capture the orators of the past as they
sounded to their contemporaries. Certainly a Hitler or a William
Jennings Bryan must be understood in terms of their speaking ability
if we are to understand their appeal to the masses. The voices of
less well known figures also help to create a feeling for the past
which cannot be conveyed by the written word. Eelco N. van Kleffens, the former President of the United Nations General Assembly,
said in an address before the American Academy of Arts and Letters

> ... the written word is merely the spoken word preserved in
> a dormant state, capable of becoming sound at any time
> in the mouth of man or in the phonograph, and of being
> transferred from generation to generation, further expands
> the significance of the spoken word a hundredfold.

While many other historians would agree that sound docu-

ments have a value for the study of history, there are major problems which have prevented the use of this material in the past.
Until recently, the United States has lacked a central depository for
sound materials. This need has been partially met by the Library
of Congress, which has the sound collections of Emile Berlinner,
Sigmund Romberg, and the radio and television program "Meet the
Press." Yale University has collected the recordings of famous
musicians, and the University of Washington, under the direction of
Professor Milo Ryan, has preserved the wartime broadcasts of the
Columbia Broadcasting System. The National Voice Library, under
the supervision of G. Robert Vincent, is now housed at Michigan
State University. Syracuse University has started a program of re-
issuing some of the Edison wax cylinders.

Despite the current upsurge in interest, several major difficulties have prevented historians from utilizing this material. The
lack of a master list of commercial recordings issued during the
past seventy years, as well as the difficulty in locating privately
made recordings, has hampered research. Much of the material
stored in archives is not made available to scholars. Such hoard-
ing of material can lead to the destruction of these rare documents
because of improper storage. Duplication of rare items is the best
guarantee of their survival for the use of future generations. Records, unlike books, do not last for centuries without constant care.

A second problem has been the lack of professional studies
on the authenticity of the recordings available. Only one doctoral
dissertation has been completed on this subject; Raymond Edwin
Fielding's "A History of the American Motion Picture Newsreel"
(unpublished doctoral dissertation, University of Southern California,
1961). Fielding noted that from 1927 to 1932 newsreels featured
unmanipulated sound film interviews with famous politicians, but after 1932 technological changes created the possibility of tampering
with the films. Certainly more research is needed in this area so
that the historian can evaluate the usefulness of recorded sound materials. The Association for Recorded Sound Collections was or-
ganized in 1966 to help create and maintain standards in preserving
and evaluating sound materials, and at their second annual meeting,

in November, 1968, at UCLA, the problem of the spurious records was discussed.

Chelsea House Publishers have produced a teaching aid called The History Machine which offers forty selections of audio-visual material for classroom use. Such a device can help to promote student interest in history, if it is well done. Recently, the American Historical Association has started a committee on feature films with the hope of using commercial films as a classroom aid. The Oral History Association has also helped to set standards in this field.

A major problem that has impeded the use of sound materials by historians has been the paucity of copies of the master recordings. In printed documents, historians have the use of rare items available at most large libraries or these documents can be obtained in microfilm. Unfortunately, sound material is not available in that manner. Only a comparatively few records are commercially available and many of these do not give the source of the original recordings, and, what is even more reprehensible, these commercial products often present only excerpts of the master record. Recordings in other languages often suffer the fate of having a distracting narrator's voice superimposed on the original like a fungus which destroys the recording for historical use.

Fortunately, several historical record series do exist which are designed to help the historian. Each of these series has a distinct point of view and purpose which deserves to be studied at some length.

The Western Electric public affairs office has recorded an outstanding album, "Dialogues on Democracy," which studies the American Presidency from 1892 to 1960. The album is divided into three sections: 1. Conventions and Elections, 1892 to 1960, with the voices of many of the contenders; 2. Presidential Power, a talk by Professor Richard Neustadt of Columbia University; and 3. The Meaning of Freedom, a talk by Professor Sidney Hook of New York University. The narrator is Richard D. Heffner. Each album is accompanied by a written text. This is the best historical series available and many of the selections come from the Library of

Congress and the National Archives collections.

The C. B. S. Legacy Collection has produced a fine series on various historical events, which offer the recollections of surviving participants, coupled with music of the period. One of the best of these is "The Russian Revolution" which has an excellent recording of Lenin's voice as well as the voice of R. H. Bruce Lockhart, Solomon Schwarz, W. Lyon Blease and others. Each record is accompanied with a transcript and, at extra cost, a book is provided giving a history of the period.

A different approach is followed by Rococo Records, a Canadian firm which has started a series of reissues of recordings of famous people of the pre-World War I era. So far two records have appeared: the first, #4001, "England Before the First Great War"; and the second, #4002, "Authors and Actors." Both records are accompanied by full notes on the original recordings and a text of each speech. These records are not narrated but each selection is uncut. The series presents the voices of Leo Tolstoy, Rudyard Kipling, V. Sardou, Sir Henry Irving, T. Salvini, Lloyd George, Asquith, and many others. Anyone interested in the history of public speaking and styles of acting of the past hundred years will find these records most welcome.

Word Records' W 3076-LP, "Yesterday's Voices," performs the same service for Protestant religious leaders of the past that the Rococo records do for actors. Unfortunately, the record notes are much briefer than in the former series but it is possible to hear the changing style of oratory as it developed between 1860 and 1950. Among the speakers heard are Dwight L. Moody, Ira Sankey, Billy Sunday, General William Booth and Peter Marshall. The narrator is Paul Harvey.

Still another approach is offered by Gotham Records in a two record set, "History Speaks," produced in cooperation with Syracuse University from Edison Cylinders. The selections are not presented in chronological order and the narration and background music are distracting, but the selections include such rarities as the voices of Robert Browning, Lord Tennyson, and Gladstone. The reproduction of more of these early cylinders would be useful.

A very interesting idea is presented by The Academic Recording Institute, which has produced a series known as "Time for Ideas." Several scholars present their ideas in depth; each one has ten LP records devoted to his ideas. The series contains the views of Samuel Eliot Morison, John Mason Brown, Charles Frankel, Ashley Montagu, and C. Northcote Parkinson. This series can be used by future generations in understanding how twentieth century scholars viewed their work.

"The Brains Trust" (Argo Records, DA 38) is composed of selections from a B. B. C. Forces Program that caught the popular imagination in 1941. A panel of experts would extemporize on questions submitted by listeners. The quality of the panel is in evidence from their names: Sir Harold Nicolson, Barbara Ward, Sir Malcolm Sargent, Sir Julian Huxley, Philip Guedalla, Professor C. E. M. Joad, Commander R. T. Gould, and Commander A. B. Campbell. The selections include such topics as modern biography, conducting an orchestra, Dunne's Time Theory, and Eastern and Western philosophy. This is one of the most stimulating records to appear in recent years.

"Tom Edison's Greatest Hits" (United Artists 3547) is listed in the Schwann Catalog under humor but the record jacket is very misleading. All of the selections are spoofs but the unwary buyer is not informed of this fact by the jacket. Instead he is led to believe that the selections are from rare cylinders that were discovered in the Edison laboratories by an old employee. The dust jacket blurb is almost a paraphrase of Mr. Vincent's discovery of Edison Cylinders. Any novice collector who purchased this record would lose interest in the subject or never buy another record of historic voices again. The dust jacket should be changed to insure against misrepresentation.

We are still far behind the European record companies in the use of recorded sound material. The one hundred "Lecture Records" on a variety of topics, issued on 78 disks in the nineteen thirties by an English company, has no American counterpart, nor have American companies shown as great an interest in preserving the memories of statesmen and authors as have Odeon, Pathé, Lon-

don International, or the B. B. C. issues.   Much more work needs
to be done in this field so that the historian may use recordings as
a tool in his research.

Another area which has been neglected by social historians
has been private recordings of family groups.   During the eighteen
nineties many families used their cylinder machines to record the
voices of friends and relatives.   Unfortunately, much of this material is still in private hands, but hearing these recordings brings
the past to life.   In the United States recordings of this type have
grown enormously since the twenties and they deserve serious study.

Another area that should receive more attention is the private recordings made from radio broadcast interview programs.
These are valuable for biographers, not only because of the contents of the program but also for the voice of the guest.   Before
the invention of the phonograph many biographers tried to convey to
the reader the sense of the speaking voice of their subject.   It is
due to the efforts of Suetonious, Einhard, and William Maclay that
we have some idea of the voices of Nero, Charlemagne, and George
Washington.   Surely, with our superior recording instruments, we
should make use of this aid in writing biographies.

Tasks that need to be done include:

1. A master catalog of recording archives.

2. Reproductions of rare recordings made available to scholars and laymen.

3. The proper preservation of recordings and the prevention
of frauds.

4. The continued recording of contemporary personalities for
future use.

5. The issuing of more and better anthologies.

The invention of the phonograph fulfilled a desire expressed
in the seventeenth century by Cyrano de Bergerac in his "Comic
History of the States of the Moon," in which he describes the moon-
men preserving their history on talking machines.   We can do no
less than further Cyrano's dream.

For further reading:

1. Eelco N. van Kleffens, "The Spoken Word," Blashfield Address, Proceedings of the American Academy of Arts and Letters and National Institute of Arts and Letters, second series, no. 6 (1956), 13-21.

2. Oliver Read and Walter L. Welch, From Tin Foil to Stereo (Indianapolis, Ind., 1959).

3. Milo Ryan, History in Sound, (Seattle, Washington, 1963).

4. Association For Recorded Sound Collections, Journal and bulletin, 111 Amsterdam Avenue, New York, N. Y. 10023.

5. Ogilvie Mitchell, The Talking Machine Industry (London, n. d.) [rare].

6. The Oral History Association, Newsletter and Proceedings.

XI. Oral History

Louis M. Starr, Columbia University

Oral history--like social security a misnomer now hopelessly embedded in the language--occupies a relatively small but well-defined area in the vast world of recorded sound. Oral history pertains to the creation of historical information by means of interviews, usually tape-recorded interviews. In most instances, however, the end product is not a tape but a typewritten transcript that has been edited for accuracy, indexed, and deposited in a research library for the benefit of future scholars. Why is the emphasis on the transcript, rather than the tape? For one, because scholars want the assurance that the person interviewed has reviewed what he said and has had a chance to verify it. For another, because the black and white of the transcript facilitates indexing, to say nothing of accurate note-taking. For a third reason, because many oral history interviews are conducted in series. Scores of the oral memoirs at Columbia, for example, exceed 1000 pages, a good deal more than one would care to listen to.

While most scholars using oral history collections for their research show no interest whatever in listening to tapes, another generation may find them fascinating--a thought that has led most oral history repositories to save segments of their taped interviews or, in many cases, all of them. Few, unfortunately, are stored under ideal conditions, and until recently, the quality of the recordings was low. To economize in the early years, tapes were commonly re-used, and thus erased. The outcries of the sound collectors put a stop to this.

The modern oral history movement began without any recording device save a pencil, the first interview being conducted in 1948 by Professor Allan Nevins of Columbia with a graduate student serving as amanuensis. The result left so much to be desired that the idea might have gone into limbo had not Nevins learned of the wire-recorder toward the end of that year. This in turn was soon replaced by the tape-recorder, the salvation of oral history. (Even today, however, the few respondents who balk at being recorded are interviewed in the old way.)

The oral history idea spread to other institutions--gradually through most of the 1950's, then with increasing rapidity in the 60's. In 1965, the Columbia office published the results of its state-by-state survey, "Oral History in the United States." The next year, James V. Mink of the University of California, Los Angeles, summoned a meeting of those listed in this report and other interested parties. At Lake Arrowhead, the UCLA conference facility in the San Bernardino mountains, some 75 persons concluded a four-day colloquium on oral history by resolving to form an association. Since then, the Oral History Association has attracted some 400 members, held national meetings each fall, published the proceedings, issued a quarterly newsletter, adopted some recommended guidelines, and published a bibliography.[1] More pertinent to the readers of this volume, its meetings have served to sharpen interest in obtaining higher quality recordings, and in preserving them against the day historians may become more aurally inclined than they appear to be today.

Historians, of course, are not alone in their interest in oral history. The method has been brought to bear in many subject areas, literature, medicine, forestry, the fine arts, and pure science among them. Columbia's Oral History Collection, the largest, reflects this diversity. Now approaching a third of a million pages, it includes both full-length biographical memoirs and "Special Projects," or clusters of interviews with a number of respondents about a single institution (e. g., the Carnegie Corporation), administration (e. g., the Eisenhower years), industry (e. g., the pioneers of radio), epoch (the Occupation of Japan), or leader (Robert A. Taft, Adlai Stevenson), most of these being specially funded. A majority of the 100-odd oral history projects in the United States today are topic-oriented rather than biographical, like Tulane University's oral history of jazz or The Pennsylvania State University's labor collection; but the trend is toward the double-barreled approach developed at Columbia. A few institutions, largely for want of means, do not transcribe, their collections consisting of tape alone.

In general, oral history's practitioners understand and appreciate highly the value of sound libraries of poetry, speeches, radio interviews and the like, but draw a clear distinction between these and oral history collections, which consist of source materials brought into being expressly to illuminate some undocumented (sometimes confidential) area of human activity for the benefit of future scholars.

1
For further information or publications, write Box 20, Butler Library, Columbia University, N. Y. 10027.

A. & M. Records, 1416 N. LaBrea Street, Los Angeles, California 90028

Abbey Audio Vision Development Oxford, Ltd. , Eynsham, Oxford. (Available through Discourses.)

Allegro Elite, 315-317 Oxford Street, London W. 1, England

Angel Records, c/o Capitol Records, 1290 Avenue of the Americas, New York, N. Y. 10019

Argo Record Company, 113 Fulham Road, London, S. W. , England

Audio-Fidelity TransAtlantic Records, Ltd. , 120-2 Marlebone Lane, London, W. 1, England

Audio-Rarities (Audio Fidelity), 770 11th Avenue, New York, N. Y. 10019

B. B. C. English by Radio, Bush House, London, W. C. 2, England

B. B. C. Radio Enterprises, Broadcast House, London, W. 1, England

Britam Agencies, Inc. , 245 Fifth Avenue, New York, N. Y. 10015

British Drama League, 9 Fitzroy Square, London W. 1, England

Caedmon Records, 461 8th Avenue, New York, N. Y. 10001

Calliope Records, 53 Pinckney Street, Boston, Massachusetts

Capitol Records, 1290 Avenue of the Americas, New York, N. Y. 10019

Carillon Records, 520 Fifth Avenue, New York, N. Y. 10036

C. B. S. Records, Ltd. , 104 New Bond Street, London, W. 1, England

C. M. S. , 12 Warren Street, New York, N. Y. 10007

Columbia Records, 799 Seventh Avenue, New York, N. Y. 10019

Command Records, 1501 Broadway, New York, N. Y. 10036

Cook Laboratories, 101 Second Street, Stamford, Connecticut

Decca Records, 445 Park Avenue, New York, N. Y. 10022

Discourses, 102 High Street, Royal Tunbridge Wells, Kent, England

Discurio, 9 Shepherd Street, Shepherd Market, London W. 1,
    England

Dover, 180 Varick Street, New York, N. Y. 10014

E. M. I. Records, Ltd., E. M. I. House, 20 Manchester Square,
    London W. 1, England

Folkways Records, 165 West 46th Street, New York, N. Y. 10036

Gramophone, 177-9 Kenton Road, Kenton, Harrow, Middlesex,
    England

Harvard Vocarium, Harvard University Library, Cambridge,
    Massachusetts, and National Council of Teachers of English.

H. M. V.-E. M. I. Records, Ltd., 20 Manchester Square, London W. 1,
    England

H. Roach, Spoken Recordings, Box 4162, Grand Central P. O. Sta-
    tion, New York, N. Y. 10017.

Jupiter Recordings, 140 Kensington Church Street, London W. 8,
    England

Lexington Records, 1 Claremont Avenue, Thornwood, New York

Library Editions, Request Records, 66 Mechanic Street, New
    Rochelle, N. Y. 10801

Library of Congress, Music Division, Recording Laboratory,
    Washington, D. C. 20025

London Records, Inc., 539 West 25th Street, New York, N. Y.
    10001

Major-Minor, 58 Great Marlborough Street, London W. 1, England

MGM Records, Loews Inc., 1540 Broadway, New York, N. Y.
    10036

Millers of Cambridge, Sidney Street, Cambridge, England

National Council of Teachers of English, 508 South Sixth Street,
    Champaign, Illinois

National Voice Library, Michigan State University, East Lansing,
    Michigan

Nealon Records, Radio Eireann, Dublin, Ireland

Philips Records, Ltd. , Stanhope House, Stanhope Place, London
    W. 2, England

Prestige-Lively Arts Records, 203 South Washington Avenue,
    Bergenfield, New Jersey

Qualiton Records, Vistula Export & Import Company, 164 Old
    Brompton Road, London S. W. 5, England

R. C. A. Victor Record Division, 155 East 24th Street, New York,
    N. Y. 10010

Rococo Records, Toronto, Canada

Scottish Records, 52 Bon Acord Street, Aberdeen, Scotland

Selection Records, Ltd. , 39 Greenford Gardens, Greenford,
    Middlesex, England

"77" Records, Keith Prowse & Company, 202 Tooting High Street,
    London S. W. 17, England

Spoken Arts, Box 542, New Rochelle, New York

Spoken Word, (Dover), 180 Varick Street, New York, N. Y. 10014

The Living Shakespeare, 100 Avenue of the Americas, New York,
    N. Y.

Theatre Masterworks, 20 Rockefeller Plaza, New York, N. Y.
    10020

Vanguard, 71 West 23rd Street, New York, N. Y. 10010

Variety Recordings, 225 West 46th Street, New York, N. Y. 10036

Vocarium Records, F. C. Packard, Jr. , R. F. D. #2, Brunswick,
    Maine

Wren Records, Llandybie, Carmorthenshire, Wales, England
    (Available through Discourses, Ltd.)

N. B.   Argo Records are processed in the United States through
        McGraw-Hill and Spoken Arts, and Jupiter through Folkways
        and Spoken Arts. Caedmon may be found in England under
        Philips Records, Ltd.

Publications of Special Interest

Association for Recorded Sound Collections: Quarterly, David
     Hall, Editor.   Rogers and Hammerstein Archives of Re-
     corded Sound, New York Public Library, Lincoln Center,
     Amsterdam Ave. , New York , N. Y.

British Institute of Recorded Sound: Recorded Sound, A Quarterly,
     Patrick Saul, Editor.   29 Exhibition Road, London S. W. 7,
     England.

Gramophone, Spoken Word, an annual.   Gramophone, 177-9 Kenton
     Road, Kenton, Harrow, Middlesex, England.

The Gramophone, Monthly.   Gramophone, 177-9 Kenton Road, Ken-
     ton, Harrow, Middlesex, England.

285